THEODORE DREISER, 1928
(Photo by Macgregor)

Letters of
THEODORE DREISER

A SELECTION

VOLUME TWO

Edited with Preface and Notes by
Robert H. Elias

Consulting Editors
SCULLEY BRADLEY *and* **ROBERT E. SPILLER**

Philadelphia
University of Pennsylvania Press

Printed in the United States of America

Letters of Theodore Dreiser

1922

WILLIAM C. LENGEL
[TLS]

P. O. Box 181
Los Angeles, California
February 26, 1922

Dear Lengel:

Thanks for your letter and wire in regard to Long.[1] I looked him up at the Ambassador and found him a very different person to the youth I encountered in Chicago,—more cosmopolitan, quite your equipped man of the world. I liked him and we seemed to get along in regard to material for the magazine. In fact he contracted with me for six studies of women after I had outlined two of them rather carefully so that he could see exactly what he was getting. I am to send them on as fast as opportunity will permit and you, I believe are destined, as usual, to see that they are pruned to the various needs of the magazine. One of these days I think I shall have to buy you a fur coat or something, just to show that there is in me a remembrance of courtesies extended.

He was also interested in the proposed study of a small state legislature by me and said that he would seriously recommend it to Hapgood and that he hoped that it would come about that I did it. He talked of an essay that he had in mind which he wanted me to do but I think in the pressure of the other discussions I must have given him the impression that I was not very much interested to do it. I felt it to be a good general subject and one that I could do. I even thought of a title for it—*The Female of*

[1] Ray Long, vice-president of International Publications, Inc., and editor (with Norman Hapgood) of *Hearst's International*.

the Species, but somehow, it became lost and nothing more was said. I am writing him to say that at any time, if he really wants it done, and by me, I will put my hand to it. But with this other material coming along he may not think it so important to him now.

The play proceeds apace.[2] I have just finished act three and am now meditating on the end. Ditrichstein is to be here in April or May,—April, I think, and we may give the thing a tryout in San Francisco. Wish you were going to be out here. I would take you to S. F. and show you that man's-size town. Every real person likes S. F. He can't help it.

> Regards and best wishes.
> Dreiser

To Arthur Carter Hume
[CC]

Dreiser had sought Hume's legal assistance in solving the many problems connected with bringing together his works under a single imprint.

> P. O. Box 181
> Los Angeles, [California]
> March 30, 1922

Dear Mr. Hume:

Thank you for your very kind letter and I will try and make as clear as I can where I stand in regard to Dodd-Mead.[3] I had a letter from Mencken—yes. A long and very clear statement of his views. He is for having me tie up with Dodd-Mead on the ground that if I don't I will never get either *The Bulwark* or *The "Gen-*

[2] See Dreiser to Lengel, January 23, 1921, n. 15.
[3] Dodd, Mead & Co. had succeeded to the contracts of the John Lane Co. in the United States when Lane gave up its American branch.

ius" matter straight.[4] Now I would be very glad indeed to tie up with Dodd-Mead if I thought they were really liberal minded men with some interest in letters over and above the average American publisher's will it sell fifteen minutes after it is out credo. No American publisher unless it is Harper appears to me to have the faintest conception of the wisdom of taking a man who has a possible future and helping him to build himself up in any way which will make him and them some money in the future or themselves money once he is gone. They have no faith in anyone, really. They live from day to day and from hand to mouth. I can get twenty-seven different American publishers to "take a chance" on some trashy third rate work that might possibly sell a few hundred or at the most three or four thousand copies and nine times out of ten they will lose their money and think no more about it. You can go into any old book store and find thousands of books on [which] scores of American publishers have taken a chance and on which they have never made a dollar, really,—piffle not worth the paper it is printed on. But approach any one of them with a genuine enduring proposition on which they might proceed with safety if they had a trace of vision and they are terrorized by the thought that they may not get their money back the same fall or spring in which they issue the work. And they want nothing to [do] with anything that smacks of having to build up and consolidate the reputation of a man. He must build up and consolidate himself, a la Twain and Whitman

---

4 Lane had advanced money against *The Bulwark* and retained rights to *The "Genius"*, which it had withdrawn from circulation out of fear of prosecution by the New York Society for the Suppression of Vice. Mencken, on March 14, had conferred with Hume and Edward H. Dodd concerning Dreiser's difficulties and on March 16 had written Dreiser that Dodd was eager for *The Bulwark*, was willing to reissue *The "Genius"* "with the reasonable cuts you yourself suggest, or to free it so that you will be able . . . to bring it out yourself," and was ready not to cut Dreiser's royalties provided Dreiser would settle Lane's claims. Mencken stood ready, he had concluded, to negotiate with John S. Sumner concerning republication of *The "Genius"* and urged Dreiser to secure a release from Liveright. On March 22 Dreiser had replied that Dodd, Mead were "not publishers of liberal books. They approach me about [as] a Baptist snouts a pervert." He agreed to consult Liveright, but saw "small hope. If I can't release *The 'Genius'* I can't. But I can do other books which they can't touch and that is what I shall have to do I presume."

and then they will come in and grab the expired copyrights, if they can. And in the meantime they want nothing to do, or very, very little, Mr. Henry L. Mencken to the contrary notwithstanding, with anyone who does not square with their conception of what an author should write about and how he should write it. That has been my quarrel and my trouble with the American publisher from the beginning and that remains my trouble to-day. I cannot find a publisher of any means who doesn't want to look over my shoulder and tell how and how not to do.[5] Having come so far along the path and having at last secured a fairly respectable body of adherents you may well guess that I am in no particular mood to have additional conservative publishers tell me what they will do for me,—usually damned little, you may be sure, if only I will take their advice and let them tell me how I am to write my stuff. They always have the honor of their ultra respectable publishing houses to consider first. Their standing as American gentlemen and church members, possibly, comes before anything else. Hence it is that they will publish, and gladly, the works of seventy commonplace imitators of yours humbly and others like him and ignore the man whom the imitators copy. The imitators listen to their advice and accept their limitations which they prescribe. The original will not.

Having exuded this profound wail I repeat that I am very dubious as to whether the Dodd-Mead Co. would prove of any real value to me. In the first place I doubt whether they bought out Lane at all. I think it is more likely that they are handling his books on lease with the ultimate say-so still in the honorable Lane's hands. In the next they are not really interested to publish my books as you will find. If you doubt it sound them out for yourself. I have a book which I am now preparing and the title of which will certainly help greatly in selling the book. It is a work about women a la *Twelve Men*. It will be as frank and direct and sincere as *Twelve Men*. It will discuss the morals of

[5] For instances of Dreiser's earlier attempts to solve his problems see his letters to: George L. Wheelock, November 17, 1920; Horace B. Liveright, December 3 and 21, 1920, March 11 and April 20, 1921; L. E. Pollinger, [after December 9, 1920]; Curtis Brown, March 25, 1921; and William H. Briggs, April 9, 1921.

women and their private attitude toward the same about as *Twelve Men* discusses the professions of the men therein presented. Will the Dodd-Mead Company say offhand that they will publish such a work. Ask them. If they stall around with a few select ifs, ands etc. you may know that they are not for me. I want none of them. I will get the book published and the publisher who gets it will be delighted to get it. And he will come to the front and do some talking about it. Will it be an old line publisher. I doubt it. I doubt it very much.[6]

If you are going to be good enough to follow this matter up for me and really wish to know whether they are the right people for me or not, ask them if they are interested in the suggestion I made them regarding a four-volume work to be entitled *The History of Myself*. This is no thin dream. Two substantial volumes of the same are finished and a third one under way. Some chapters from volume two have already appeared in the *Bookman*,—safe chapters. Would the Dodd-Mead Company be interested in those volumes? Would they approach them in a liberal spirit, knowing before hand that a very liberal stand will have to be taken in regard to the material therein contained. I asked them if they were interested. No reply. They want *The Bulwark*. Why? Because Lane claims he advanced me some money against it? I can scarcely see another reason. They approach me with a tricky offer to knock off one thousand of the alleged Lane claim if I will reduce my royalties and by the process they will make more than they will lose. Outside of that they will advance $1,000 when I can go to Harper or Liveright now and get $3,000. And this offer of theirs is really tentative. They will look at *The Bulwark*. If it isn't too radical for them and I will make such changes as their conservatism would dictate then the aforesaid offer holds good.

Frankly, Mr. Hume, I can't see it. All I see here is the same old picky, sniffy stuff that I have enjoyed for twenty years now. In spite of it all I have done pretty well but no thanks to any American publisher but one that I have ever dealt with[.] Never-

6 Horace Liveright published the two-volume *A Gallery of Women* in 1929.

theless, I am willing to believe that something can come of this Dodd-Mead offer. At any rate I am going ahead arranging with Liveright to drop in the hope that ultimately I can induce a publisher of prominence to take over all of my books. When I have something definite from Liveright, I will let you know. In the meantime, assuming that I do not care to take the terms offered by Dodd-Mead do you suppose they could be induced to release my several books including *The "Genius"* to me for a moderate sum. I would be glad to hear from you as to that. And I am very much obliged to you for your very kind interest.

I think I told you that I wrote Mr. Dodd suggesting that *The "Genius"* be cut so as to eliminate the objections raised by Sumner but that to that letter I received no reply. Naturally you can see that they may well be too conservative for any good to me.

To Arthur Carter Hume
[CC]

Replying to Dreiser's letter of March 30, Hume had asked on April 8: (1) whether he should try to bring about Dodd, Mead and Company's publication of The "Genius" *as edited by Mencken, providing publishers and editor were agreeable; (2) whether Dodd, Mead and Company should be asked for a decision about* Twelve Women *before or after they had seen the manuscript; (3) whether the same conditions should apply to* The History of Myself; *(4) what "arrangement most disadvantageous to yourself" Dreiser would be willing to make concerning* The Bulwark. *Hume had also (5) agreed as a last measure to inquire into the cost of releasing all the books from Dodd, Mead.*

P. O. Box 181
Los Angeles, California
April 18, 1922

Dear Mr. Hume:

You will find all of your questions answered below and in their order. But, before coming to them I want to make a suggestion. The easiest way in the world to find whether Dodd-Mead and Co. will make good publishers for me is to do as you suggest,— try them with something. I am prepared to do that. I mentioned a book that I am doing. We will call it *Twelve Women*, though that is not to be the title. I propose to take one of the more daring and honest studies and send it to you. You read it, or not, as you choose, but submit it to Dodd as a sample,—one of the more drastic studies which the book contains. See what he says. If he is dubious of such a book all bets are off. Not that I shall think any the less of him for refusing to publish a book of the sort but because there is nothing in his place for me. I want a whole-hearted sponsor,—not one who is sniffing nervously at everything handed him. And he may find it impossible not to sniff. It depends upon his private as well as his public attitude. To make haste with this matter I am enclosing the study [7] and will thank you to let Dodd look at it and then return it to me as speedily as may be.

Now to your letter.

1. Mencken will see Sumner, get his views and make such changes as are necessary providing Dodd-Mead are interested to bring out *The "Genius"*.[8] And I am willing that these changes should be made by Mencken and that you should see Dodd as to this and arrange for the publication of this revised version whether any other arrangement of any kind is made with them or not. Here is a P.S. to this of which I wish you would make a note. There is now in existence a short version of *The "Genius"* made

[7] "Olive Brand," the first of the sketches to be completed for what became *A Gallery of Women*.

[8] At the same time (April 18) Dreiser was writing Mencken that he would see to it that the work would be done by others; it would simply be submitted to Mencken for approval when completed.

for magazine purposes. It is only 100,000 words long and contains nothing objectionable. I would rather have the long version edited by Mencken and published but in case Dodd-Mead are not interested in that, ask them about this short version,—whether they would be interested to see it. In case they are call up William C. Lengel, Mgr. Editor of *Hearst's International Magazine,* 119 West 40th Street, and ask him for the loan of that short version.[9] He will send it over to you. Don't let them keep it long and see that they return it to Lengel. It is an only copy and valuable.

2. Your second question regarding *Twelve Women* is answered above. Show them the enclosed ms. if you think it advisable.

3. *The History of Myself* in three volumes will be as frank as this paper entitled "Olive Brand." I have two volumes ready. I can submit one. But before bothering them with it I would like to know whether they feel that they have the courage to bother with strong material. There is really no use dickering with people who are constitutionally opposed to calling a spade a spade anywhere or at any time. I have no recollection of any worthwhile frank book having ever been published by Dodd-Mead and Co. If they have published such a work by a living American author I should like to hear of it. If, after reading "Olive Brand" they are still interested to see one of the volumes about myself—seriously interested,—I will be glad to have it sent over. There is a copy of one volume now in New York City.

4. In re *The Bulwark.* I can get a clearance paper from Liveright in regard to this book. I owe him $1,300 against all of my books which he publishes. It would simplify matters if this thirteen hundred were paid. This could be accomplished if Dodd & Mead were to make me an advance of $3,000. They would not need to give me any cash but could cancel the balance due Lane —if you say so—($1,597.92) and the amount due Liveright,— ($1338.13). For this sum I would give them either *The Bulwark,* which is not yet completed or another novel of equal merit. This other novel is also under way. But, in case a general arrangement

9 Lengel was the abridger.

is entered into I want this Lane and Liveright matter cleared up now. If a general arrangement for all of my books is not entered into I will not transfer *The Bulwark*. But I still will be glad to have them publish *The "Genius"* as outlined above.

5. In case you cannot come to terms with Dodd-Mead do as you say,—see if they will not let me have all of my books back for as low a lump sum as possible.

Now my sincere thanks for your kindness in this matter. I wish something worth while might come of it all but I am very skeptical. While you are talking to them will you ask them to let me have new Dodd-Mead contracts for *A Hoosier Holiday, The Titan,* and *Plays of the Natural and the Supernatural,* providing this will not interfere in any way with your suit against the Lane Co.[10] You have my copy of the Lane *Hoosier Holiday* contract. May I have that back if you are done with it.

Regards and best wishes.

To H. L. Mencken
[TLS–NYP]

Mencken had come to agree with Dreiser's views of Dodd, Mead and other publishers as set forth in Dreiser to Hume, March 30, and argued that Dreiser would never conclude his difficulties by remaining in Los Angeles.

---

[10] On Hume's advice, Dreiser had claimed California residence and brought his case up in equity in the Federal courts, claiming $20,000 in damages for Lane's failure to continue publication of *The "Genius"* after 1916. Eventually, in December 1922, Dodd, Mead & Co. as Lane's American successor decided against reissuing the novel and agreed to turn over their rights to it if they were paid for the value of the plates, bound copies, and copyright, if they were reimbursed for advances allegedly made by Lane against *The Bulwark,* and if Dreiser would give up his suit. Liveright paid Dreiser's debts and reissued *The "Genius"* (uncut) in the spring of 1923.

P. O. Box 181
Los Angeles, [California]
April 18, 1922

Dear Mencken:

Don't worry about the Dodd matter or anything else in connection with the books. Have been intending to write you this for weeks, it seems. I am fairly well satisfied that the Dodd Co. and myself will never hit it off. But no harm. We can live without each other. As for Liveright he is certainly a poor fish but a port in a storm. He has rendered me one service and another and I am not ungrateful. One of these days I may be able to finance my own works and then they can all kiss my royal standard, such as it is.

Your noble words about the demise of the puritans make me laugh.[11] No doubt for others the ban may have been lifted [but] for yours humbly it seems to hold up fairly well. The Dodd gentlemen seem to teach you nothing. And the enduring attitude of Mr. Sumner, nix. You forget that from time to time I attempt to market various things in places other than the *S. S.* and that even through a Los Angeles fog I can discern certain things, albeit dimly. The critical reception of *The Hand of the Potter* proves clearly that all the old-time puritanic rage has been blown out of the land and that we have a body of liberal critics capable of viewing all serious things at least tolerantly. The notices of the play in the *Freeman,* the *New Republic,* the *Dial,* the *Independent* and such like liberal critical institutions prove as much.[12]

[11] Mencken's letter with the "noble words" is missing, but his sentiments appear in his reply to Dreiser, April 22: "With all due respect, Tush! Even Doubleday would print *Sister Carrie* today; Briggs, of Harper's, told me not two weeks ago that they would be glad to have *The Titan. Some* progress has been made, and maybe a damned sight more than you suspect. You are shut off from human society, and apparently read nothing. Worse, you are befogged by your weakness for *The "Genius".* I could get it past Sumner easily, with not a dozen changes, all of them unimportant. But while it was on the stocks I'd be hot for cutting out whole reams of words. There we would quarrel."

[12] See *New Republic,* XX (October 8, 1919), 297; *Dial,* LXVII (September 20, 1919), 276; *Nation,* CIX (September 6, 1919), 340—(comments in the *Freeman* and *Independent* cannot be found). Their consensus had the effect of praising his sincerity and even his understanding of character but of labelling him artistically inept because of his melodramatic incidents and editorialized conclusion.

Hail to the new day. Darwin wins by fifty-one to forty-nine in the Ky. state legislature [13] and the *Atlantic Monthly* announces that it would not publish *Sister Carrie* even now.[14] You certainly have sound reasons for your optimism.

Dreiser

However I have all the bootleg I need[.] [15]

To H. L. MENCKEN

[TLS–NYP]

Dreiser had requested Mencken on April 18 to consult with Sumner concerning making changes in The "Genius" *that would permit reissuance. Mencken on April 25 had replied: "I'll be glad to see Sumner and to arrange the cuts. I doubt that he will insist on any of much concern. . . . But, to be frank, I want to be sure in advance that after the work is done you will not buck. Are you willing to let Dodd do the book with the cuts? If there is any impediment in your mind to this plan, what is the use of going on? I doubt that any other publisher would do the book as it stands."*

P. O. Box 181
Los Angeles, California
May 1, 1922

Dear Mencken:

Of course I am willing that you should purify *The "Genius"* and grateful to you for being ready to perform the service. My willingness only extends to what must come out to satisfy the Boy Scouts, however. In your last letter but one you announced

---

13 "An Act to Prohibit the Teaching of Darwinism, atheism, agnosticism and evolution as pertaining to the origin of man" was rejected by the Kentucky House of Representatives, 42-41. (See *New York Times*, March 10, 1922.)

14 Dreiser's statement has eluded verification.

15 Postscript in Dreiser's hand.

that in case you set to cut it at all that you should proceed to cut reams and reams or words to that effect.[16] Hardly. And as much as I may pretend to love you. Your approach to the book is not mine and while I respect your zeal I reserve all rights and prefer to hold the work as it stands. Don't forget that the book is already established as it stands, and such cuts as are now made will be but temporary anyhow.

I was about to polish you off in a screed of great delicacy and point but now prefer to rack my lance for the present. As in the case of the story of the English lock man, I will say one thing: you stand at the head of the class for making assertions and then trusting to the bass drum to silence the reply. We shall see.

I wish you would let me see exactly (seriatim) the changes demanded by Sumner. I have his old list,—some seventy-seven in all.

Dreiser

To H. L. Mencken
[TLS–NYP]

Mencken on May 31 had met with Sumner and, as his report to Dreiser the next day showed, secured some modifications of the vice society's original demands. Descriptions of Bouguereau's paintings of nudes, discussions casting doubt on the existence of the Deity, and scenes of unashamed illicit desire were eliminated, although Mencken had succeeded in saving sentences where Sumner had sought to cut out entire pages and in saving paragraphs where Sumner had sought to cut out entire chapters. In the conversations between Witla and Suzanne that Dreiser refers to, Sumner had demanded the cutting of four and a half pages, while Mencken had managed to preserve all but a few paragraphs in which Dreiser was making explicit that Eugene's

---

[16] See Dreiser to Mencken, April 18, 1922, n. 11. (This letter was written before the request of even date referred to in the headnote.)

desires were physical and that Suzanne was responsive. In the discussion of Angela's motive for wanting a child—that of controlling Eugene through the sobering effects of fatherhood and the bondage of family responsibility—Mencken, however, had consented to complete deletion.

P. O. Box 181
Los Angeles, [California]
June 8, 1922

Dear Mencken:

Well, I have just finished checking up the solemn labors of yourself and Sumner. To many of the cuts I make no objection since if cuts must come I think you have done as well by me as could be. The items which strike me as fantastic are those which relate to the conversations between Suzanne and Witla—pages 534, 539, 541, 553, 557.[17] Also the cut which explains [that] [18] Angela wanted a child and why.[19] Since this is a definite point in the dramatic structure of this tale,—the one thing that gives it real point in view of her death afterwards by reason of this wish and effort I cannot see how, logically, it can come out. And I cannot see how it can be written so very differently if the same point is to be made. As for the thing being immoral that is too crazy for words. The discussion of child-bearing and the reasons therefor is almost a commonplace today. I cannot see this and I feel that this point ought to be rediscussed. If the thing is taken up as

---

17 For full details see *The "Genius"* (New York, 1915):

Original Demand of Sumner:		*Compromise of Mencken and Sumner:*
P. 534	omit entire page	omit "He went back" to "lingering over the name."
P. 539	omit entire page	omit " 'We must be careful' " to "Why did she let him?"
P. 541	omit entire page	omit " 'Come to me, Suzanne' " to " 'No,' she said. 'No.' "
P. 553	omit " 'At last?' " to foot of page	omit " 'At last?' " to " 'How long can you stay?' "
P. 557	omit entire page	omit from top of page to "dominate her mother's?" and from " 'Yes, we must think now' " to bottom of page.

18 Dreiser wrote "why."

19 A cut of four paragraphs, beginning with "It was at this time" on p. 445 and comprising all but the last line of p. 446.

definitely elsewhere in the book I do not know it. And just now I haven't time to reread the work to see. But there is certainly nothing prurient or salacious about that and I should like to have it stay in. Will you talk to Sumner about this.

Now as to Liveright and Dodd. The matter of *The Bulwark* has been adjusted. Liveright waives any claim as I knew he would. He never had anything to do with *The "Genius"*. Hence, he has no claim and makes none. Whether it is worth while to reissue *The "Genius"* cut remains to be seen. I wonder if any one will want a clipped copy.

Just the same I am once more your debtor for your work in connection with this. I can see that you went carefully into the matter and saved a very great deal that was asininely doomed. It surprises me to know that you could make him accept such intelligent suggestions. I think I shall have to send you a can of pork and beans for Christmas.

To be definite here is how I feel and where I stand. If you can save the cut on pages 445-446 above referred to I will accept this revised version and will see if I can induce Dodd to reissue it.[20] I would like it if he would merely black out the offending lines and use the present plates as they run, numbers and all. If you talk to Dodd or Hume, suggest this.

Dreiser

Important→Thanks[.] [21]

To H. L. MENCKEN
[ALS–NYP]

On October 28 Mencken had asked whether it was true that "you are thinking of doing an unexpurgated edition of The 'Genius'

---

[20] On June 16 Mencken was able to report that "Sumner agrees to let pages 445 and 446 stand. But in order to give him something I have suggested cutting out one sentence. It is unimportant."

[21] Postscript in Dreiser's hand.

next year. . . . If it is, I'd like to know it in advance, so that it may not appear to Sumner that I was fooling him about the cuts. He acted very decently. . . ."

16 St. Luke's Place
New York, [N.Y.]
November 5, 1922

Parding, Captain, this long delay in answering your several courteous notes & inquiries. I have been slaving—unpacking barrels, boxes & crates & rearranging them as is our human way. In another week I hope to have this accursed joint presentable.

In re Sumner. Various discussions here with Hume, Dodd, Briggs, Liveright & others have led me to know that if I publish an expurgated version of *The "Genius"* it will not sell. Expurgated versions of anything do not sell at all and I will have had the mealy pleasure of seeing the book issued & forgotten in that secondary form. Besides Liveright is now having certain lawyers & other vultures of the local District Attorney's staff look into the possibility of defeating Sumner in a fight which is to begin with the publication of the book as it is. I did not ask him to do this. He asked me if I would not prefer to have the book reissued as it stands. Of course. Then he asked permission to look into the chances of winning via a process of fixation—I believe. I have given that permission. If he weakens I may let Dodd-Mead proceed. Hume knows my point of view. I went to his office & told him what I had heard & how I felt. You can tell Sumner as much of this as you think is wise—giving my chances as much consideration as you please.

In re *Sister Carrie*.[22] I do not ask you to sell the book. As a matter of fact if approached again—even with an offer of $2,000 I wish you would rest until you hear from me. Certain things

---

[22] Knowing of an offer for the manuscript that Dreiser had given Mencken, Dreiser had on October 28 asked Mencken not to accept less than $2,000, in order not to undersell Dreiser, who was trying to dispose of the manuscripts of others of his works. Mencken had replied on the same day that although the *Sister Carrie* manuscript was not for sale, he "might be induced, by suitable arts, to hand . . . [it] back to you. Let us be frank. If you are short of money, it is yours, now or at any time. But no other scoundrel ever gets it."

have developed here which make a high priced sale entirely possible[.] If I should arrange a deal such as you personally could
not effect and it meant a round sum & you wanted to take over
some ready cash would you split the returns. Your share should
be over $2,000. Same to me & something to a third mysterious
grafter.

Glad you are back & hope to hear that Germany is feeling better. N. Y. to me is a scream—a Kyke's dream of a Ghetto. The
lost tribe has taken the island. I plan to return to Chicago permanently I believe next year. There is a Spaghetti joint over the
way. Drop down & I will have them weave a spaghetti overcoat
for you[.]

Simon—called Peter.

To H. L. Mencken
[ALS–NYP]

16 St. Luke's Place
New York, [N.Y.]
December 6, 1922

Dear Mencken:

Yes, I received *Prejudices III* & read in it several hours[.]
Such things as "Spangled Men," "Memorial Service," "Five Men
at Random" and "Advice to Young Men"—or a part of it—I had
read before. I like such things as "On Being an American,"
"Huneker," your defense of the critic as an artist, and "The
Novel." All of the stuff is really vastly entertaining[.] You always
muster a brisk and refreshing style & brisk and refreshing
thoughts. That the people you openly attack in "On Being an
American" don't retaliate is a marvel to me. I assume that your
aim is to goad them into action.

In regard to the critic as artist—you never were a critic really.
You have as you say—a definite point of view & a philosophy &
you have used the critical role to put it over[.] Your comments

on life have always been vastly more diverting to me than your more intensive comment on books. I notice the freer brush strokes the moment you set forth your direct observations on men & things.

It's a good book & ought to sell. I presume all of your things do. But I still think you ought to do a cynical slap-stick political farce with all our stuffed figures galvanized into action. If you want to dine with me call me up when you come—Telephone Spring 8376. I have one now. Don't give my address to a soul[.]

Dreiser

1923

To Sidney Kirkpatrick
[CC]

Kirkpatrick was "Herod" in the Colored Folk Theatre production of Salome.

16 St. Luke's Place
New York, [N.Y.]
April 29, 1923

Dear Mr. Kirkpatrick:

I had the singular and exquisite pleasure this past week of witnessing at the Lafayette Theatre two performances of *Salome* by the Colored Folk Theatre company [1] with yourself, Solomon Bruce, Evelyn Preer and Laura Bowman, not to mention any of the other members of this very distinguished company in the cast. Out of the general silence,—in white critical circles I mean, —that appears to have attended this surprisingly valuable artistic presentation I wish to extend to you personally and to all these others my grateful and deep appreciation of the grace, the culture and the abiding beauty of this presentation. I have seen many presentations of *Salome* in New York and elsewhere,—none that I feel to be the peer of this. My first and second and remaining impression was and is that it was flawless,—a very, very great deal to say. I was especially impressed with your own high artistic fervor and understanding. Also with that of Miss Preer, Mr. Bruce and Miss Bowman. May I say this as forcibly as possible.

---

[1] The Ethiopian Art Theatre is the name by which Percy Hammond refers to the company in his column "Oddments and Remainders," *New York Tribune,* May 14, 1923, where Dreiser's letter is reprinted in full.

If artistic criticism in New York and America, for that matter were not the thin and anaemic thing that it is all of you and the Colored Folk Theatre would have been hailed within the week. I trust that your laurels will not long be delayed. My own sincere wish is that you maintain this artistic integrity uncorrupted indefinitely.

To Rex Beach
[TCS]

As chairman of a special committee of the Authors' League of America, Beach on April 26 had sent out a form letter beginning: "The Authors' League assumes you will welcome an opportunity to help in a definite plan to advance the artistic and cultural standards of motion pictures, and, consequently invites your participation in a proposed international two days' congress on motion picture arts to be held in New York City on . . . June 7th and 8th. . . ." The proposal had, it appeared, originated with the moving picture producer, Adolph Zukor.

16 St. Luke's Place
New York, [N.Y.]
May 5, 1923

Dear Mr. Beach:

The Authors' League of America is wrong in assuming that I would welcome an opportunity at this time to advance the artistic and cultural standards of motion pictures. Not that they do not need to be advanced. But, for the reasons which I am herewith presenting I do not care to participate.

My mature opinion is that the Authors' League of America might be much more appropriately concerning itself at this time with calling conferences of such forces as it can muster to make safe the cultural and artistic privileges and necessities of serious letters, than which there is nothing more important at this time.

To be sure the arbitrary and inquisitorial Clean Books League Bill has been temporarily scotched in the state senate at Albany, but how long will it be before it will be before that body in another form, or before some one of the other forty-eight state legislatures. This issue is pressing,—a genuine menace;—whereas the other is not. Motion Pictures, buttressed by full financial bunkers and encircled by well paid lawyers and such literary assistants as their intelligence will permit them to employ can wait.

In the teeth of the present situation it strikes me as not only deplorable but significant that at the first hearing of the Clean Books League Bill at Albany, than which no more sly, malicious and intellectually throttling legislation ever came before an American legislative body, no representative of the Authors' League was present either to protest or to counteract in any way the plans of the various forces, always active, that are seeking permanently to destroy all artistic and cultural privilege in this country. And what forces? I call your attention to the following groups, all present by their representatives and all savage and uncompromising: 1. The Salvation Army, 2. The Roman Catholic Archdiocese of New York, 3. The Federated Catholic Societies, 4. The Holy Name Society, 5. The League of Catholic Women, 6. The Protestant Episcopal Church of the State of New York, 7. The Y. M. C. A., 8. The New York State Federation of Churches, 9. The Society for the Suppression of Commercialized Vice and—10. The Minerva Club, whatever that may be, not to mention other minor and unimportant bodies of a like complexion. Opposed to these, if you please, and that after days spent in attempting to waken the literary and artistic interests of the city and the nation to the enormity of the present proposition were one lone publisher, Horace B. Liveright, and four authors, there at their own expense, as I understand it. The Authors' League, as I have since learned, did send a protesting telegram that same day or several days later.

And yet in the face of this, and at the crook of the finger of Mr. Adolph Zukor and other motion picture impressarios to

whom such a situation as this is apparently meaningless, the Authors' League of America and you, Mr. Beach, hasten to summon or, at least, enthusiastically endorse, and the Authors' League does not hesitate to expend its funds to further, an international two days conference to advance the cultural and artistic standards of motion pictures. And you have the effrontery to ask me to give of my time and my suggestions to further this soul-shaking cause. Upon my word.

Pardon me for not availing myself of the invitation. It strikes me as trivial and unimportant,—in the face of this other, I mean. If at any time the Authors' League should espouse a cause worthy of the name it can command me, of course.

Bows, hand-kissings, profound and various gestures and genuflections.[2]

Theodore Dreiser

To Gelett Burgess
[TC]

Burgess, vice-president of the Authors' League, had made a statement to the press on May 18 replying to Dreiser's letter to Beach of May 5. According to the New York Telegraph *of May 19, he accused Dreiser of ignorance of the League's efforts and said: "If he should devote as much time to furthering the cause of literature as he does to seeking personal publicity, he wouldn't need to ask an association he doesn't belong to to help protect his dubious sex-fiction." The League, he remarked, opposed literary censorship and personal publicity, both, and had done much at Albany quietly, helped by George Creel. Dreiser sent copies of the following letter to the papers as his rebuttal on June 2 and was quoted fully in the* Jersey Journal, *June 6.*

2 Dreiser's refusal to help the moving pictures reach a higher level was widely quoted in the press, and on May 16 printed in full in the New York *Globe and Commercial Advertiser.*

16 St. Luke's Place
New York, [N.Y.
between May 19 and June 2, 1923]

Dear Mr. Burgess:

Your reply to my letter to the Authors' League, furnished to the newspapers direct, has been called to my attention by these same papers with the request that I make some comment. Because of the nature of your various assertions, I find this unavoidable. But first let me say my primary reason for writing the Authors' League the letter that I did, was because in so far as I know the Authors' League, from its inception to this day, has never at any time throughout the various censorship attacks on books of varying artistic and intellectual import, come forward to say one word or spend one penny to either ameliorate the cost of such attacks, or hearten the author or publisher as against the ever increasing and censorious band of vice-crusaders. Roughly I think of such books as: *Leonardo da Vinci* by Freud; *Hagar Revelly* by Daniel Carson Goodman; *Susan Lennox* by David Graham Phillips; *Jurgen* by James Branch Cabell; *Homo Sapiens* by Artzybashev; [3] *The God of Vengeance* by Sholem Asch; and my own work, *The "Genius"*.

No one of these, or their authors or their publishers, in so far as I know, ever received one word of encouragement or one dollar of cash from the Authors' League of America. On the contrary, the general impression among the intellectually enlightened and liberal is that your organization runs safely and only with those who concern themselves with the safer and more popular forms of light fiction. Your roster of membership will, I think, bear me out. Then why approach me for service in connection with your plans and grow angry with me because I fail to see the value of co-operating with you in your issues.

But to continue. You say that because I am not a member of the Authors' League, and because I did not personally attend the State Senate hearing on the Clean Books League Bill in Albany, I could not possibly hear or know of the work done or not

[3] The author's name is Stanislaw Przybyszewski.

done by the Authors' League of America, in the matter of disposing of that obnoxious measure. Wrong. I did not attend the hearing in question because I was advised that my presence under the circumstances might prove more of an aggravation than otherwise, my own work, The "Genius" having previously been the subject of censorship meddling, as you and your organization well know.[4] But the presence or absence of any single author could scarcely have the significance or weight of the presence or absence, by representative, of a body that is supposed to represent a majority of the writers of this country. Or do you refuse to agree?

However, let me present you with some interesting details. On Wednesday, April 11th last, Horace B. Liveright, your publisher and mine, learned through Denis Lynch, the New York Tribune correspondent in Albany, that the Clean Books League Bill was slated to pass the Assembly on the following Friday and would be brought up the following Monday in the Senate by Senator Cotillo,[5] where it would also undoubtedly pass. Thereupon Mr. Liveright phoned to five leading book publishers in New York City, including the President of the National Book Publishers Association, and was told by all of them that the bill would undoubtedly pass and that so far as they were concerned, it could pass. As you know, he telephoned to you, and you did want to go to Albany but felt that your President, Mr. Ellis Parker Butler, should be the one to take official action. Mr. Butler referred Mr. Liveright to your secretary, Mr. Eric Schuler, who said that committee action anent who should go, would have to be taken. Friday the bill passed the Assembly as scheduled. By this time Park Commissioner Gallatin [6] had been retained to represent a small group, no part of which was the Authors' League.

At that time, as you may or may not know, Senator Cotillo was amazed that any opposition whatsoever to his bill, as shown

---

4 Beach and Burgess had been among those to sign protests against the "suppression" of The "Genius".

5 Senator Salvatore Cotillo was a co-sponsor of the bill.

6 Francis Gallatin was a partner in the law firm of Fay, Rubin & Gallatin.

by Liveright and his group, had manifested itself. He thought there was no real opposition. If you doubt this, ask Senator Cotillo. In view of this opposition, however, the Senator finally agreed to hold a public meeting on the bill in Albany on the following Wednesday, April 18th.

I have before me at this writing, a 245-page document, the minutes of this hearing, at which no member of the Authors' League was present in any official capacity, although your League through its Miss Wilcox, absolutely promised that Arthur Somers Roche, of your League, would join the delegation at Harmon-on-the-Hudson. When he did not make his appearance either in the train or in Albany, Mr. Gallatin of counsel for Mr. Liveright and others, telephoned twice to the Authors' League, where everyone seemed to be in committee meeting or outside of the premises. However, finally the League did telephone back to Mr. Gallatin that Mr. Roche at the last moment, found he had another pressing engagement. And in addition, I may add, the minutes here before me show that two of the proponents of the bill asked many questions regarding the non-presence of any official representative of your League. In other words your absence by representative, was a point and a significant one.

But to continue. In your letter and in your Authors' League *Bulletin,* you scoff at Albany delegations. Excellent! However, four members of the judiciary committee now state that the bill positively would have passed the Senate on Tuesday, April 19th, had it not been for this delegation. It is true that Mr. George Creel of your League wrote a strong and wise letter to Senator Cotillo, whom he knew personally and intimately during the war, when he was in charge of government publicity in Washington. It is also true that the Authors' League sent two telegrams to Albany. However, there were thousands of letters and telegrams sent to Albany. How much more weight than these other letters and telegrams, yours had, extending to them their proportionate credit, is not for me to say. But in spite of these letters and telegrams, Senator Cotillo and his group stuck to their guns and refused to make a motion to re-commit the bill.

And subsequently voted for the bill, thus showing the direct influence on Senator Cotillo of the Creel letter.

Mr. Liveright and Mr. T. R. Smith, his associate, and Mr. Gallatin, their counsel, Mr. Fred Hume, Secretary of the National Association of Periodical Publishers, and Mr. William A. Deford, attorney for Mr. William Randolph Hearst, made five or six trips to Albany between April 18th and May 2nd, the date on which the bill was killed. It may interest you to know that on several occasions during this time, when a tentative poll was taken, as many as twenty-four senators, were in favor of the passage of the bill, which if put to a vote at an inopportune time, would undoubtedly have been overwhelmingly passed. Some of the above mentioned gentlemen spent most of their time in Albany for three weeks, talking to legislators, and by argument, logic and persuasion, brought a sufficient number of them to see the light. Although several requests were made that they cooperate in this work, again the Authors' League took no part.

In the face of this, in your Authors' League *Bulletin* for May, I read, after the writer has troubled to take a shot at Heywood Broun for having given credit to Horace B. Liveright, where it belongs: "We are willing to bet the next good cigar that somebody gives us, that Mr. Creel and his letter and Mr. Schuler and his letter and the organization behind them, are entitled to most of the credit for the bill's demise. Here's to them!" Indeed! Then let me add my congratulations, also.

And now, much against my taste and will, Mr. Burgess, I am compelled to turn to other matters most unfortunately obtruded by yourself at this time, for they have nothing to do with the censorship propaganda one way or the other. You say, "He (I) would not need to ask an association he does not belong to, to help protect his dubious sex fiction." Really! Just when, where, how have I ever asked the Authors' League of America or any other association or person here or the world over, to help protect either my fiction or myself. Your League, as you may or may not know, invited me via Rex Beach, if I am not mistaken (circa 1914) to become a member. I declined at the time because I did

not feel the need of the services of the League and I was satisfied, of course, that it did not need me. Subsequently, at the time of the censorship attack on *The "Genius"* (1917) [7] your League, without suggestion or hint from me, invited me to appear before its executive committee, a body of six or ten members, with a view, as I understood it at the time, of supporting me in my contention that *The "Genius"* was not an immoral work. My publishers, the John Lane Company, as was well known at the time, had deserted the work because of the expense involved and I was compelled to proceed alone. However, although as result of the conference, a bare majority vote of your executive committee brought me a tentative endorsement, I learned later that the passage of this resolution by a bare majority vote was looked upon by a majority of your membership as, to put it mildly, unfortunate. The book, as they saw it, was not moral and I was not a writer to be upheld. At any rate, I received no further aid of any kind from the Authors' League, and I fought the *"Genius"* issue single handed for five years. [8] And I am still fighting it—single handed.

More recently, as you know, and again via Mr. Beach, I was invited by your League to participate in the coming conference to be held under its auspices, the purpose as was stated "to advance the artistic and cultural standards of motion pictures." I declined, as you know, and for reasons that are now of record. But I did not ask your League to do anything for me. On the contrary, you were asking me to do something for you. I merely stated that I declined to be associated with it in a minor enterprise when I felt that there was a major one to which it was blind. Hence all this pother.

But your savage and very personal comment upon me and my fiction, indicating, as it does, your own, as well as the League's

[7] 1916 was the year when the attack was launched and the controversy over it was most active.

[8] On May 31 Mencken reproached Dreiser: "With all due respect, you lie like an archbishop. Young Hersey sweated for you like a bull, and there was a critic in Baltimore who, as I recall it, laid out $300 in cash to round up the authors of the United States on your side." On June 2 Dreiser admitted being "a victim of the archepiscopal failing."

reaction to the same, leaves me but one recourse. Inadvertently, you have placed yourself in a very questionable, and to me amusing, situation. You have referred to me in various newspapers as the author of "dubious sex fiction." Very good. Granted, we will say, for the purpose of argument, anyhow, that this is true. What then, however, would you think of a writer and an executive of the Authors' League, who holding this opinion of the work of a fellow writer and broadcasting it to the world over his signature, would nevertheless find it artistically and morally possible to importune that same shameless writer on behalf of the fiction of his wife, to wit; that he read the same, and give him and his wife, his honest critical opinion in order, presumably, that said wife might feel encouraged to persevere in her artistic ventures. I am not pointing definitely to anyone. I am merely posing to you an odd question.[9]

Once more, and as I said before, bows, etc., etc.,

Theodore Dreiser

N.B. Returning to the other matter of the Clean Books League Bill, I must add that no one individual active in this matter, Mr. Liveright least of all, feels that anything he might have done, could have proved effectual without the loyal and hearty support of all the newspapers of New York City, and in particular the wonderful work of Charles Hand of the N. Y. *World*, Robert Watson of the *N. Y. American* and Denis Lynch of the *N. Y. Tribune*, all Albany representatives of their respective papers.

P. S. Personally I would like to know what is the artistic, intellectual or critical attitude of your organization to such works as: *Essays in Love and Virtue* by Havelock Ellis; *City Block* by

9 As recently as March 14 Burgess had written Dreiser:
    My dear Dreiser:
        Estelle has a story in the March *McClure*['s] that she is very desirous of having you read and give her your most brutal criticism. It is "Eleanore the Second Hand" by Estelle Loomis.
    Will you get it and let her know?
                                                    Yours sincerely,
                                                    Gelett Burgess

Waldo Frank; *Leonardo* by Sigmund Freud; *Many Marriages* by Sherwood Anderson; *Sons and Lovers* by D. H. Lawrence; *The God of Vengeance* by Sholem Asch; *The Triumph of Death* by Gabriele D'Annunzio; *Susan Lennox* by David Graham Phillips; *The Dark Flower* by John Galsworthy; *Jurgen* by James Branch Cabell; *Casanova's Homecoming* by Arthur Schnitzler; *The Revolt of the Angels* by Anatole France; *The Pretty Lady* by Arnold Bennett; *Memoirs of My Dead Life* by George Moore; *Homo Sapiens* by Artzybashev; *Nana* by Zola.

To Fremont Older
[TC]

Older, editor of the San Francisco Call and Post, *had just read* Sister Carrie *and on November 20 had asked why the book should ever have been suppressed: "What . . . so offended the 'good' people?"*

> 118 West 11th Street
> New York, [N.Y.]
> November 27, 1923

Dear Mr. Older:

I feel like beginning " 'tis a sad story, mates." [10] I finished *Sister Carrie* in the spring of 1900. It was written at 6 West 102nd Street, N. Y., by the way. I was a free-lancing magazine contributor at the time and was over-persuaded by a young literary friend of mine who was convinced that I could write a novel even when I knew that I couldn't. Once done, however, after many pains and aches, I took it to Harper and Brothers, who promptly rejected it. Then I took it to Doubleday, Page & Co. At that time Doubleday had newly parted from McClure and

---

[10] Compare Dreiser's account here with the one that emerges from the correspondence between Dreiser, Arthur Henry, Walter H. Page, and F. N. Doubleday, July 19, 1900—[after September 4, 1900].

had employed Frank Norris as a reader of manuscripts. It was Norris who first read the book. He sent for me and he told me quite enthusiastically that he thought it was a fine book, and that he was satisfied that Doubleday would be glad to publish it, but that more time for a final decision would be required. Subsequent to this, because he wanted to go on record in the matter, I presume, he wrote me a warm and very kindly letter praising the book, which I still have.

About a week or ten days later I had a letter from Walter H. Page, the late ambassador, who asked me to call. And when I came he congratulated me on the character of the work and announced that it was to be accepted for publication, and that he would send me a contract which I was to sign. Also, because he appeared to like the work very much, he announced that no pains would be spared to launch the book properly, and that,— (the glorious American press agent spirit of the day, I presume) —he was thinking of giving me a dinner, to which various literary people would be invited in order to attract attention to the work and to me. Being very young, very green, and very impressionable, this brought about very ponderous notions as to my own importance which might just as well have been allowed to rest, particularly in the light of what followed.

For this so stirred me that I decided to be about the work of another novel,—to join the one a year group, which seemed to be what was expected of me. And to this end I scraped together a little cash and retired to the country. Frank Doubleday, the head of the house, was in England at the time. In my absence he returned and hearing, as I was afterwards informed, that the book was much thought of, decided to read it or, at least, have it read for himself. Accordingly as Norris, and later William Heinemann of London, informed me, he took the book home and gave it to his wife. Being of a conventional and victorian turn, I believe—(I have always been told so)—she took a violent dislike to the book and proceeded to discourage her husband as to its publication. He in turn sent for me, and asked me to release him from the contract which had already been signed. His

statement to me was that he did not like the book and would not publish it.

My personal wish was to take the book under my arm and walk out, of course. But before his letter had arrived I had been reached by Frank Norris as well as some other individual then connected with the house,—a second reader, I believe, both of whom, for some strange reason urged me not to take the book away but to stand on the contract—of all silly things—and insist that the house publish it. Norris's argument was that once the book was published and distributed to the critics the burst of approval which was sure to follow would cause Doubleday to change his mind and decide to push the book. He even took me in to Walter Page, who announced after some discussion that he thought this course might not be inadvisable. He appeared somewhat uncertain, but since Norris was so interested, he thought it might be all right.

And for this reason, and no other, I decided to do as Norris said, feeling, however, as I did at the time, that my position was wrong—ridiculous. It was true that the summer had been allowed to go by and the date of issue was comparatively near at hand, but still I might have easily gotten the book published elsewhere if I had not been so silly as to do this. And Doubleday finding that I wished to stand by the contract, announced very savagely one day that he would publish the book but that was all that he would do. I returned to Norris, who said in substance, —"Never mind. He'll publish it. And when it comes out I'll see that all the worth-while critics are reached with it. Then, when he sees what happens he'll change. It's only his wife anyhow, and Page likes it."

When the book came out Norris did exactly as he said. He must have written many letters himself for I received many letters commenting on the work and the resulting newspaper comment was considerable. However, as Mr. Thomas McKee, who was then the legal counsel for Doubleday afterwards told me, Doubleday came to him and wanted to know how he could be made safe against a law suit in case he suppressed the book—

refused to distribute or sell any copies. And McKee advised him that he could not be made safe—that I had rights under the contract which could be enforced by me if I were so minded.[11] Nevertheless, as he told me, Doubleday stored all of the 1,000 copies printed—minus three hundred distributed by Norris—in the basement of his Union Square plant, and there they remained, except for a number abstracted, until 1905, when I, having obtained work as an editor, finally decided to buy the plates and all bound copies. In the meantime, I had carried the bound book from publisher to publisher hoping to find someone who would take it over without cost to them, but I could not find anyone. In turn Appleton's, Stokes, Scribner's, Dodd,Mead, A. S. Barnes, and others promptly rejected it. In after years I heard many curious details as to the internal commotion this particular work caused in all of the houses.

But here is an interesting bit for your private ear. At the time of my last conversation with Frank Doubleday I referred to the fact that not only Norris but Mr. Page were heartily for the book, and that Mr. Page had told me that not only would he be pleased to publish the book but that he proposed to make quite a stir about it,—in fact that he had suggested getting up a dinner for me. This seemed to irritate Doubleday not a little, and walking into the next room where Page was sitting at the time at his desk, and asking me to follow him, he said: "Page, did you say to Mr. Dreiser that you really like this book very much and that you intended to make a stir about it and give him a dinner?" And Mr. Page calmly looked me in the eye and replied, "I never said anything of the kind."

He was a man of about forty-five years of age, I should have said, at that time. I was just twenty-nine and not a little over-

11 According to Thomas H. McKee (letters to present editor [RHE], March 23, 1949, and October 12, 1956), he had suggested that Doubleday offer Dreiser the plates to buy peace. When Dreiser had refused, McKee had informed the publishers that "publish" meant the duty to manufacture the book, offer it for sale publicly, and deliver it when asked for. Doubleday, who disapproved the book on his own, quite apart from what his wife may have thought, did decline to spend money on advertising because he declined to go against popular taste and what he construed to be an adverse critical tide.

awed by editors and publishers in general. In consequence, although I resented this not a little, I merely got up and walked out. It seemed astounding to me that a man of his position would do such a thing. At the same time, I gathered from his manner and facial expression at the time that he stood not a little in awe of Doubleday. Also that finding Doubleday violently opposed to the book, he did not think it worth while to quarrel with him on this score. It was easier to dispense with me in the above manner.

Afterward—in 1901—Norris, personally, sent the book to Heinemann in London. And he published it. And it was much talked of there. Later Heinemann came to the United States and looked me up and gave me a dinner. At that dinner he told me how only the night before he and Mrs. Doubleday had actually quarreled over the book, principally because he made it plain that he considered her opinion of no great import. He stated that for some reason she appeared to be very bitter in regard to it all. Adverse critical comment, I believe.

In 1907, having by then laid aside sufficient cash for the purpose, I bought a third interest in the B. W. Dodge Company, then being organized, and, as a member of the firm, took the liberty of reissuing the book from the old plates. It sold about ten thousand copies.[12] The next year a ten thousand edition was printed by Grosset and Dunlap, and sold at fifty cents a copy.[13] In 1910, having finished *Jennie Gerhardt,* I took the book to Harper's, and that firm asked to be allowed to reissue *Sister Carrie* as a companion volume to *Jennie Gerhardt,* and at that time it sold some seven thousand copies more—at $1.50 per copy.[14] Since then it has sold continuously, the average annual sale being something over a thousand copies.

To this I set my hand and seal.

Theodore Dreiser

[12] Records in Dreiser's handwriting indicate 8,000.

[13] From 1908 to October 1, 1910, Grosset & Dunlap sold 8,178 copies.

[14] According to royalty statements, during 1912 and 1913 Harper's sold 2,247 copies, including 256 in England. Until Dreiser in 1917 contracted to let Frank Shay reprint *Sister Carrie,* Harper's sold a total of 3,284 copies.

1924

TO SHERWOOD ANDERSON
[TLS–New]

118 West 11th Street
New York, [N.Y.]
January 10, 1924

Dear Anderson:

Only the other day I received a copy of *Free and Other Stories* with your foreword in it.[1] That pleased me very much. It is so simple, straightforward and sincere, a homely, Lincolnian foreword.

Previous to that Huebsch sent me your book *Horses and Men.* In it I read "I'm a Fool," "The Sad Horn Blowers" and "The Man Who Became a Woman." (So far[.]) I liked those. But I like all of your short stories. And I liked *Many Marriages,*—very much. In *Horses and Men* I noted the several dedications or compliments. I never know quite what to say under such flowers and usually wind up by saying nothing at all. However, last year when I met you I said this man is like his books. It is his personality shining through his books that is capturing the fancy of his readers. It is a groping, artistic, sincere personality. I hold to that. And what I want to say now is that I am glad to have such a man as yourself compliment me. It means more than many compliments.

I hope we meet again and have another talk.

Theodore Dreiser

1 The Modern Library reprint.

To William C. Lengel

[TCS]

Lengel was arranging for the publication of Dreiser's "The Irish Section Foreman Who Taught Me How to Live"—an account of Dreiser's illness and recovery in 1903—in Hearst's International, *XLVI (August 1924), 20-21, 118-121.*

118 West 11th Street
[New York, N.Y.]
March 6, 1924

Dear Lengel:

My actual experience in the matter of losing and regaining my health was somewhat as follows.[2] Owing to a malignant appendix, the true condition of which I did not solve finally until 1907 my early physical condition was poor. I had stomach trouble in various forms and remained very thin until after the appendix was finally removed. Coupled with this—probably in part taking its rise from it was a kind of morbid psychology or hypochondria which was heavily accentuated by living difficulties due to the fact that beginning with 1898, or about the time I began to find myself in a literary way, I was trying to write a type of thing which few if any magazine wanted. Hence my literary pickings were small and my way for the most part thorny. Ye hall bedroom.

However, by 1900 I managed to write *Sister Carrie* and because of considerable private praise I based great hopes on that. They were dashed. What is more, I was cut off from most of the writing avenues that up to that time had been open to me. I found myself very much up against it, out of funds and what with the normal physical strain due to said appendix, I presume, I went under. I developed not only neuresthenia in a sharp form but also a lung spot as present x-rays show,—an old scar. I found

[2] The most complete account—and probably most reliable—is in Dreiser's unpublished *An Amateur Laborer.* See also Dreiser to H. L. Mencken, March 27, 1943.

myself unable to work. Hence unable to earn. And I went down and down. Too long to relate here.

However, at the bottom, when I began to think that according to Hoyle I should cash in either via the knife or the river I decided that I wouldn't. Instead, having given up the only room I had and with about twenty-five cents between me and nothing I paid my ferry passage from Brooklyn to N. Y.—don't forget that hall bedrooms are—or were—cheaper in Brooklyn than in Manhattan, checked my lorn bag at the Grand Central parcel station and went up to see the President of the New York Central R.R. My object was to convince him that he ought to give me a job out in the open air somewhere which [would] feed if not clothe me and incidentally save my life. But he would not see me, as I found. I couldn't even begin to get by a whole row of underlings. But I was told that if it was work of any kind that I wanted I might see the Superintendent of Maintenance of Way who was the man with more men under him than anyone else,— all kinds of men,—50,000 no less. He might do something for me. But when I went to see him he was out. I wrote something on a piece of paper and left it for him, saying that I was coming back and would try to see him. I then went out and with one more nickel, my last, I think, bought a loaf of bread because I wasn't sure how soon it would be before I would be able to eat again. A half of this loaf I then and there ate. Then fortified I returned, later to see the Superintendent. He was still not in. Before going into his office I laid my half loaf, well wrapped on a window ledge outside. When I came out it was gone. I took it for a bad sign. However, an hour later I returned, sent in my name and he saw me. Interesting incident here,—too long to narrate here. But I got a job. Only I had to report at Yonkers. But I had no money wherewith to get to Yonkers.

However, an idea struck me. I walked to the old Provident Loan at 4th Ave. and 23rd St. My plan was to tell the man my story and offer to hock my overcoat for a loan. However, he confused me a little by demanding to know quickly what I wanted. So I said I'm down and out. I have a job on the New York Cen-

tral if I can get to Yonkers. How much will you give on this coat. It was April and still cold. He looked at me fixedly for a moment and then said "I don't want the coat. But write me an I.O.U. for ten and I'll loan you the money." I wrote "I owe you ten" and he gave me ten. So I went to Yonkers.

The rest is a story of amusing day labor. A part of it only is in "The Mighty Rourke." [3] But I worked nine months,—first for fifteen, then for 17½ cents an hour and carfare. The Engineer of Maintenance of Way and I exchanged friendly letters from time to time. Once he stopped off to see me. Anyhow I got well and plunged into new literary difficulties,—Street and Smith, *Hampton's Magazine*,[4] the Butterick Publications and all within the space of four years.

Is this anything like what you mean.

And what do you expect to pay for this stuff.

The original sufferer.
T. D.

If it's the day-by-day details of the work itself and the particular 17½ cents per hour rooming house life, that can be easily supplied. But just assume that it has color. An article would give a mere outline of it all.

To Louise Campbell

[ALS]

Mrs. Campbell was helping prepare the manuscript of An American Tragedy *for publication.*

---

[3] In *Twelve Men.*

[4] A later title of the *Broadway Magazine*, published by Benjamin Bowles Hampton and edited by Dreiser in 1906-7.

118 West 11th Street
New York, [N.Y.]
May 2, 1924

You Very Dark Flower:

I predict that if you can combine chapters 1 & 2 in one morning you could at the same rate combine the other 28 in 14 days or less. And have only 14 chapters to re-copy all told. By the same process of elimination the whole thing might be done in a day. However I would not like to encourage you too much in that direction. After all I am writing a novel. But kidding aside. I wish you could see your way to either cutting out or at least indicating proposed cuts. If you were to retype one copy—cutting as you went it would be easier & shorter and it would assist yours truly enormously. For they are yelling for this book and there is a deal of labor ahead of me yet. Nevertheless—and thou kinst not, thou kinst not. And I'm deeply grateful for the work already done. In token of which I am sending by registered mail 1 Rolls-Royce—Tom Thumb size. Be on the lookout.

As for L.I.—if you're coming over we'll discuss that then. You might save time for it. What or no[.]

T.D

To H. L. Mencken
[ALS–NYP]

Mencken had asked Dreiser to write an article on contemporary novelists for the American Mercury.

118 West 11th Street
New York, [N.Y.]
May 12, 1924

Dear Menckhorn:

Just as soon as I get the time I'll be glad to try my hand at such an article. I hesitate to criticize the younger group even though I dislike some of their efforts, because they are working

in the right direction. I like Evelyn Scott's trend though not her bitterness. I dislike a book like *Paint* because it's pretentious—grandiose[.] The writer is thinking more of himself than he is of life. I like *Weeds*. Also Rose [5] Suckow's things. But she isn't half as significant as is Sherwood Anderson of whom I heartily approve—the most original of them all. Ben Hecht thinks more of his phrase & Ben Hecht than he does of the spectacle of life itself. So it goes in regard to many. But I'm afraid I would make many useless enemies. And I haven't any now.

Did you ever read a short story of mine entitled "The Mercy of God." It is right out of life & should have appealed to you[.] [6]

Sorry you're ill. And I hope it's nothing serious. I won't mind your dying in 1935[.] But as yet 'tis bissell geschwindt.

I have two very large rooms here now and am thinking of staging a high-brow feast. Do you & Nathan want to come.

                                   Dreiser

TO LOUISE CAMPBELL

[ALS]

                          118 West 11th Street
                          New York, [N.Y.]
                          June 30, 1924

Dear Louize:
    Done!
    I mean—I will gladly—*(joyously* would [be] more poretic)—pay said fare to & fro. (Cash in hand on delivery) Have just turned over part one to B. & L.[7] Threw out the last chapter entirely—freight car stuff. Think it adds pep so to do. My regard for you—

[5] Ruth. *Paint* (New York, 1923) is by Thomas Craven; *Weeds* (New York, 1923), by Edith Summers Kelley.
[6] Mencken printed "The 'Mercy' of God" in the *American Mercury*, II (August 1924), 457-464.
[7] Boni & Liveright, then preparing *An American Tragedy* for publication.

AS AN EDITOR—grows apace. (AS AN EDITOR) [Dreiser has, beneath these last three words, drawn some musical half-notes on a four-line "staff."]

Nevertheless, love, affection, good will, kind feelings, interest[.] Pleasant thoughts. Heaven will reward you.

T.D

I am sending chapters 30 & 31 which please condense with others[.]

To George Sterling
[TLS–SU]

On May 16, 1923, Sterling had written Dreiser: ". . . some of your cosmic gropings in Hey Rub-a-Dub *have inspired me to write an essay that (so far) I call 'Life.' It will shed light on some of the dark roads we are following. As soon as I've got it out as a pamphlet, I'll send you some copies." On June 27, 1924, he had sent Dreiser a manuscript copy, saying:*

Don't drop dead: this doesn't *have* to be read. It's only an attempt on my part to give you light in some of your intellectual gropings, to try to answer some of the questions you have put to the Darkness. I am having it printed as a pamphlet, soon, and want to dedicate it to you, so, if you're afraid that it's not the stuff you care to be godfather for, you *may* have to glance over it. This is not quite an up-to-date copy: I've made some additions in improvement. But there's nothing in them you'd object to, if you can stand for my main thesis. The printer has my only complete copy.

Of course you may not care for my altruistic ending: but I've conjured up such a cosmic nightmare that I thought it needed a little amelioration. I don't care to afflict my fellows with the full weight of my pessimism.

118 West 11th Street
New York, N. Y.
July 15, 1924

Dear Sterling:

Read your philosophy, so carefully condensed, and am impressed. How darkly you brood on the nature of the All. There was much of this in *Lilith* and your poems. Actually you are a philosopher after my own heart, so why wouldn't I be pleased and flattered to have you dedicate the little booklet to me. But just how many do you expect to interest in these spacious and solemn broodings. I wonder. Nevertheless, dedicate it to me and send me a copy for my birthday. I'll treasure it.[8]

By the clippings I see that you have been entertaining Anderson.[9] I found him most interesting and what is better from a social point of view, delightful. And I'm glad that you have been piloting him around S. F. He will enjoy it. And he probably realizes how fortunate he is to have you do it, you most hospitable and bohemian of poets. How I would like to return to S. F. I treasure every scrap of memory connected with it. And one of these days I am going to be there again. Will you have a few dinners with me?

I see your friend Abrams [10] died and I have wondered in what shape he [left his] work,—that is whether it can be pushed on to the point of recognition now that he is gone. Did your faith in his ideas and deductions remain as strong as it was when you first spoke to me about him? At your leisure, sometime, I would like to know.

Am working on a novel which will be done, pretty soon, now,—then I expect to travel some and plan now to pass through S. F. Helen is not here. She is in L. A. Jack Powys and his brother

[8] Sterling did not print it. During 1926, the year he committed suicide, he was still revising it, changing the title first to "Pleasure and Pain" and then to "Intimations of Infinity."

[9] Sherwood Anderson, who had been living in Berkeley during a visit in California.

[10] Dr. Albert Abrams. See Dreiser to Llewelyn Powys, July 19, 1921.

Llewelyn whom you sent to Abrams lives right around the corner in Patchin Place. He never had any more lung trouble.

Ah, George, would that I were in your charming city and presence this day.

Th.D.

Shall I mail this ms. back or just keep it here? [11]

To Esther McCoy
[ALS]

Miss McCoy, an undergraduate at the University of Michigan, had begun a correspondence with Dreiser in May.

118 West 11th Street
New York, [N.Y.]
September 24, 1924

Well, it's nice to get your new address but 'tis a sad tale you relate. I swear I can scarcely grasp the stupidity of men, at times, as much as I have witnessed & even been the victim of it. So called *mind* seems to me for the most part an illusion. The actions of men have little to do with it or its primary principle—logic. In fact men act & react by some system of responses—chemic or psychic which has nothing to do with what we have been dreaming of as mind. So when you tell me of your Dean & and his comments on Dostoyevsky, Turgenev—& others I see him as a chemic or psychic sign of his time—little more. And the average run of professors is but symbolic of some mass mood. They thumb over books & harvest unrelated notions. Your explanation of your un-academic mind was wonderful. But he didn't get it, of course.

But you know. I can't tie up your letters with your picture or your reported age. Is this a hoax? Are you one? And are you just kidding me? If so, I'll laugh—I'll have to. And the joke will be

11 Handwritten postscript.

on me. If you aren't, you're the oddest combination of girlhood & wisdom that has come down the track in my experience. What's the *real* answer? Are you a myth?

I got the little green cloth *Alice* & liked it for the inscription. I got your nice letter saying sure you would come down here. But now—because of the Dean—you seem to regret being so near. Why didn't you try Columbia or N.Y.U.? There's opera here. And you must tell me when you're interested to come and I'll send you your trip. Haven't been feeling so well, recently, and can't get what it is. Weary nerves, maybe. I'm very tired—too much so—& prefer to sleep—or lie about to anything else. Am thinking of going to the country for a few days—to a work-farm like Muldoon's used to be to see if I can be pulled into shape.

Meanwhile you must write me more about yourself. I've had five different annual invites from student groups in Ann Arbor to lecture before them, but I never have—or will I guess—since I can't bring myself to feel that I can lecture. Writing is my game —and that's about all—books & an occasional play.

I hope when this reaches you you'll be feeling better—liking the University better. If not—come down here & see what you can find to study here. I'd like to talk to you. All my best wishes for you[.]

T.D

To H. L. Mencken
[ALS–NYP]

"Some time ago," Mencken had written on October 31, ". . . I met Edgar Lee Masters for the first time. He struck me as a capital fellow. Why not a party for the three of us some day?"

118 West 11th Street
[New York, N.Y.]
November 6, 1924

Mine Herr:

I'm a little off Edgar Lee. Ask me not. Years ago when he had written nothing & was thinking to kill himself he was exquisite[.] It was I who persuaded him to crystallize his bitter broodings into the *Spoon River Anthology*. He sent most of them to me & I took them to Lane who rejected them. Reedy began to publish them after they were sent to me. You do not recall my writing you of him I suppose—in 1913—or 14? [12]

There is an amusing follower of yours whom you should know, Allen Benson. (Very able in a purely practical unpoetic way) He has a charming house & good car in Yonkers. Any day, on demand he will get it out & cruise us all over lovely Westchester among the lakes. I will arrange for the luncheon & dinner. Bring the walled-in Nathan & we will make a day of it—showing him a few brown November leaves[.] Benson will be delighted to put us up for the night. And these are the perfect days in which to go[.]

D

12 See Dreiser to Mencken, [after February 19, 1913]. Since Dreiser's letter of introduction was presented to Mencken, Mencken's recent meeting was probably not the first, unless the letter was never presented by Masters in person. In a reply ([after November 6, 1924]) Mencken wrote: "I remember the Masters matter very well."

1925

To Louise Campbell
[ALS]

Mrs. Campbell in Philadelphia was continuing with the editing of An American Tragedy.

118 West 11th Street
New York, [N.Y.]
January 9, 1925

Dear Louise:

I owes juice several apologies. Here they are all nicely wrapped up[.] I got your card & letters & on receipt of each I said now I'll write Louise a nice sweet note today which she will prize highly & file among her archives. (What the devil are archives?) (Hives—chives—archives) But—as you may have noticed by now I didn't. Still, Louise, I've been working hard & have had many worries. Ah, my worries. And I still have a few worries & much work. I average 8 worries to the hour, normally. Work—not so many. But I have thought of you (Thanks—Theodore) and wished I might see you. It's the Gods. But I haven't seen you. Once—between Xmas & N. Year's I was just on the verge of getting off at Philly & saying hello. And I may be over this month yet. There is an article that calleth. Soon—I want you to read Part II & tell me about it. I'm actually through with it[.] (This book will be a terrible thing) And are you ever coming this way soon—or at all. And if so—willest thou kindly look up the Author of the Song of Songs. Do. Due, due, due[.]

T. D

To Louise Campbell
[ALS]

[Brooklyn, New York]
March 12, 1925

Dear Louise:

Yes. I had a slight relapse. Went on perspiring & coughing (should that be coffing or coufing?) until yesterday, really. And very weak. Staid in bed 3 days more. But I'm up now & once more doing. The ant, the bee & myself. Have completed chapters 1 & 2 of part III. Looked over all your correcting line by line. Decided they were very intelligent and advantageous—done in the spirit of the book itself. It was fine of you to come over & help me out. Decided also that with 3 or 4 chapters re-written I could just black out your cuts & let the ms. go as you fixed—which same I'm doing[.] Hope to turn it in tomorrow. Please make a novena for the success—not the repose—of the completed book. And when you blow the $500 you won—think of how I would like to be doing it for you.

Regards—respect—undying love.

T. D

To George Sterling
[ALS–SU]

[New York, N.Y.]
July 25, 1925

Dearest Sterling:

Mencken writes that he hears you are ill in a hospital. I hate to think of you ill. You are in my private Pantheon and before you burns a sacred light. Get well. Take this five & get some one to get you a drink or two & drink with me *to you*. My regards, my compliments. All my best wishes. If ever I strike a roll I will make you a handsome present because I admire you so much.

Theodore Dreiser

I think of you always[.]

To Louise Campbell
[ALS]

Room 1516
[Guardian Life Building
Union Square
New York, N.Y.]
November 25, 1925

Dear Louise:

Here is the outline of *The Bulwark*. In a separate package I am going to deliver what has been done. Make me a copy of this. Although the book [1] is done I am very much rushed and tired. Want to come over Saturday if I can but may have to put it over. I want to see you—sure.

T. D.

To H. L. Mencken
[ALS–NYP]

In order to confirm certain details in his forthcoming An American Tragedy, *Dreiser had sought permission to visit the Sing Sing death-house. Failing, he had asked Mencken, shortly before November 14, to use his influence with the New York* World *to gain him entrance. The newspaper had successfully come to Dreiser's aid. Claiming receipt of a tip that one of the prisoners was about to make a full confession, it had secured a court order granting Dreiser access as a special reporter. But because the judge issuing the order had subsequently heard of the novel-in-progress and become suspicious, the editors had asked Dreiser to write an article that would confer sincerity on the assertions they had made before the court. When Dreiser had then set a price on his authorship, Mencken, November 28, had*

[1] *An American Tragedy.*

wired him: "World *complains that after getting you permit with great difficulty by saying you represented it you now demand money*[.] *This puts me in a nice hole indeed,*" *to which Dreiser had immediately replied:* "*The* World *lies*[.] *Your telegram is an insult*[.]" *Finally, December 1, Mencken had written:* "*The episode has a classical finish. The innocent bystander is belabored by both sides. On the one hand the* World *bawls that I let it in for trouble, and on the other hand you denounce me for libelling you. May the great pox consume you both.*"

> Hotel Empire
> Broadway at 63rd Street
> New York, [N.Y.]
> December 3, 1925

Dear H.L.M.

The ways of the Honorable—the American Press. I ask you as a favor to me to use your influence with the *World* to aid me in getting the physical lay of the Death Block at Sing Sing. You ask the *World* as a favor to you to do what it can. Presto—the *World* sees a 5000-word signed article by me—*for nothing*[—] which it can *syndicate.* But no word of this in the courteous preliminary negotiations. I am to be permitted to look into the Death Block. Incidentally—(and I wonder why at the time) I am to be permitted to interview Mr. Pantano. *But I have no need to interview Mr. Pantano!* Nevertheless I am being sent two bundles of clippings relating to the Pantano case, which I am to read. Also a court order permitting me to see him. Why—I finally & distinctly ask. Because I now know—the *World* wishes to know whether he is ready to confess—or how he feels *now.* Maybe I will be good enough to tell them—or write something. When I hear write (— *I am in the midst of packing & moving an office & an apartment*) I reply—very good—but I cannot say. I will see Mr. Pantano. If anything important appears I will report—come & talk to Mr. (The City Editor)[.] *Tell him* (not write) what I have seen. I have no time to write now. I go. See Pantano. The material is fairly interesting. I report by telephone. Presto. Enthusiastic interest.

I am to write a 5000-word article for the Sunday *World* to be used at once & *syndicated*. Excellent. But I have no time now. Such an article will take a week at least. My price will be $500. *"But we had the idea you would do it for nothing."* "You are mistaken. Nothing was said about my writing anything. I will be glad to see you—or a reporter & tell you all I heard & saw." Silence. A telegram from you *charging me* with extorting money from the *World*. Upon my word. Have I ever exacted anything from you—for a favor. The thing makes me laugh. The editors of the *World* give me a large pain[.] Why couldn't they have said in the first place—"so much for so much." At that they got a feature.[2] And as for myself—my imagination was better—(more true to the fact)—than what I saw.

My regards—

I touch the floor with my forehead.

Th. D

To Louise Campbell
[ALS]

The Ridgewood
Daytona, Florida
December 28, 1925

Dear Louise:

Here I am at Daytona and I know a lot more about Florida at this writing than I did before. Blew in here Saturday from St. Augustine. There's a charming place—historic & beautiful. The Ponce de Leon and Alcazar hotels occupy something like a long New York block. And the Spanish fort brings back the middle ages & the Inquisition[.] It's enormous.

This burg is all talk. It has the climate—most days. Saturday & Sunday were warm—delightful. Today cold. Take a tip. Don't

---

[2] An account of Dreiser's visit to Sing Sing, written about him rather than by him, had been featured on the front page of the *World*, Monday, November 30, 1925.

come down this way without winter things. You can wear white & silk undys one day but you'll need a fur coat the next. Warm at noon. Cold at night. Occasionally cloudy & rainy[.] Have had but an Xmas card from you so far. There's a *mail* crush at Jacksonville. 50 cards undistributed. Outside the P. O. at St. Augustine a large van load of mail (a moving truck full) lay unopened when I left. Insufficient help. There's a mail queu (how the hell do you spell *Cue?*) at St. Aug.—40 people long all day long. And only 1 clerk on the job. Rooms are high—there & here in any public hotel. Four to $8 per person[.] The restaurants here are nothing. I haven't found a smart one. But cars by the hundreds. (Thousands I might say) Palms, flowers, live oaks. And they're stealing all California's house designs & names "San Jose"[,] "Santa Rosa," "Santa Barbara" et cet. I'm going on down to Miami now. I'm having *mail* sent to *General Delivery, Ft. Lauderdale, Fla.* That's about 25 miles north. No more Cues if I can help it. Write me there. What about *The Financier*.[3] If you're coming down send me your address. If I leave, I'll leave a forwarding address at Ft. Lauderdale. This hotel is the best here (in the city.) It's very palmy & flowery. Ormond Beach—about a mile or so from here—(the coast of this burg) is marvellous. 27 miles long. 200 feet wide[.] Hundreds of cars race up & down the sands— as hard & smooth as concrete. I went along it yesterday & stopped at a club. Cocktails 1.50 each. But you can still get a hot dog for a dime. And a cup of coffee ditto. Wheat cakes & sausage are still 50 cents.

Yours respectfully

T. D

The real estaters! They occupy every third store and deal in clouds, rainbows & castles in the air & in Spain[.]

3 Mrs. Campbell was to revise *The Financier*. The new edition was published by Boni & Liveright in 1927.

1926

To Louise Campbell
[ALS]

[Ft. Lauderdale, Florida]
January 14, 1926

Dear Louise:

Regards—compliments: Since my last letter I've toured the entire state. Nix! Nix, Nix! I fear you would die down here. Millions of realtors and all hick-dom from Wyoming & Texas to Maine—moving in. California not a patch. Beauty here—but not to my taste,—yet. Not enough romance. I liked California oh, ever so much better. But Miami! A swarm of realtors shouting about their subdivisions. Boca Raton, Coral Gables, Indrio, Hollywood-by-the-Sea—mere realty divisions—and except for Coral Gables & Hollywood—nothing done—mere plans on paper. The bunk. And Coral Gables advertises 40 miles of water front & has no water front at all! Believe it or not[.]

But I can't stand it. It's cold. Very. *Today.* Ass that I was I left my fur coat in N. Y. I'm coming back in about 15 days to little old N. Y. where I can get warm in a hotel. Do you know of a nice studio anywhere in Philly that I could lease by the month. I may stay there for 3 months. But here—Nix. In about 10 years one might come back & find something—maybe. But if the hicks are going to fill it up with Methodist churches, rotaries, Kiwanians et cet.—Nix.

Mail addressed here up to the 20th will probably get me—or be forwarded. After that—61 W. 48th St.[1] Have had a lot of excited

---

1 The address of Boni & Liveright.

letters about *An American Tragedy*[.] Liveright wires me that it's selling well.[2] Do I see you on my return? If so I'll take *The Financier* along. I think I'll drop *The Bulwark* & finish *The Titan* trilogy[.]

T. D.

To Arthur Davison Ficke
[ALS–YU]

Las Alas Inn
Ft. Lauderdale, Florida

My permanent address
is ℅ Boni & Liveright
61 W. 48th St, N.Y.

January 14, 1926

Dear Ficke:

I am down in this real-estate madhouse known as Florida. No doubt when Ponce stepped ashore it was a flowery Paradise. Today it is a row of real estate signs (shouts!)—and oil and hot dog stands. And with the unquenchable determination of being a bigger and brighter Riviera—personally guaranteed by the middle west. Needless to say I am just leaving for the chilly & unregenerate north.

However despite many movements your letter reaches me here—at Ft. Lauderdale[,] Florida. This is 30 miles north of Miami. And it may interest you to know that it's the first letter concerning the book so far[.] Ten days before its publication I fled to avoid a deluge of knocks—and I have not seen a clipping. One telegram but now laid on my table announces that one Stuart P. Sherman has been converted.[3] Well, he's only one enemy

2 Published in December in two volumes at $5, it had by the end of the month sold 13,378 copies and brought Dreiser $11,872.02.
3 Sherman had praised it at length in the *New York Herald Tribune Books,* January 3, 1926.

less. But your letter pleases me. I don't forget your poem about
The "Genius." [4] And I've just read this "Nocturne in a Library." [5] The part that pleases me most is IV[,] "We [,the] so-
doubtful heroes of today"[.] We certainly need to take old Don as
our hero—and yet I doubt if we are worthy of him. There's something so pitifully noble about him—better than most of the illusions & dreams of this day—if any remain[.]

As for *An American Tragedy.* Well,—it's done. And that's that.
I hope it soothes some. It entertained me for many a day. It
pleases me to think that you who saw so much in *The "Genius"*
see so much in this. For though I may be a halting writer of prose
you are a good poet and you see clearly to the essentials.

Sorry to hear of your illness. I hope you get well quickly. I
earnestly do. And once you are back in Commerce Street—if I am
in N. Y. I'll look you up. And send me a poem once in a while—
as good as this one[.]

Theodore Dreiser

To H. L. Mencken
[ALS–NYP]

*When late in December 1925, en route to Florida, Dreiser had
stopped in Baltimore to visit Mencken briefly, Mencken's mother
had been critically ill. The next day she had died.*

[?New York, N.Y.]
February 2, 1926

Dear Mencken:

It was only this morning that Liveright told me of your
mother's death. Lost in the wilds of Florida I never heard. I
recall when my own mother died that the earth seemed truly

---

[4] See Dreiser to Ficke, October 17 and November 29, 1915.
[5] First published in the *Saturday Review of Literature,* I (June 20, 1925),
833-834, this poem opened Ficke's *Selected Poems* (New York, cop. 1926).

black and rent. The ground shook under me. I dreamed sad, racking dreams for years. These things are in the chemistry and the physics of this immense thing and *"wisdom"* avails not at all. Yet fortitude is exacted of us all whether we will or not. I offer— understanding.

Dreiser

To Louise Campbell
[ALS]

[Hotel Pasadena
Broadway at 61st Street
New York, N. Y.
March 17, 1926]

Where do you think *The Bulwark* ought to start? What about the start in the Real Estate office. Might not that be best—& then revert back to the marriage, etc.

No. I'm not at the Empire but at the Pasadena—61st & Broadway. I'm sticking around because they're making a play of the *Tragedy* & there's something else in the wind. Why not come over some day when you're strong for a party[.]

T.

Excuse this fierce paper. I found it here.

To Horace B. Liveright
[CC]

At a luncheon meeting with Jesse L. Lasky and Walter Wanger, to discuss the sale of the moving picture rights to An American Tragedy, *Liveright had accused Dreiser of lying and Dreiser, inviting Liveright to stand up, had thrown a cup of coffee in Liveright's face when Liveright had remained seated.*

[?Hotel Pasadena
Broadway at 61st Street
New York, N. Y.]
March 23, 1926

My dear Liveright:—

The facts connected with the *American Tragedy*-movie transaction are a little too drastic to be dismissed with a "sorry." I feel that I am entitled to a written apology based on the facts and the following are the facts.

You will recall that just before leaving your office at noon of that day [6] in order to meet Mr. Lasky and Mr. Wanger I had signed a contract with you for the dramatization by Patrick Kearney of *An American Tragedy*. A very vital part of that contract reads as follows:

> "In consideration of the fact that *An American Tragedy* is a play made from a successful novel written by Theodore Dreiser, the manager (Horace B. Liveright) agrees that the terms on the division of the motion picture rights shall be as follows: No share of the motion picture rights is to be received by the Manager, providing *that before the date of production* (of this dramatization) *the picture rights shall have been sold by Theodore Dreiser for a sum of $30,000 or more.*"

You will also recall that in a supplementary clause or letter to a four-year general publishing agreement dated Jan. 1, 1923 between yourself and myself, it is stipulated that in case you, as agent, should at any time sell or cause to be sold for dramatic or picture purposes any one of my books, you were to be entitled to a commission of ten per cent. Yet in arranging for the dramatization of this play by Mr. Kearney you were anxious to exact from me a half and latterly 30 per cent of the moving picture rights of the book before production, regardless of whether the play planned by you was a success or not. When I took exception and refused to allow that the clause above quoted was inserted.

[6] The contract was dated March 19, 1926.

Now preliminary to your remarks at the luncheon—and to which I took and still take most violent exception, I wish you to recall that before I had signed the above play contract between yourself, Mr. Kearney and myself, you were urgent in your assurances that the moving picture rights could not be sold for more than $35,000; that you had consulted with Mr. Lasky about this book; that he was not interested in the least and could not be until you had explained to him that you were about to do it as a play—whereupon he had said that only in case it should be done as a play would he be interested. Also that I should be glad to get $35,000 and that if I would accept that sum you still might be able to close with him. Afterwards, however,—but only afterwards, and after I had exacted that until the play had been produced and proved a success and not before—should you claim a third interest in the moving picture rights (feeling from the start that I could sell the book as it was without a play being made from it), and had then signed the contract, was it that you announced that what you had said concerning Lasky's attitude was not true—that, as a matter of fact, he was anxious then and there to sign for the rights without waiting for the play and that for three days he had been trying to get in touch with me (which, afterwards, Mr. Lasky himself confirmed), and that for that same day at one o'clock you had an appointment with him at the Ritz to discuss terms—yet apparently without consulting me. You also said that if I would go along and would take a determined stand in regard to such price as I might have in mind he would pay it, you were sure.

Then and then only was it that you asked what I really would take—and I said $100,000 and gave you my reasons for it, although you personally suggested $60,000. You then and there agreed that if I would go to the luncheon and affirm my determination to take no less that you were sure that Mr. Lasky would pay it. And then and then only was it—and that in the face of just having tried to get me to sell for $35,000 (and also in the face of the agreement just drawn and signed in which you waived any interest in the proposed sale price) you announced that I was "to take

care of you"; that you were sure I would; but just how you did not say. And only when I finally inquired what you meant by "take care of you" you announced that I should take 70 per cent of whatever was paid and you 30—at which—in view of the contract just signed and the sharp practice so openly confessed, I merely smiled—said nothing at all. Later, on the way over, and to your assertions that you were sure that I would take care of you, I merely replied that I would do so. But certainly not according to your proposed division since by the clause inserted in the contract before it was signed, and which is quoted above, this had been excluded. There was no such thought in my mind at any time.

Now let us be quite frank. In view of what took place in your office and that luncheon afterwards, I consider that I have been most outrageously insulted and sharply dealt with into the bargain. Neither commercially or socially have I ever lied to you. On the contrary I have been of immense commercial and literary aid to you and you know that. From time to time you have talked bravely of what you would like to do for me. I have just clearly seen what you would like to do for me. And I shall not soon forget it.

But to return to this matter of that luncheon. When at the table in the Ritz—before Mr. Lasky and Mr. Wanger—you announced that it was agreed between yourself and me that you were to have 30 per cent and I 70, you know that you were lying. I had not said so. As I explained to Mr. Lasky and Mr. Wanger then and there—it was all news to me. Next, when later you announced that I had agreed on the way over to the Ritz from your office to sell the movie rights for $60,000 and that you knew that I would double-cross you—you were lying. I had no intention of double-crossing you—was actually seeking to persuade them to pay you fifteen or twenty thousand and finally did insist on the $10,000 you are about to receive.[7] It is due to my insistence and to none other. Get that straight.

Under the circumstances the least that can be done or accepted

[7] Dreiser got $80,000.

by me is that you acknowledge these facts either in writing or by Ok-ing this letter.[8] I have done you no wrong. I have merely protected myself against you who have insisted over and over that you were seeking to protect me.

TO JOHN COWPER POWYS
[ALS]

[Hotel Pasadena
Broadway at 61st Street
New York, N.Y.]
March 24, 1926

Dear Jack

Where art thou? Walking to & fro in the earth? We are at the Hotel Pasadena 61st & Brdwy. (Telephone Columbus 7127) I have read your book.[9] (Marvellous!!) I did not read it until recently because I was so wearily enmeshed or submerged in my own that I could not. But once to it I could not let it alone and soon reached the end. I like it because it is so interpretive of your viewpoint—so full of, I will not say a brooding so much as a warrior melancholy. A group of such books would most certainly place you in a noble frame. And how about the serpentine Kansan.[10] Has she decamped or can she be lured by a Hindoo flute? Helen [11] says that she can & will get up a grand supper or

8 On March 26 Liveright, while explaining his position, said he should not have spoken that way to Dreiser, especially before strangers. Then on April 2 he added: "It's a darn shame that now that fortune is, after so many years, spilling gold into your lap, instead of merely reaffirming its pronouncement of many years, that you are our great literary figure, . . . what has happened between us should have arisen. These are the days when we should be riding around together in bandwagons with champagne flowing and beautiful slave girls fanning us with peacock feathers."

9 Probably *Ducdame* (New York, 1925).

10 Phyllis Playter, an intimate friend of Powys's, who had lived for some years in Kansas but was actually a native of Kansas City, Mo.

11 Helen Richardson.

dinner to be served in this suite and we can argue even as Rook and Hastings. Wilt come? Or, artist in Fez or Dahomey? At any rate write. A word. I would like to hear. Better to see. And Helen says the same to both of you.

I bow—
I beat my head upon the floor[.]

Dreiser

To John Cowper Powys and Phyllis Playter
[ALS]

Hotel Pasadena
Broadway at 61st Street
[New York, N.Y.]
March 26, 1926

Fairest Jack!
Oh Serpentine Kansan!

The deal is on for Tuesday night. You are to report at 6:30. If you can endure drinks—drinks you shall have. And boisterous and threatening argument—as to the temperaments & intentions of binderskeets dancing on the fifth invisible ring of Mercury. (Trans-galaxite spaces.) And the modern sphinx from the banks of the Kaw will look us all down with inscrutable and tolerant eyes.

Well, that's that. It [is] fine to know you are here & coming.
Bows—
Genuflections
Hand kissings
Profound & vigorous swaying of the smoking censer[.]

Dreiser

To Louise Campbell
[ALS]

Dreiser had gone to Europe briefly to talk with his foreign publishers, make a visit to his father's birthplace in Germany, and collect material for his final volume about Cowperwood.

Grand Hotel
Wien, [Austria]
August 27, 1926

Dear Louise:

Thanks for your several letters. Since I wrote you last I have been here & there—Stockholm, Copenhagen, Hamburg, Berlin, Prague & today I am leaving here for Buda-Pest[.] I have been intensely interested by the changes since the war. A new democratic era has set in and America is now the little tin Jesus. They want to be like America—but still not like America—themselves for instance with American improvements. But they're all nervous & times are jumpy. This city *Vienna* is real[ly] a shell. No doubt it was swift and gay in 1913. Today it's a weak shadow. The socialists are in charge. You can get a studio for 13.00 a YEAR! A morning breakfast—coffee with cream, 1 egg, rolls, marmalade, butter—costs about 16 or 17 *cents*. (The Austrian shilling (our quarter) is worth about 14 cents[.)] Only the American at the big hotels pays. The rates for a room with bath American style average $6 to $8 and all hotel service in proportion. So if you want to come over here & live cheaply take a studio. But a dyed in the wool American couldn't live here or anywhere in Europe permanently. There isn't enough doing. I haven't seen Paris yet—but I hear that even there—eventually—it palls after N. Y. Glad you're so well & strong. I'll be back around the 5th or middle of October —I think. I was about to cable you to send the revised *Financier* ms. to me at Paris but have decided to wait & clean it up finally in N. Y. When I get back I'll see you there & we can talk things over. And do them—also. From the tone of your letter!! Enclosed is the $100.

T.

1927

To Sergei Dinamov
[CC]

*The Russian critic had asked, on December 10, 1926, whether
Dreiser had been inspired by Frank Norris and Stephen Crane,
what he would propose in place of the capitalists and capitalism
that he plainly did not like, and what he thought of Soviet Russia, which Dinamov hoped Dreiser would visit.*

[?New York, N.Y.]
January 5, [1927] [1]

My dear Mr. Dinamov:

I want to thank you for your very interesting letter of December 10th, together with the article which you have written about
me. I am having the latter translated so that I may fully understand and appreciate what you have said.

I, too, regret that I was unable to come to Russia this summer,
but my time was very limited, and it was impossible to include
your country in that particular trip. I hope some day to make
an exhaustive trip to Russia. [2]

As to your questions: To say that any writer is influenced or
inspired by another is, I believe, hardly ever a conscious process.
Certainly there are temperaments which think and see in com-
patible terms—with the same understanding and sympathy for
life, and when two or more such temperaments set their thoughts

[1] Misdated 1926.
[2] Before the end of the year Dreiser had been officially invited to visit the
U.S.S.R. and gone there.

449

on paper, people immediately suspect or imagine that one is influenced by the other. But in many cases it has so happened that they were not even familiar with each other's work. In the case of Frank Norris, I first became acquainted with him and his work, when he was a reader for Doubleday-Page and Company, and I took *Sister Carrie* to them to be published. He was most enthusiastic about it, and during all the trouble which ensued from that connection, he stood steadfastly by me, so that I should say, in the strictest sense, he sponsored my first work, rather than inspired it.

And now in regard to your questions of social conditions, I can only say that I have no theories about life, or the solution of economic and political problems. Life, as I see it, is an organized process about which we can do nothing in the final analysis. Of course, science, art, commercial progress, all go to alleviate and improve and ease the material existence of humanity, and that for the great mass, is something. But there is no plan, as I believe, from Christianity down, that can be more than a theory. And dealing with man is a practical thing—not a theoretical one. Nothing can alter his emotions, his primitive and animal reactions to life. Greed, selfishness, vanity, hate, passion, love, are all inherent in the least of us, and until such are eradicated, there can be no Utopia. Each new generation, new century brings new customs, new ideas, new theories, but misery, weakness, incapacities, poverty, side by side with happiness, strength, power, wealth, always have, and no doubt, always will exist. And until that intelligence which runs this show sees fit to remould the nature of man, I think it always will be the survival of the fittest, whether in the monarchies of England, the democracies of America, or the Soviets of Russia.

In conclusion, I want to say that I know so little of the truth of conditions in Russia I would not venture an opinion as to the ultimate result, but I do hope that something fine and big and enduring does come out of it.

Sincerely yours,

To Ludwig Lewisohn
[A&CCS]

Lewisohn, on December 16, 1926, had sent Dreiser his The Case
of Mr. Crump, *saying that for the first time in his life he had
achieved morally and artistically something that warranted asking two or three of his most distinguished contemporaries for a
helping hand: ". . . if it strikes you hard, not otherwise, say so
in a letter to me with the privilege of repeating what you deem
fit to say."*

[? New York, N.Y.]
January 6, [1927] [3]

My dear Lewisohn:

Having just finished a careful reading and examination of *The
Case of Mister Crump,* and before venturing an opinion or criticism, may I ask you one or two questions—questions which I
would ask you to ponder long and seriously before you answer
me.

First, do you believe that you are far enough removed, in time,
from the actual events about which this book is written, to approach them with the clear, uncolored, unemotional viewpoint
which any writer must have when fictionizing that which lies
nearest his heart? Do you think you have brooded long enough
about those years of your life, which you have dramatized here,
to be able to set them down without bitterness, without hate,
and without distortion? Personally I don't believe you have.
When you let such lines as "That foul and treacherous old hag
would try to drag him into her own slime" (p. 420) mar the perspective of true psychologizing, you are too close to your emotions, to honestly portray any character.

Do you not think it wiser to let the years mellow your viewpoint? For it is obvious—far too obvious—that you have suffered
keenly throughout the years of your first marital existence, and

3 Misdated 1926.

that self-evident fact is embittering the tone of your work. It is hard for any of us to stand on the sidelines and view ourselves with impartiality, but is that not necessary in transcribing our temperaments to fiction? And can that fiction have real power— real force—reality itself, until we have reached that stage of objectiveness which gives us an honest, or at least unbiased, viewpoint.

Strindberg was many years removed from his suffering before he wrote *The Confessions of a Fool*—I myself waited eight years before *The "Genius"* [4]—and here you are, only barely four years away from the strife which so embittered you, trying to review it calmly. I don't think it can be done. And until it can be done, you are not qualified to attempt this kind of thing.

For instance, on p. 137, you state casually enough, "their long talks out in the open resulted in their most harmonious moods. Such hours were the only truly pleasant ones that Herbert could recall out of their long companionships, the only ones without a bitter or an acrid aftertaste." That sentence in itself seems to justify at least the incipiency of the relationship, and had you given this early phase of it its true color, as it was to you in those days, you would have at least justified yourself for the entanglement which followed. For every contact must have a first justification. You cannot deny it, and you cannot evade it. This is only a hint of the quality which I believe you will be able to infuse into the book if you will wait a little while and then rewrite it.

Of the writing, the vivid, incisive style, I have only praise—its intensity—its facility—its compelling interest, are undeniable. I quarrel only with the harshness, the vulgarity, the bitterness, the one-sided-ness,[5] the psychological astigmatism, which transfuses

4 The evidence shows that it was within a year after his difficulties on the *Delineator* that Dreiser completed the first draft of the novel that included an account of the events and that it was within five years that the final version (changed mainly in its ending) was published. William C. Lengel and other friends of Dreiser's at that time had given him advice that is almost indistinguishable from Dreiser's to Lewisohn.

5 For Dreiser's complaints about one-sidedness, see his comments in the *Literary Review of the New York Evening Post*, November 17, 1923, p. 255, and *New York Times Book Review*, December 23, 1923, p. 7.

it. This eradicated, I think the work will prove arresting to many —very many. And I would be among the first to endorse it as you now desire me to do. As it stands I cannot honestly say more than I have said in this letter & that, of course, is not what you want. If you think I am entirely wrong will you tell me just where[?]

Theodore Dreiser

To Franklin and Beatrice Booth
[ALS]

Dreiser had begun a walking trip. Booth, an artist and a fellow-Hoosier, was the illustrator of A Hoosier Holiday *(1916).*

[The Court]
Somerville, New Jersey
March 25, 1927

Heigh-ho!—you two. I did 10 miles on Wednesday [6] (late start) & 15 miles yesterday. But made a mistake & walked 5 miles in the wrong direction. Had to walk it back. Chased 3 dogs with rocks and refused 3 offers to ride. It was grey & cool—but not cool walking. All the spring things are under way. I saw a flock of 10 catbirds in some bushes along the Raritan. My route as I figure it now will be Phillipsburg, N. J.[;] Easton, Pa.; Bethlehem, Allentown, Reading[,] Lancaster, York & Gettysburg (old Pa.)[.] When I get there I'll decide what else. Regards to you both. I was so tired last night I went to bed at 7.30. Oh, the good old hay!

Dreiser

This hotel—*The Court*—is directly opposite the court house in which they tried Mrs. Mills.[7]

[6] March 23.
[7] Scarcely. Mrs. Eleanor R. Mills and the Rev. Edward W. Hall had been murdered in 1922, and it was Mrs. Hall who, with her two brothers, had been tried, in 1926.

To FRANKLIN AND BEATRICE BOOTH
[ALS]

Hotel Traylor
Hamilton at Fifteenth Street
Allentown, Pennsylvania
March 28, 1927

Dear Franklin & Beezie:

Reached here tonight at seven after doing 22 miles between here and Easton. My speed is improving and I'm feeling better already. Tomorrow I set out for Reading—36 miles & should get there Wednesday noon. Then on to Lancaster—36 miles more and I should be there by Friday or Saturday morning. That's within a few miles of the Susquehanna. I've always wanted to follow that stream—north & south. It goes South to Havre de Grace—North to Harrisburg. And the country through here is beautiful. If you should be moved to make a trip sometime try this. If you should be moved to come to Lancaster over the week end & cruise along the Susque you might wire me at Lancaster c/o Gen. Del. At any rate remember it. I like this country. It's beautiful. I don't feel like a million as yet—but say a half million—with a million as the objective. Regards to both of you[.]

Dreiser

The worst thing about this hotel is this outside envelope.[8]

8 The envelope to which he refers has a large print of the hotel occupying half of the face of the envelope, with "The Pride of Allentown" over the print.

To Carl Van Vechten
[ALS–YU]

The Berkshire
Reading, Pennsylvania
March 30, 1927

Dear Van Vechten:

There is something quite marvellous about a cross-country junket at this time of year. I have done something like 150 miles so far, have enjoyed the spring time scenery, lost weight and re-gained a jaded appetite. Besides I have moved up my speed from 10 to 20 miles a day. I shall certainly make the Blue Ridge in West Va. easily in a month—perhaps sooner. I write this merely to testify to the charm of the reality & to suggest it to others as a very beneficent experience. Try it some time. Come out & do a day with me. My route is through Lancaster[,] Pa., York, Pa.—Gettysburg[,] Pa., Hagerstown, Maryland; Martinsburg[,] Virginia & so on. I was sorry not to be able to accept your invitation that day but when I get back around May 1—maybe you will renew it. And my best regards to Fania Marianoff[.] [9]

Dreiser

An invitation is no good without an address. Allow 3 days each between each of these towns—counting Lancaster as Saturday April 2nd. Anyhow I leave forwarding addresses & B. & L.[10] would reach me.

[9] Fania Marinoff, the actress, who was Mrs. Carl Van Vechten in private life.
[10] Boni & Liveright.

To Louise Campbell

[ALS]

The George Washington
Winchester, Virginia
April 10, 1927

Dear Louise:

Porgy [11] arrived at Martinsburg—and I read it at a sitting. It's one of the few American novels I really like because for once it is colorful & revealing. We know so little about the intimate life of the blacks & this somehow conveys a breath of it—and the fine natural drama of life itself. It's a book to keep I think.

Since Lancaster—well, miles and miles. I walked 27 in one day to York. Then 23—out of 32—the next to Gettysburg. Then a lazy 10—to Emmitsburg because I stopped to go over the Battlefield. Then 32 to Hagerstown, 21 to Martinsburg, 23 to here & so it goes. This morning I am off for Woodstock—30 miles away and then New Market, Pa. This is the Shenandoah Valley. Along the road I go today Sheridan rode that alleged ride. The signs say so. Missed you after the train pulled out much—but will see you in N. Y. one of these days soon. It has rained & snowed days at a time but today is perfect. And so was yesterday.

Love
T.D

Don't miss the enclosed check[.]

11 The novel by DuBose Heyward (New York, cop. 1925).

To Franklin and Beatrice Booth
[ALS]

The George Washington
Winchester, Virginia
April 11, 1927

Dear Booths:

That interesting razor came at Hagerstown, but I was so knocked out there by a 32 mile walk that I gave over the idea of acknowledging it there. Yesterday for the first time I used it and like it very much. It seems more pliable than the Gillette. . . . .[12] Missed you two greatly after you left. Walked all day in the rain to York & the next day to Gettysburg. Since then have been moving down the Shenandoah Valley—Hagerstown to here[.] This morning I start for Woodstock[.] Saturday—at Martinsburg it snowed all day—but yesterday was perfect—and this morning from this hotel window the Garden of Eden *as I last saw it* is brought to mind. I have only a few more towns to go and then I'm through. But I won't be sorry to get back to New York for I like that as much in the spring as any other place I have seen.

When you two mix a good cocktail think of me[.]

Dreiser

To Jack Wilgus
[CC]

[? New York, N.Y.]
April 20, 1927

My dear Mr. Wilgus:

I found your letter of April 6th most interesting. And in so far as it is possible to explain the genesis of any creative idea, I shall be glad to tell you how *An American Tragedy* came to be.

---

12 Dreiser's punctuation.

I had long brooded upon the story, for it seemed to me not only to include every phase of our national life—politics, society, religion, business, sex—but it was a story so common to every boy reared in the smaller towns of America. It seemed so truly a story of what life does to the individual—and how impotent the individual is against such forces. My purpose was not to moralize —God forbid—but to give, if possible, a background and a psychology of reality which would somehow explain, if not condone, how such murders happen—and they have happened with surprising frequency in America as long as I can remember. I don't know what more to say to you, but I do wish you much luck.

Very truly yours,

To Dwight Sidney Gaffney
[A&CC]

[? New York, N.Y.]
May 22, 1927

Dear Mr. Gaffney:

I regret very much that the stress of other matters has caused such a long delay in answering your letter. Then too, there was the natural delay of going over your interesting pamphlet and poems. Unfortunately, even now I lack the time to go into any special details, but I will frankly say that you apparently have the ability to write and a vocabulary to express yourself, that is quite unusual for one of your age.

You have asked me to answer several questions which seem important to you in your work and I will give you my thoughts on these matters, but naturally they will have to be brief and to the point.

You desire advice as to whether you should continue your education. I believe it would be better to do so, if possible, and then pursue your cherished ambitions. As a matter of policy, I

do not care to criticize the literary efforts of anyone and espe-cially those just beginning, but having your best interest at heart, I will say it is apparent that the exuberance and ardor of your diction indicates a lack of maturity and of actual contact with realities. Your pamphlet is well written and seems to express your earnestness. It also contains a high poetic truth, not as yet sufficiently clearly or forcibly expressed by you. But this subject meditated upon and then restated by you should prove of real value and charm. The subject about which you write will always be a matter of general debate and no doubt interpreted by indi-viduals according to their own ideas and desires.

You refer to your lack of interest in journalism. I question the intrinsic value of a smattering knowledge of this, or any subject. But the value of a thorough knowledge of the fundamental prin-ciples of journalism, to a person seriously considering the avoca-tion of writing, cannot be overemphasized. A journalist sees many aspects of life and finds his experiences in that field a valu-able adjunct to the correct expression of thought. Many of our most eminent authors have been journalists.

The criticism of your college professors, that you are too young to write on the subjects on which you have written, seems to have embittered you unduly. It should not. Your faith in your own ideas & dreams must not waver. All writers are, and must expect to be, criticized.

Since you feel this decided bent towards literature and that it is a part of you, no doubt you will keep on writing, and should for I think you have—or will have—presently something to say. The fact that thousands of writers never reach the heights of their ambitions is neither here nor there. You may[.]

Lastly, I am interested enough in what you have sent me to wish you a real and genuine success.

Sincerely yours,

P. S. I am returning the poems you sent me.

To Franklin and Beatrice Booth
[AL]

The Booths were then in Carmel, Indiana.

[New York, N.Y.]
June 24, 1927

A plug of tobacco!
A plug of tobacco!
To bacco!
To bacco!
Plug—
Plug!
Yet what would a plug want with—?
No, No.
Or tobacco with a—?
No, No.
Mystery—
More mystery—
My Brain!
My Brain!

To chew—?
To chew—?
Tooch—ooo!
Chew-chew!!!
To chew-chew!!!
Ha, Ha!
To choo-choo!
But where?
Ha—
Mystery—
Yet on the trail—maybe.
Or—
A plug chew?

A plug choo-choos?!!
No, no.
Yet—
A plug chews.
A plug chews what?
What could a plug choose?
Oh! Ouch!
A plug chews—!
A plug chews!
A plug chooses.
A plug chooses to choo-choo!
Oh-oh!
God—
Help!
Plug—
Ug!
g.
Oh—g.
!!!!+×—*psst—f353—!!?! [13]

To Franklin and Beatrice Booth
[AL]

[New York, N.Y.]
June 25, 1927

By rights a spittoon should have come with that plug.

To Franklin and Beatrice Booth
[ALS]

Dreiser was on his way to visit the U.S.S.R. at the invitation and expense of the Soviet government.

[13] The end of this line contains a wide splatter of lines.

Hotel Adlon
Unter den Linden 1 am Pariser Platze
Berlin W., [Germany]
October 26, 1927

Dear Booth & Beatrice:

Thanks to the Bolsheviki and the downtrodden workingman—
here I am and in a suite. I'd really like to know how a moujik
would take the news that a critical guy was smashing around at
his expense at the Adlon. And with no other intention than to
look him over. And riding de luxe here and there. However,
<in> Russia—and once out of the hands of these government
agents I will prove more simple—even to the extent of riding
third class with him & sleeping on a mat[.] I thought that up
here I would find cold weather but they tell me that almost summer weather has reigned so far. And that even in Moscow where
they eat ice & snow for breakfast it is still pleasant. God must
have arranged this. I may be able to discard my fur coat which
weighs like a scale.

I hope both of you are well. Being led here & there by individuals whom one doesn't know & discussing theories of Government & life has its drawbacks & contrasts poorly with the happy
intimacies of those you are closest to in your daily life. *Worse,*
travel is really hard work[.] This business of changing—soften it
up as much as one will,—is a steady pull on the strength & the
nerves. I had group companionship over on the boat [14]—Ben
Huebsch, the publisher, Judge Muller of Holland,[15] Max Ernst [16]
(the N. Y. Lawyer & his wife)[,] Diego Rivera, the Mexican
painter & others, but still I was under a strain. Muller, Rivera,
Huebsch came as far as Paris. Rivera & Huebsch are here with
me in Berlin, but from here on I lose both, & take up with strangers. It doesn't cheer me much and I wish I were strolling into
your place instead. Since that cannot be I hope the place will

14 The *S.S. Mauretania,* which had left New York, October 19.
15 Judge Nicholas Muller, a criminologist with particular interest in children's
misbehavior.
16 Morris L. Ernst.

still be there when I return. My address, in case you want to use it at any time is care the *Torgovo-Promyshlenny Bank,* Moscow, U.S.S.R. I hear it takes about 2 weeks for a letter to come through. And much of the time I will not be in Moscow or Leningrad either. But if you take a notion to drop a line—either of you—it will cheer up yours humbly

Dreiser

Regards to the composer[.]

To Louise Campbell
[ALS]

Hotel Adlon
Unter den Linden 1 am Pariser Platze
Berlin W., [Germany]
October 28, 1927

Dear Louise:

Regar-hards! I'm sick in bed in that dear Adlon—but I'll be better tomorrow I hope. The doctor just left. The enclosed [17] will give you a little idea of what's doing. I was met by a delegation of these German Moscovites last night and addressed—etc. Flowers for your Uncle Dudley among other small incidents. Leave Sunday—or Monday—(if I'm up) for Moscow. (Two long days!) What I wish to say is shortly I will mail you an article which I agreed to write for Max Elser of the Metropolitan Syndicate of N.Y.[18] It's not so good—but you shape it up.—(You ought to know) & send one copy to him & keep one copy for me.

[17] A clipping from the Paris edition of the *New York Herald,* October 27, 1927, headed "Theodore Dreiser Here on Way/To Study Results of Sovietism" and telling of his plans, his opinions of Mencken and Upton Sinclair, and his view of the American attitude toward religion.

[18] "Dreiser Analyzes Rebellion of Women" (February 5, 1928) was part of a series of articles on America under the general heading *Love, Women and Marriage* printed in such papers as the *New York American, San Francisco Examiner, Dallas Morning News,* and *Oregonian* between April 10, 1927, and March 11, 1928.

And please do a good job. It's on the restlessness of women these days. Incidentally send me a few kind thoughts up there in the snow. All I'll have is Vodka and Borscht I fear—maybe cabbage soup. But that's not enough, as you know. This meeting people though—that's why I'm sick this day. And of course Berlin bores me. But Paris on Wednesday was delightful—a perfect fall day. And how many people I saw.

So long. Love & skisses

The Nubian

Sinclair Lewis & Ben Huebsch are due here to sit & smoke I suppose at 9:30[.]

To Franklin and Beatrice Booth
[ALS]

Grand Hôtel
place du Revolution No. ½
Moscow, [U.S.S.R.]
November 23, 1927

Dear Booth and Beatrice:

Here it is Nov. 23—and I am still in Moscow. It is due to the tempo of official life here. I am [interviewing] [19] the Russian chiefs [20] and it takes time. However by Tuesday next I hope to move,—first to Leningrad, next to Novgorod on the Volga; next to Omsk, Novosibirsk and Kuzbas in Siberia; then back to the Volga and down it to Samara, Saratov to Tiflis in Georgia, Baku in Aserbistan [21] and Batum. The last two are (Baku) on the Caspian and (Batum) on the Black Seas. Then I cross to the Crimea (Sevastopol)[,] Odessa, Kiev, and Kharkov as well as the Don Basin—now a great steel center. From there I either return to

---

[19] Dreiser's text reads "interfering."
[20] Nikolai I. Bukharin and various lesser commissars.
[21] Dreiser's transcription of "Azerbaidzhan."

Moscow & so Berlin—or through Odessa to Constantinople and take the transcontinental to Paris. Expect to leave Odessa by Jan. 10—Paris or London by Jan. 20th for New York. Life here is very interesting to me—more interesting really than in most European capitals[.] To see communism work is an experience. And to see the hundred or more Asiatic types drifting in and out of this burg is still more amazing. I never weary looking at them. Saturday night I went to Tolstoy's old home Yasnaya Polyana— about 130 miles south of here. It was really fascinating. They— (his daughter [22] & niece as well as the villagers) were commemo- rating the 17th year of his passing. I stood by his grave & heard the peasants sing "There is no Death." He lies among tall pines. No stone or mark of any kind. There was deep snow but they had covered the grave with evergreen & strewn it with flowers. I liked their voices. All Russians love to sing in chorus & they achieve a natural harmony. All soldiers—whole regiments—sing as they march. After the ceremonies I spent the day with his daughter & niece seeing the school, hospital, agricultural farm etc. which they conduct. And all his old keepsakes. Also I heard his voice on the phonograph in English, German & Russian. Finally they took me in a Russian sleigh eight miles in order to make a fast train. It was bitter cold and I was bundled up in a Shuba which is another name for eight blankets made into a great coat. Still I was cold. But I peeped out now & then at ham- lets, wastes of snow, a modern village and finally at Tula—a city of 200,000 with electric lights, street cars, a great depot, buses, etc. So I began to see how things are changing for it is more modern than Moscow;—more like a city in America really. It has been my first venture out so far. But soon as I say I am going. The Government publishing house here has just taken over all my books (six are already published) and Stanislavsky of the Moscow Art Theatre is taking *An American Tragedy* and *The Hand of the Potter*. We have become good friends.[23]

Well—so much for now. I have only five minutes in which to

22 Alexandra Lvovna.
23 They had met on the afternoon of November 19 at the Theatre.

dress. But I wouldn't trade my trip here for any previous experience. It is new and I have gotten a light on certain things which are not visible in America. The difference in the two lands & temperaments make them invisible there.

All my best thoughts to both of you[.]
Dreiser

My address here is care
Torgovo—Promyshlenny Bank[.]
It will forward all mail[.]

1928

To George T. Bye

[CC]

Bye, an agent who often handled Dreiser's contributions to periodicals, had written on May 31 that Frank Phelan, a staff writer for the New York World, *wished to interview Dreiser on the subject of "Modern Life."*

> [200 West 57th Street
> New York, N.Y.]
> June 6, 1928

Dear Mr. Bye:

In regard to the request for an interview by Phelan of the New York *World* I have this to offer. To me the American newspaper is intellectually bankrupt. Apparently downright constructive thought on any topic is not what they want. They are after feature stunts; the playing up of a personality as they would some exotic animal. I have not the least interest in that sort of thing and for the last year have refused interviews. If it were possible to conceive of some American newspaper being interested in a radical discussion of money or religion or government, and who would dare to publish independent of the Catholic Church, politics, Wall Street, and the business office such an article[,] I would be interested. But I know from long experience it is too much to hope for.

I note the letter from Andrew H. Dakers of April 24th.[1] Do

---

[1] Dakers was a British literary agent, who hoped to represent Dreiser in London, with a view to establishing a newspaper feature there for him. However, Dakers retired from his agency in 1929 and does not recall whether he was instrumental in placing Dreiser's lone contribution to the *Daily Express*, January 23, 1930, one of the essays in the symposium *Divorce as I See It*. The symposium was reprinted in book form in both New York and London, 1930.

you still feel that the *Daily Express* would be interested in the article described? If so I think I might prepare it.

Very sincerely,

To Louise Campbell
[AL]

Upon his arrival home in February Dreiser had asked Mrs. Campbell to help anew with his work, beginning with Dreiser Looks at Russia.

200 West 57th Street
[New York, N.Y.]
June 21, 1928

Dear Louise:

The magnus opus arrived & I am reading & revising. So far I have revised five chapters and am now on my sixth[.] Much re-typing is right ahead of you. I like what you have done—particularly in setting forth new chapters and am taking those and building them up. However, the G.P.U. stuff will have to be set off by itself as a separate chapter[.] It concerns a kind of thing which the Russians love—terrorism & will have to have the psychology of that discanted on. It is all over Russia[,] fear of the secret police.

Also I feel that a new arrangement of the chapters should be made. On the enclosed slip I am showing you. Apart from this I think of nothing to change. The work so far as I have gone is supremely intelligent. The only thing I can think of is this— that you should be over here. There is so much to do & no one but you appears to be able to do it for me.

How is mother dear? I hope no more scares. And how about moving up to Mt. Kisco? Don't forget that as soon as this is over the entire *Gallery of Women* is to be dumped on your table for final examination & revision—16 separate studies. They have to

be ready by September 15th[.] So don't plan any distant trips until that is over[.]

I now eat 1 meal a day & weigh—stripped 178. Have no trouble in holding that[.] [2]

Why not come over next week and bring my note book? [3]

To Franklin and Beatrice Booth
[ALS]

Dreiser was at the Woods Hole Marine Biological Laboratory.

[Woods Hole, Massachusetts]
July 7, 1928

Dear Booth and Bee:

Cape Cod is the exquisite sea place[.] It is so much a part of the ocean that the weather changes as it does at sea—sunshine, clouds, fog, rain[,] moonlight all in the same 24 hours. And the air is salty and light as in England and San Francisco. I am amazed at the road improvement here—good roads everywhere. And smart little towns, hotels, beaches. I have been wishing this last week that we three might make a tour of some different sort of place—Maine or the Adirondacks or Nova Scotia[.] Also I have been wishing that in my absence you two would go up & use the cabin.[4] It is so beautiful there. If you do—and please do—write & tell me if the pond is done, if they have put the gravel on the bottom, as agreed and the first log cabin is done. If so see that a good strong lock has been put on it—also copper screens in the windows & door. Then try it out to see how it works.

I am hard at work here extracting information from biologists. There are some 283—big & little—and I have uncorked about 12. But I am seizing on special cases. They are all mecha-

2 This paragraph and the final one are marginal notes.
3 Probably the journal of his trip to the U.S.S.R.
4 At "Iroki," Dreiser's place in Mt. Kisco, N. Y.

nists & in so far as life is concerned hopeless[.] It is a good show—
sometimes—but ends for man here[.]

The other night we motored through Cotuit—and I looked
for the "First Church of Christ Scientist"—but didn't find it.⁵
Then I tried *Mashpee*. Finally we wound up at a charming restaurant in Hyannis—which lovely place I commend to you both.

Today all is bright here—blue waters, white gulls, lovely sandy
beaches. I have room 225 in the Marine Biological Laboratory
from the windows of which I can see a part of this charming
fishing town harbor. Drop me a line there. And let me say that
even here I still miss the B & Bee—or F & B as you will restaurant
—the best meals in N. Y. I've been very busy reading proofs on
my Russian book, looking through microscopes, interviewing
biologists, swimming, driving[,] eating—and all mostly in a hurry.
But this salt air! Try it sometime—or let's us try it. There used
to be billions of mosquitoes here but now there appear to be
scarcely any. Increase in population I think. The whole Cape
is being turned into a charming salty seaside paradise[.]

Dreiser

Do use the cottage[.]

To Franklin and Beatrice Booth
[ALS]

Room 225
Marine Biological Laboratory
[Woods Hole, Massachusetts]
July 16, 1928

Dear Beatrice and Franklin:

Thanks for the two pictures.⁶ They arrived in time. And I
have turned one of them in. But in spite of the delightful fogs

---

⁵ Franklin Booth was a Christian Scientist.

⁶ Dreiser had requested for the Laboratory newspaper *(The Collecting Net)*
photographs Mrs. Booth had made.

& mists of this place and the fairyland which lies just below the microscope in all of these rooms I am planning to leave here next Monday—or *Tuesday* [7] rather—arriving at Mt. Kisco Tuesday night. Wednesday I expect to run down to New York & if you two are not busy that evening would like to take you to dinner. I wish I might bring a microscope & a biologist and his material. I have met and listened to and cross-examined some fifty men,—a fascinating group. They are not all mechanists, tell Franklin. Some are agnostics, some mystics, some of a reverent and even semi-religious turn. Personally I am awed and so amazed by the processes visible to the eye that I grow decidedly reverent.

I hope you two go to the cottage this coming week-end. Noyes, the contractor tells me that coarse sand is best for the bottom of the pool as it will not let the mud through as gravel would. So coarse sand is to be put in this week. Try the place—you two. Regards to both of you.

Dreiser

I've had six long distance calls from New York here at the Laboratory in one week.

To Michael Gold

[P–*New York World-Telegram,* September 25, 1936, p. 23]

Gold, editor of the New Masses, *had asked Dreiser to recommend him for a Guggenheim fellowship and sent him two selections printed in the magazine from his novel in progress,* Jews without Money: *"On a Section Gang," IV (July 1928), 8-9, and "The Gangster's Mother," IV (August 1928), 3-6.*

[7] July 24.

[200 West 57th Street
New York, N.Y.]
August 7, 1928

My Dear Gold:—

I read your two contributions to the *New Masses* and found them very interesting. Personally, I never can see Protest as literature and in these two Studies while I find some Protest, I find more of that detached observation of reality which no one with Protest only as a reason for writing can achieve. I feel that you are more the Artist than the Social Advocate and should see where your fine gift lies. Now as to the Guggenheim Foundation Letter. Assuming that I will write a letter what should it say— that you cannot write and that it would be a crime to waste money on you? Let me know.

Theodore Dreiser

What particular thing is it that you hope to do that the Guggenheim Foundation might approve of? Supposing you write your own letter and let me see it.

To Louise Campbell

[ALS]

Mrs. Campbell was editing the manuscript of This Madness, *to be published as a serial in* Hearst's International-Cosmopolitan, *February-July 1929.*

200 West 57th Street
New York, [N.Y.]
August 31, 1928

Dear Louise:

I'm sorry to scratch up this grand work of yours in this ruthless fashion, but so it is. The sketch will be the better for it. Besides I note that you grow more & more—not moral but publicly squeamish—a bad sign. I fear the worst. You will rejoin the church. In God's name why cut out the little youthful stuff in

wretched family parlor. I'll put it all back in the galleys. Fie!
Fie! Shame! Shame! That life zest & its courage should so depart
from one. Oh, how reducing to my spirits.

Otherwise good work and today came the additional bit of
"Sidonie." [8] I'll clean it all up & forward very presently, maybe
Monday or Tuesday.

Am sending this to 135 North Bartram Ave. But if you're gone
no doubt it will be sent on to 4730 Warrington, Phila.

Love,
T.D

To Michael Gold
[TLS–RHE]

Dreiser in a statement of belief for the Bookman, *LXVIII (September 1928), 25, had written:*

I can make no comment on my work or my life that holds either
interest or import for me. Nor can I imagine any explanation or
interpretation of any life, my own included, that would be either
true—or important, if true. Life is to me too much a welter and
play of inscrutable forces to permit, in my case at least, any significant comment. . . . In short I catch no meaning from all I have
seen, and pass quite as I came, confused and dismayed.

*Acknowledging Dreiser's letter of August 7 Gold had commented
on this credo:*

I have always worried over your philosophy because it makes a
revolutionary philosophy seem trivial. But the more I think about
you & your writings the more I feel your confusion and pessimism
comes from a very profound and honest *social pity* & without letting
this emotion work fully & consciously—that is, working for it, finding
social reforms to express it—one must feel as bad as if one consistently repressed sex or other desires. . . . Your Protestant individ-

[8] Part 3 of *This Madness: Hearst's International-Cosmopolitan*, LXXXVI (June
1929), 83-87, 156-168; LXXXVII (July 1929), 86-87, 179-186. Part 1 was "Aglaia,"
LXXXVI (February 1929), 22-27, 192-203; (March 1929), 44-47, 160-166; Part 2,
"Elizabeth," LXXXVI (April 1929), 81-85, 117-120; (May 1929), 80-83, 146-154.

ualism has created a conflict with it inside you & that is what projects itself as "confusion" in your credo. . . . But is the artist only a wonderful & special mirror of nature—& nothing more? That's what your credo implies but I don't think that is the whole truth about the artist-man. I think his measure of creation always lay in the special twist & improvement he lent nature.

> 200 West 57th Street
> [New York, N.Y.]
> September 19, 1928

My dear Mr. Gold:—

The trouble with you and all reformers for that matter is that you regard humanity—(the human race) as a very kindly and much imposed upon organism—not only exteriorly as to nature, but interiorly as to fractions or divisions of its membership—the strong against the weak, say, or the rich against the poor. As a matter of fact humanity as a whole—the human race, no less, is a predatory organism, fighting and killing to not only save but advance and even luxuriate itself at the expense of and as against every other type of organism. If you don't believe it walk to the nearest butcher shop or visit the Chicago stockyards.

And nature's way in a bad situation is by no means, as you say, to do the most hopeful—if by that you mean helpful or kindly thing. If you mean the self-helpful thing, however cruel it may be, I agree. Witness war—the late war; the brutal fights between capital and labor—or rival trade organizations. Again in Russia the ruthless suppression of individualism by communism is a fair illustration of what I mean—peace and prosperity under a gun.

In short my pessimism springs not only from pity for the minute individual attempting to cope with so huge and difficult a thing as life but also from the obvious futility of man as anything but a pleasure seeking fly. And in the face of a few thousand years—let alone eternity—what are either fame or achievement? And as for security or luxury for which so many strive, how much do they avail against chance and change and how many have or

maintain them for so long as ten years, let alone a lifetime. And how do they avail against mental or physical misery?

Power? Another asinine illusion. A form of slavery. The strong toiling for the weak and incompetent—slaving for means in order to aid them. As for benefiting a race that lives by murder of weaker things—well it may be a glorious aim. I don't know. If I had faith to believe that man could or would ultimately change the character of nature—I might applaud. But can he? Has he? Where is the evidence. The time to enthuse will be when you can produce data to show that man is now modifying or ever has the outstanding cruelties of the creative impulse. So far I have come upon no convincing evidence.

Certainly I pity the individual when he is weak, defeated, put upon. But I also cease to pity him when I find him strong, selfish, vain, cruel or brutal. And I note that to make him into either requires no more than the addition or subtraction of a very little material success—so little that it is pathetic, really. Furthermore, only the outside pressure of nature—as cruel and as indifferent as himself—appears to enforce on him (man) the necessary humbleness or sense of equation or balance, without which he is unable to function socially at all.

In the face of this a certain amount of philosophic pessimism is certainly in order. But that actually from day to day in my ordinary working life I am made at all miserable by the thought of this I deny. Life has used me personally well enough and continues to do so. It is only that philosophically I refuse to substitute illusion for what I can easily spy out for myself.

Regards—
Theodore Dreiser

To Sergei Dinamov

[CC]

Dinamov had written Dreiser, September 24, that Gosizdat would publish A Gallery of Women *and would surely pay and that*

Dreiser should send his manuscript or proofs either to him or direct to them.

> 200 West 57th Street
> New York, [N.Y.]
> October 14, 1928

Dear Dinamov:

You are very flattering. I don't know whether it will sound very vain if I say that I hope you are right. I am glad you received the books safely. I assume that the only things of mine that you haven't in your possession are *Plays of the Natural and the Supernatural, The Hand of the Potter, Twelve Men* and *The Color of a Great City*. If I am wrong let me know and I will send you anything else that you haven't.

If you really want to do me a real service though, you will clear up my business relations with Gosizdat. As you know, I made a contract with him, which is on file with that authors' union there in Moscow. You can see it at any time you please or, I suppose, at Gosizdat. According to that they were to take over most of my books—new and old—and pay me an advance against each one as issued. Furthermore, they were to take over any new thing that I might write, on the same terms. The only exception was to be *A Gallery of Women,* against which, on receipt of the manuscript, they were to pay $1,000.00. I mention this particularly because the manuscript is now ready and can be forwarded on order from you, but before doing so I would like to know how they feel now about this relationship. You know these Russians and their ways, how commercially careless they are. For instance, according to my contract, I should have had a July statement before this but I have not received a statement of any kind and by January 1st there will be another statement due, and unless you do something about it, it is not very likely that I shall receive that either. Therefore I feel that it is important that you or someone over there look into this matter for me and straighten it all out. Awaken them to the fact that they are really doing business with me, and persuade them to act promptly in

regard to their obligations as they fall due, otherwise I certainly am not willing to turn over any new works as they shall be completed.

Judging from letters that I am receiving, the books must be making a fair stir. If such is the case, Gosizdat should enter upon the work of publishing all of my books with a clear understanding of what it implies. For instance, in issuing *The Financier* and *The Titan* they should understand that these are two parts of a trilogy which is still to be completed. Part three is to be called *The Stoic,* and I am about to begin work on that now. It should be ready in a year at the most. When it is ready, and if by that time Gosizdat shall have published *The Financier* and *The Titan,* it should be announced as the third volume of that series and then the whole series sold as one, that is, a three-volume set. That is the way it is being done in Germany and that is the way it is being done in England and there is no reason why the State Publishing Company shouldn't do the thing as intelligently in Russia.

There is another set which is already partly done and which should be looked into and handled as a set as well as per volume. This set is to be called *A History of Myself* and will consist, when completed, of four or more volumes. You already have in your possession Volume II of this set. It is called *A Book about Myself.* The real title of it, however, is and should be *Newspaper Days.* It was so entitled at first but Boni & Liveright, who issued it over here without waiting for Volume I or the rest of the set, insisted on changing the title to *A Book about Myself.* However, Volume I of this history of myself is now done and ready for publication. It is entitled *Dawn* and should precede the publication of *Newspaper Days* or *A Book about Myself.* As soon as I am through with *The Stoic* I propose to write Volume III of this history of myself and to entitle it *Literary Experiences.* There may be even two volumes of *Literary Experiences,* but certainly one. It is therefore most important, as I see it, that Gosizdat should see this series as a whole and not assume that *A*

Book about Myself is a separate work but only as Volume II of this series.

If you understand this and can cause Gosizdat to do the same, I wish you would take up this idea of this complete set in volume order with them and write me how they feel about it. All told and when completed it will make as clear and intimate a picture of the more or less allegorical development of America since 1875 as is likely to come out of this country in my day. Being my personal reactions to the American scene from that time on, it will be much more of a painting than a history,—the actual mentality and movement of the country. As that I should think it would be of the greatest importance to Russian readers and probably have a wide sale. However, as I say, I am not willing, unless this matter of my relations with Gosizdat is very clearly defined and looked after by someone, to send on Volume I, which is now ready, or Volume III when it is completed. Hence my solicitude for your help in this matter. You said you would like to be my agent and I most certainly would like to have you represent me over there. If you still feel that way I wish you would give this situation of mine your earnest attention and let me know the result as soon as possible. Meantime I need not reassure you as to my deep personal feeling for you. I think you take your emotional disappointments too keenly. You are a very big man, Sergei, and, unless I miss my guess, you are going to be called to some position of importance under your Government. Any career of real importance is more or less of a sacrifice. You have suffered not a little already, and before you achieve what you are probably called on to achieve you will suffer a lot more. It is the only way that we learn. But there are big things ahead of you and that intellectually and spiritually you will be rewarded I haven't any doubt at all, in fact, I am absolutely sure.

If at any time you want a vacation and can get out of Russia and into the United States, come over and stay with me, and if you want to lecture I will see that you are provided with the opportunity to lecture anywhere you please in this country.

Affectionately,

To William C. Lengel
[AC]

[200 West 57th Street
New York, N.Y.
October 16, 1928]

Dear Lengel:

My books including *A Gallery of Women,* which is now ready, number 19. Printing *A Gallery of Women* as two volumes—that makes 20 volumes all told.[9] There is also ready for publication *Dawn*—which is Volume one of *A History of Myself.* This is to be a four or five-volume history of which *A Book about Myself*—(the proper title of which is *Newspaper Days)* is volume II. Two additional volumes in this series will be entitled *Literary Experiences,*—1 and 2.

Then there will be *The Stoic*—volume III of the Cowperwood Trilogy.

Also *The Bulwark.*

Altogether a set—when done of 25 volumes[.]

Now I have never been satisfied [   ] [10] is the man to handle the set whenever it is ready and that should be reasonably soon. He never was the publisher of my choice. I came to him by accident and after John Lane had refused to continue *The "Genius"* or publish *The Hand of the Potter.* Even Liveright refused to publish that, at first. In short I am where I am without much aid from any publisher and I am because of a special kind of contract drawn with Liveright at the time I went there free to go if not exactly now—and I can even arrange to do that,[—]then in three years from this date[.]

The reason I am writing this to you is that I would like a good offer from the *Cosmopolitan* Book Corporation and the reason I say a good offer is because I already have two offers from less financially if not editorially famous concerns. I refer to

---

[9] If *An American Tragedy,* also originally printed as two volumes, is similarly counted, the total should be twenty-one volumes.

[10] Name omitted by Dreiser.

Harper & Brothers & Simon & Schuster. I can show you (personally) both the Harper and Schuster offers in writing. Harper's, to make a long story short, offer to take in the works as an agent and market them for me at a profit of only 10 per cent to themselves—all expenses,—advertising[,] agents' commission etc.—open to all. But in marketing these they proposed to advance & spend for advertising $75,000. My current books—plus necessary advertising are to be handled in the same way.

Simon & Schuster approach the matter somewhat differently. They propose a regular guaranteed payment of $16,000 a year for 10 years—or a total of $160,000—and this regardless of sales. $50,-000—or the first three yearly payments would be paid on the signing of the contract. After that there would be no payment of any kind for three years. In addition they propose to set aside & spend for advertising during the first five years $50,000 or ten thousand a year. After that special advertising for special things. A third offer is made by Liveright. He offers fifteen thousand a year for ten years and one hundred shares of Boni & Liveright stock at $100. The price of the stock today is 275.00. This is equivalent to a bonus of $17,500 on the signing of the contract.

Of all these Liveright's seems as good as any. None of them as I see it take into sufficient consideration the value of good will which in this case is considerable. The value of the name & the books as a property has been created not only by me but various publishers, Doubleday, B. W. Dodge, Harper's, Lane, & Liveright. Now whoever takes the ultimate set [and] any future books such as *A Gallery of Women, The Stoic, The History of Myself, The Bulwark* takes all of this accumulated good will or public standing plus the increasing sales likely to follow on a change, advertising, the publishing of a set. Besides today I have a growing stand in Europe, Australia, and South America. This if emphasized here would mean larger sales here as well as abroad. I suggest $25,000 a year for ten years,[11] but with a renewal option

11 From 1923 to January 1, 1927, Dreiser had had a contract with Liveright under which Liveright guaranteed him $4,000 a year.

for the next ten years at 12,500 per year and a straight fifteen per cent royalties throughout.

Do you think you can get me such an offer.

To Thomas J. Mooney
[ALS–UC]

Dreiser had recently become actively interested in attempts to secure a pardon for the celebrated victim of the miscarriage of justice, still imprisoned at San Quentin.

200 West 57th Street
New York, [N.Y.]
November 10, 1928

Dear Mr. Mooney:

Please do not imagine that the data you sent me is not being considered. I am preparing a letter to Governor Young which I hope may obtain some results as soon as it is in his hands[.] I will send you a copy.[12] My compliments. I am sorry for your plight. But don't forget you are not forgotten. Also that you are the essence of a great issue. How many people—outside, free—have no way of making any least interesting thing of their lives[.]

Theodore Dreiser

To C. C. Young
[CC]

Young was governor of California.

---

12 On November 15 he sent Mooney the letter of that date he wrote to Governor Young (see letter immediately following this one).

[200 West 57th Street]
New York, [N.Y.]
November 15, 1928

Dear Sir:

Recently letters relative to the case of Thomas J. Mooney have come to my notice. Although I knew something of the case, I was unprepared for the unanimous repudiations by the jurors and the presiding justice, Judge Griffin [13]—to say nothing of the Captain of Detectives Matheson,[14] Captain of Police Goff,[15] and others directly concerned in the case of Mooney's guilt. In consequence I am deeply interested to know why you refuse to pardon him.

In one of these letters, from you to Mr. Paul Scharrenberg, dated September 19, 1928, answering what I assume was a request for a pardon, there is this statement: "I have never been able to bring myself to a belief of the innocence of the accused."

In view of the apparently conclusive character of the evidence of Mooney's innocence submitted to you, would it seem proper to ask for a statement of what facts, known to you and not in the evidence given you, warrant such a declaration? There is such overwhelming concurrence on the part of many people whose honesty and acquaintance with the facts appear to be unquestioned.

I cannot believe that you would personally and for reasons which you would refuse to make public permit any inexcusable delay in reviewing the case of a man now in his twelfth year of confinement where there is the slightest possibility of his innocence. In a letter to Mr. Chester H. Rowell, dated September 24, 1927, in saying that you could not grant a pardon, you indicated that you might be favorable to a parole. Yet in a letter to Mr.

13 Franklin A. Griffin, the judge before whom Mooney was first brought to trial on January 3, 1917, and now judge of the Superior Court of California, had suspected as early as April 1917 that there had been perjury. (See *The Mooney-Billings Report—Suppressed by the Wickersham Commission* (New York, cop. 1932), p. 4.) Warren K. Billings had been convicted in September 1916.

14 Captain Duncan Matheson had been in charge of the parade at the time and scene of the explosion.

15 A Sergeant in the party, led by Chief of Police White, that arrested Billings.

Scharrenberg a year later, of which I have spoken, you implied a possible doubt in your interpretation of the case.

For that reason it is that I would like to know what your private reasons are[.] [16]

Very sincerely,
Theodore Dreiser

To Emma Goldman
[CC]

The Russian-born anarchist was remembered mainly for complicity in Alexander Berkman's attempt to assassinate Henry Clay Frick during the Homestead strike in 1892 and for pacifist activities that culminated in her deportation from the United States in 1919. She was now living in the south of France.

200 West 57th Street
New York, [N.Y.]
December 15, 1928

Dear Emma:

I would like very much to write something about you which I could include in my next book, *A Gallery of Women*. Already I have considerable material concerning your life drawn from files of the New York *World* and other papers, and as you see, for I am sending it to you, it is unescapably dramatic and colorful. But what I wish more is to include certain of those dramatic incidents which relate to your arrival and early life in New York, your vivid interest in the unsatisfactory arrangement of society, and your determination to furnish the world with an illustration of what was wrong by personally slaying Henry C. Frick. You once told me this and some other things, and apart from this I have vivid memories in connection with you in your work and I

[16] In a reply, December 8, Governor Young indicated that he was anxious to study the case, but noted that not everything else could be put aside to devote the needed time to the task. At the same time he enclosed a copy of a letter of even date to Judge Griffin, explaining in detail the reasons for his hesitations.

can hardly call it private life, for you were more a public person than private even in your own room—perhaps jails would be better.

I have the feeling that the thing I propose writing will be of considerable value not only as a forerunner to the biography [17] I know you are writing, but as an avenue to a publisher and a popular success which otherwise might not follow easily. More, feeling as I do about you and knowing how I would proceed with my interpretation, I have the feeling that its publication would result in your return to this country. I think I might be even more able to justify you to society than you yourself would, because I have always felt that I knew, not exactly why you are as you are mentally or chemically, but being what you were, why you did as you did.

At least I would like to work out my thoughts in that connection. But to do the thing properly I will have to have a few essential and condensed pivotal incidents around which I could throw all the rest. The sketch when done would not be more than nine or ten thousand words. You will have a permanent place in one of my most valuable and truthful books, and I would be so glad to have you there. My feeling is that the result should be entirely favorable to you in every way.

Will you reply at once furnishing me such material as you feel is truly dramatic and pivotal, and believe me,

Always,

N.B. Presently I am going to Washington and it is my intention to use my influence with certain personages now in power to have the ban on you lifted. You really belong on Thirteenth Street near Fourth Avenue.

17 Her autobiography, *Living My Life* (New York, 1931).

1929

To Covici, Friede, Inc.
[CC]

*The publishers on January 14 had sought Dreiser's comment on
the legal banning of Radclyffe Hall's* The Well of Loneliness.

200 West 57th Street
New York, [N.Y.]
January 16, 1929

Gentlemen:

There is apparently a process in Nature which favors the division of the race into men and women and their desire is each toward the other. "Male and female created He them." Nevertheless, this biological process does not appear to hold in all cases. There are and will continue to be, I assume, exceptions to the rule. Shall the rule be slain for the exception, or the exception for the rule?

If I believed that the race as I now see it is an ultimate, unchanging perfected thing, the net result of which is happiness for all, I would certainly say "Let the exception be slain for the rule." As it is, I lack sufficient evidence to warrant the belief that all that I see is ultimate and perfected or results in general happiness.

But that I favor exceptions to rules just to be favoring them is not true. Life being what it is, humanity being in the main the defeated and mistaken mass that it is, my sympathy naturally goes to those who find themselves different, defective or what you will. When, through no volition of his own, an individual finds himself emotionally defeated by Nature and rises to explain not only the nature of his condition, but to offer or not as he chooses,

485

a plea, my courtesy as well as my sympathy covers that endeavor.

I have not read *The Well of Loneliness,* but several whose judgment I deeply respect insist that it is an honest, well-written and interesting picture of this exceptional state. In view of this, I cannot bring myself to say that such a presentation should not reach the hands and the minds of those who seek it. I am sorry that the authorities are once more to the fore with a general condemnation and a definite legal ban. My feeling is that intelligently, as well as constitutionally and legally there is a better way than that. Just what that way is at the present moment I am not prepared to state, but most certainly legally and intellectually the thing should be given serious consideration and a social procedure that is intelligent and helpful[ly] devised and legally enacted. Intellectually, I personally feel entitled to read and meditate on the conditions which this book endeavors to make plain and I am not willing to deny this to others. It follows, naturally, that I protest against the legal banning of this book.

Yours very truly,

To M. Lincoln Schuster

[CC]

Simon and Schuster, about to publish John Cowper Powys's Wolf Solent, *had on February 1 sent Dreiser proofs for comment.*

200 West 57th Street
New York, [N.Y.]
March 12, 1929

My dear Mr. Schuster:

In regard to *Wolf Solent,* I have not been able to read all of it yet, not because I am not fascinated by anything that Jack writes, but because of the pressure of a lot of things which will not allow me to continuously stick to it.

The intuitively spiritual and mystical character of all of Jack's

thinking is so illuminating and so fascinating to me, so full of a great understanding and a high poetry, that it makes very little difference to me what he writes—whether it is an essay, a poem or a book—I am absorbed by him and his reactions. Even if I never concluded this book I would still be absorbed and fascinated by that portion which I had read.

The pattern of his mind reminds me of some gorgeous cloth, any bit of which might well be treasured for itself alone.

When I conclude the book I will give you my opinion of it as a whole.

To Simon and Schuster
[CC]

In reply to Dreiser's letter of March 12 Schuster had said that he looked forward to Dreiser's comment on Wolf Solent *as a whole.*

> 200 West 57th Street
> New York, [N.Y.]
> March 26, 1929

Gentlemen:

In regard to Jack's novel, I feel that it is almost impossible to list it under the heading of the novel, as we know it. True, there is a story and a good one, of West Country life in England. It has suspense, thought, character study and drama and Powys' usual intense and quite mystic feeling for the soil and vegetation of that portion of England, or anywhere, in this instance the geographical background of the people who live off of it.

As in all of Jack's novels, the style is to me a little old-fashioned, slow and dignified, sometimes too much preoccupied with the niceties of painting a complete picture, not sketchy or blunt or spectacular. At times it has seemed to me as though he were over-impressed by Thomas Hardy. At other times as though his one novel ideal was *Wuthering Heights*. As in the case of Dostoyev-

sky, whom Jack so ardently admires, history unintentionally and because of his own temperament becomes really a medium for his philosophic reactions to the whole earthly, or for that matter, universal scene.

Wolf Solent is very much Jack himself, I judge, just as in the case of *Crime and Punishment* Raskolnikov and again in *The Idiot* Prince Mishkin, and in *The Brothers Karamazov* Alyosha are none other than Dostoyevsky stalking this earthly mystery. And his great dream is to resolve, if possible, this Life Illusion, to present mentally, by means of our five limited senses, something of the final reality which lies beyond. A daring program, and as I see it, hopeless. We will never solve the mystery, though Jack might hope so. Yet the mental processes in this volume might well supply material for a college of psychologists. It holds speculations so intense, so searching and ennobling as to suggest little less than revelation—at their lowest ebb high poetry.

I think in some instances he has captured thoughts and half thoughts that heretofore have actually eluded words. I do not know because I am but minutely aware of even a part of all that has been written. Always his language is clear, exact, heartfelt. Like a mirror when it reflects something beautiful, but brutal beyond compromise when it sees the Gorgon's head.

Obviously, the facile, non-speculative reader of novels as they run will see in this amazing book a heavy, tedious something to be avoided. On the other hand, those who are temperamentally drawn to a contemplation of the mystery in which all things find themselves involved, may well find this an enduring treasure—like *The Brothers Karamazov*, like *Arabia Deserta*, even, in a more voluminous way, like *Wuthering Heights*, his dearest love.

Most of all, this book presents, to me at least, something more of the little known geography, and better yet, the rumor and mystery of that mystic and marvellous land which is the mind of John Cowper Powys.

To Grant C. Knight

[CC]

Knight was a member of the English Department, University of Kentucky.

200 West 57th Street
New York, [N.Y.]
May 13, 1929

Dear Mr. Knight:

I recall with pleasure the letter you wrote me concerning *An American Tragedy* in 1926.

In regard to *This Madness* and the request you have from the *Bookman* for a review, I would like to make a statement concerning it before you write anything.

When the material which I sold the *Cosmopolitan* has run its course, it will consist, at the most, of three-fifths of the entire book. Besides the three studies which are in the *Cosmopolitan* now, or will be, there are four which have not appeared, although two of these are written. In addition to these seven studies, there will be an introduction and a philosophic commentary at the close, which will throw some light on the book as a whole.

In addition to this, you should know that the studies as they appear in the *Cosmopolitan* are not by any means the complete text of the original studies submitted. In order to make the material suitable to the censorship in various states and possible prejudices of some of their readers—although I scarcely see how that could be—the material was cut, almost I should say a third, so you can readily see how little any review of the supposed book entitled *This Madness* and which you are about to do, will represent the text and the spirit of the completed volume. With this knowledge before you, of course, you are free to do as you please and I have no other comment to make.

In regard to the material—it is autobiographical.

When I was twenty-six I read Rousseau's *Confessions*.

Cordially,

To Claude G. Bowers
[CC]

Bowers, then on the editorial staff of the New York Evening World, *had sent Dreiser an editorial from his paper, "Congratulations to Mr. Dreiser," May 25, critical of Boston's banning of the sale of* An American Tragedy *and the Collector of the Port of Boston's confiscation of thirteen copies of Voltaire's* Candide.

200 West 57th Street
New York, [N.Y.]
May 27, 1929

Dear Bowers:

Thanks for the editorial concerning *Candide*. I suppose you saw where the Collector of the Port of Philadelphia would not allow Rabelais to be brought in there, although it is on sale all over the United States.

Personally I am convinced that this is a direct attempt on the part of the officials of the Catholic Church, with possibly the cooperation of some religious organizations of other denominations. I have stated over and over that the chief menace to the world today is the Catholic Church because it is a world wide organization and because chiefly it attacks intelligence—the development of the human mind in every country in the world—since for its own prosperity's sake it believes in mass stupidity. Hungary, although you may not know it, is the latest illustration in point. The intellectual status of the country has been shoved back about 100 years already. Something ought to be done about this noble "real estate organization"—even though you did the nominating of Al Smith at the convention.[1]

I am glad—if you are—that you and Mrs. Bowers are going abroad. Personally, I would rather think of being abroad and

[1] Bowers had been keynoter and temporary chairman at the National Democratic Convention. Franklin D. Roosevelt had, of course, been the one to place Smith's name in nomination.

coming back to New York. When you get back and your book comes out,[2] bring up a copy under your arm and we will talk things over.

To George H. Warwick
[CC]

Warwick, an English reader, had on June 25 objected to a statement in the third paragraph of Chapter 11 of Jennie Gerhardt, *in which Dreiser states: " 'Conceived in iniquity and born in sin' is the unnatural interpretation put upon the process [of conception] by the extreme religionist, and the world, by its silence, gives assent to a judgement so marvellously warped." Citing the honor in which conception was held by the Jews and the Christian Church, Warwick had insisted that the passage from the Psalms did not reflect on the process of conception and hoped Dreiser would revise the paragraph in later editions.*

200 West 57th Street
New York, [N.Y.]
July 9, 1929

My dear Sir,

I wonder if you considered when you wrote me recently that *Jennie Gerhardt* is an American novel—depicting a typically American moral view of a given situation—and that the interpretation of the phrase "Conceived in iniquity and born in sin" as set forth is the common American version and is accepted here— rightly or wrongly—as the only one that can be placed upon it. Hence my own cry out against it.

If the Church, as you state, considered natural conception as a beautiful, clean, uplifting achievement, then why the beatification of the Virgin primarily because of her "Immaculate Conception"?[3] I am very much afraid that neither the Roman Church

---

2 *The Tragic Era* (Cambridge, Mass., 1929).
3 In reply, on July 18, Warwick attempted to enlighten Dreiser as to the meaning of this idea.

nor those of Anglican or Greek extraction look upon this close, intimate relationship as being anything except unholy and unclean—only raised to the standards of decency and a sacrament through the placing of the blessing of the Church upon it—and this in each and every individual case, not a blanket condonement ever.

Further, even David, a Jew, and a link in the chosen line that was prophesied to produce the Messiah, in his humiliation and abjection in the 51st Psalm, 5, acknowledges all that this implies in his cry, "Behold, I was shapen in iniquity; and in sin did my mother conceive me."

I wish that the world and the Church might take the uplifting and elevating moral view you hold, but I am afraid that the day of its general acceptance is yet away off.

Cordially,
Theodore Dreiser.

To George Douglas
[TLS–TEH]

Douglas, literary critic and friend of George Sterling, was on the staff of the Los Angeles Examiner.

200 West 57th Street
New York, [N.Y.]
August 14, 1929

Dear Douglas:

Thanks so much for your answer with the news and especially the comment on the German-American relationship.[4]

Of course, I am glad that you have been pushed up into the Editorial Department of the *Examiner,* because I feel that that

---

[4] In response to a request, Dreiser on July 23 had sent the *Deutsche Allgemeine Zeitung* a statement for a U.S.A. number of their paper to be published in connection with the World Advertising Congress in Berlin, in August. The statement appeared on August 23, but Dreiser evidently had earlier sent Douglas a typed copy.

is where you belong. Personally, in my judgment you would make a strong editorial director and should hold that position. If you did I would subscribe for your editorial page.

Although you find Los Angeles a little trying after San Francisco—and for a time I think you will—you may also go through a period in which you will think it is ideal—almost perfect. After twenty years of New York I tried it for three years and found an ethereal something in that climate which I doubt that I shall ever be able to describe. For the first two years or more it did not make any difference to me that there was very little doing intellectually in Los Angeles—or I might say in Southern California. I was lost in contemplating the velvety brown mountains, the amazing flowers and the relaxed mood in which every one took the perpetual and to me stimulating and restoring sunshine. As a matter of fact, I owe Southern California a debt—a romantic one to be sure,[5] but nevertheless one that I shall never be able to pay.

If you ever come to New York—for heaven's sake come and stay with me.

Theodore Dreiser

To H. S.
[CC]

H. S. had read Dreiser's books and written, August 23, that he was sure Dreiser would understand his peculiar despondency and loneliness.

> 200 West 57th Street
> New York, [N.Y.]
> September 6, 1929

Dear H. S.:

I have read your letter and I sympathize with your mood. Since you ask for my advice, let me offer this: Every artist suffers

[5] It was there he had met Helen Richardson, who became his second wife on June 13, 1944.

from the loneliness and isolation of spirit that you are feeling and which you think is peculiar to you—and it must be so. All creative work is born of the travail of the spirit; every piece of sculpture, every book, every painting is a monument to the suffering out of which it was created. And you cannot be happy in an ordinary, commonplace way if you would be individual.

If you have that unconquerable urge to write, nothing will stop you from writing. You will write whether it is convenient or inconvenient, whether you are rich or poor, whether you are lonely and alone or your life is filled with friends and frivolity, for in that last event you would go out of your way to seek solitude and there give your spirit reign.

I could not, of course, advise you to give up your position if you are dependent upon it for support, for I do not know whether you have sufficient ability and only the quality of your work will show that.

I am grateful and glad if my books have been of any help to you. As you must readily surmise, though, I am very busy with my work and have almost no time to devote to my friends so my books must now speak to them for me.

I would like to leave this thought with you—Observe life directly as much as possible and prepare yourself to write by reading the really worth-while things that have been written by others and then look upon your writing as the most important thing in the world—to you—and the petty annoyances that now seem to color your whole life will quite naturally fall into their proper perspective.

I wish you all manner of success.

To Emmanuel Morris
[CC]

[200 West 57th Street
New York, N.Y.]
November 25, 1929

Dear Mr. Morris,

Your response to "What I Believe" [6] interests me—not so much that you agree with it exactly as that you are so taken by the problem as a whole and grasp it so satisfactorily for yourself.

I find acceptance of the idea of complete dissolution not so much comforting as restful. It means not a little to me to be done with bothering about the hereafter and so concerning myself with today.

To Hilary Harris
[ALS]

Dreiser was replying to the birth announcement of the son of Marguerite Tjader Harris, with whom he had recently established a friendship.

200 West 57th Street
New York, [N.Y.]
December 19, 1929

My dear Hilary:

Welcome to our best of all possible worlds. And thanks, thanks for your letter. For one so young, Hilary, you are beginning your earthly services very soon,—your earthly secretarial services. And while no doubt your mother appreciates these same, will you allow me a hint. Beware of a maternal fixation[.] It begins so,—

6 *Forum*, LXXXII (November 1929), 279-281, 317-320.

with a desire to serve. And ends, so I hear, with cramping one's manly style.

But since you find yourself so secretarily minded for the time being may I ask you to say to your mother that I have this long while been most properly and even affectionately concerned for her—have, in short, sent her many dynamic wave lengths intended to induce peace and a fortunate fruition to all of her dreams and even experiments—biologic, sociologic, scriptic. I trust she received them. Incidentally—just before your note arrived I was thinking of flowers—pansies, forget-me-nots, violets—only for novelty's sake—paper ones,—à la Russe, a little eau de Sibirsk sprinkled on for native breath's sake, so to say. But, as I say, just as I was about to look for them came word of *My City*—bound, numbered.[7] And said I in lieu of flowers à la Russe it shall be this book, most affectionately inscribed by myself and as promptly dispatched.

For, as you may or may not know, Hilary your mother took a very great interest in this work. I think you might call it a labor of love. She it was who discovered and persuaded the charming if impractical Mr. Pollak to make those lovely studies of New York for it. And for how little I should hate to say. It must have been for the love of the work, for what else he got out of it I have never been albe to learn. Besides she supervised and directed—arrangement, type, paper. Ah, your dear, capable tasteful mother. You must kiss her hands for me, Hilary.

And so this day I am sending it with my acknowledgements—and beg you, as soon as ever she looks able to endure the shock to lay the same before her. I bow: And with renewed assurances of my regard, respect, reverence even—and with hand kissings and such various gestures and genuflections as may come to you and at the time seem appropriate, ...[8] I beg of you.

Also, dear Hilary, please say that on Saturday & regardless of various sinking boats Helen & I—are off for—well—(the curse

---

[7] Dreiser's poem, originally published in the *New York Herald Tribune*, December 23, 1928, sec. 3, was issued by Horace Liveright in an edition limited to 275 copies, illustrated by Max Pollak (New York, 1929).

[8] Dreiser's punctuation.

of rum!) the West Indies to be gone until Jan. 6—or thereabout. At which time—dv—and your mother's health permitting, it will make me happy to call and say all the nice things I now think. Also more.

Believe me, my dear Hilary, with every good wish for your own & your dear mother's welfare and prosperity, I am

Theodore Chesterfield Dreiser

By Tiffany-Dobbs De Pinna, Secy.

1930

To Louise Campbell
[ALS]

Santa Rita Hotel
Tuscon, Arizona
March 31, 1930

Dear Louise:

Haven't written you because, in the main, I've been working harder than I did in N. Y. and sight-seeing! Sort of knocked out by the individuality of this world. Nothing like it anywhere that I have ever seen[.] Always 2,000 to 7000 feet above sea-level. Always mountains arranged in triangles, squares or parallel lines above the flat level of these high mesas. Always cacti or mesquite or bunch grass. Mostly a blazing sun or a cold starry night. Fairly good roads. A hundred miles without a house, sometimes with only one gasoline station. Hundreds & hundreds of forgotten and deserted pueblos or ancient Indian towns have [been] buried in the sand, perhaps thousands of them. Hundreds of live inhabited pueblos with from 300 to a 1000 Indians all farming and looking much like the Indian you gave me. And then thousands of Americanized Indians—short skirts, high heels, silk stockings—attending the state schools or colleges[.] And thousands of Mexicans, real or Americanized—and first, second[,] third & fourth generation ones—and actually the handsomest & most temperamental & vivid people out here. Then the business American—all business-machine-like—with his office building 10 or 12 [stories] high, his swell banks, baptist churches, Woolworths, Kresses, Penney's and his Hollywood houses & 1930 cars. And then le Tourist—swelling around or rolling through. And cowboys—in uniform. And ranchers. And miners. And the movies. And jazz.

498

And the bootleggers. And emigrant runners. Really is colorful. Skies like those of Italy. Sunrises & sunsets that would make you cry or go crazy with loneliness. Old missions. New large white ones with bells & towers. Thousands of wild cattle in the 100,000 acre ranches. Roaming to get fat or die of starvation as you please. No food & not too much water provided but what's left driven to pasture land (or shipped) to be fattened & then slaughtered— Chicago, Kansas City, Omaha, Dallas[.]

All told—except for business—the Americans [are] the dullest of all. Never heard of anything except congressmen & senators & Mary Baker Eddy & Volstead and Christ. Oh—well—. . . .[1] I'm planning to go to Phoenix, Yuma, Prescott[,] Williams, Grand Canyon, Flagstaff & so in New Mexico—Gallup—the Indian detour, Albuquerque, Santa Fe—and then either back east or a stay in Albuquerque. I'm here—General Delivery until—Sunday April 6. Then Phoenix until April 9. (General Delivery) then Yuma. But I'll write you again before then. How's everything? Numbskull! You sent me a corkscrew in a trunk when I can get one anywhere—in any Woollyworts for 10 cents. And their Wollyworts are nicer as ours.

I'm enclosing some views. They're too true not to send.

Love—
T.D

To Louise Campbell
[ALS]

Santa Rita Hotel
Tucson, Arizona
April 5, [1930]

Dear Louise:

This [2] will hand you a smile I know. I can't see where I am to find the mood to do this. I'll scan it if I get time. If not bad it

---

[1] Dreiser's punctuation.
[2] Apparently a request to read and, if necessary, revise someone's manuscript.

goes to you for pencil working as to what should come out. Once it's in book form I'll tell him who pencil-worked it.

—Dear, this is a wonderful climate. You never saw such mornings & evenings anywhere. In Umbria—Italy—some best mornings in Hollywood and on the Riveree. It is said to rain here occasionally. I have not seen a cloudy day. And these mesas! In Russia they would be steppes. In Kansas plains. Here they are brown, dry, warm or hot. And with cacti or mesquite or chaparral —nothing much over three to five feet high except those one arm cacti which here are as tall as telegraph poles and thicker. Marvellous! There is a forest of them near here 30 miles across. But to walk on the mesa! To lie in the sun! To watch for prairie dogs or lonely, strange birds! To watch ranchers & lone cattle and the mountains changing in the light[!] I can't tell you. The ordinary American may be dumb & all business—but oh, his land!

Love
T.D.

From April 6 to 12—Phoenix. (Gen. Del.)

To Thomas J. Mooney

[ALS–UC]

On May 30 Dreiser had visited Mooney in San Quentin and then personally made an appeal to Governor C. C. Young.

Roosevelt Hotel
West Park and Salmon Streets
Portland, Oregon
June 6, 1930

Dear Mooney:

It was exactly as I expected. The person referred to had no new thing to say. He was persistent in his insistence that there was no trace of bias. No one was influencing him. His own conscience —and his own conscience only—was his guide. And now that the

case of Billings was up for decision [3] and the trials were related his duty to himself, the public—a general sense of fairness to and respect for the court demanded that he wait IN BOTH CASES until the court's decision was rendered. I emphasized all your points but most particularly my own—his proposed action in regard to you in case the Billings decision was unfavorable. In reply to that—when pinned down—all he would say was that he must wait and read the court's opinion since that opinion might throw some light on you—favorable or unfavorable which he would need to take into consideration in justice to himself, the public, the court.

You know what I thought. I cannot sufficiently express my contempt for the petty dodging that is being indulged in.[4] But as I told you there is another and better way and I have arranged that way.[5]

Theodore Dreiser

My permanent address is
    61 West 48th St.
      New York City
    % Horace Liveright, Inc.

To Sarah Gertrude Millin
[CC]

Dreiser had recently met the author of God's Step-Children *during her visit to the United States. She was now at her home in Johannesburg, Union of South Africa.*

[3] The case of Mooney's co-defendant, Warren Billings, was then before the California Supreme Court.

[4] For a somewhat fuller account of Dreiser's interview and his reactions, consult in Dreiser's files a drafted statement of his following Young's decision, [after July 7, 1930].

[5] Possibly a reference to his attempt to interest William Randolph Hearst in the Mooney case. He later succeeded in securing coverage by the Scripps-Howard papers, to which he contributed an article in August.

200 West 57th Street
New York, [N.Y.]
July 19, 1930

Dear Mrs. Millin:

I would write you in long hand but I think you would not understand what I meant. I have been wondering about you and how you made out on your return trip and in other ways. I am genuinely sorry about your younger brother. I know how tragedy of this kind is likely to weigh on you if you let it. You speak of loneliness—all thinking people are lonely unless they prize, really, the jewel which is their mind. Years ago I let myself rather morbidly to the thought of personal loneliness although later as I look back it appeared that all that really stirs in my life grew out of my suppressed feelings of loneliness. Since then I have come to get an enormous kick out of contemplating as well as being a part of the visible scene. It does not bore me—trudging humanity whether individually known to me or not—it fascinates me. I do not have any personal pleasure which requires so terribly much more than the privilege of looking at it today and thinking about it. I am not prepared to commend anything as a doctrine to anyone but I am stating it for what it may be worth.

On a number of occasions I have been full of the intention of writing you. I wanted to say this[,] that I enjoyed your coming to America and that we achieved a companionable and agreeable time and that I was privileged to learn so much about South Africa through you and through your books. You ask me whether I have read one of your books. I told you how much I had enjoyed your ethnographical and sociological study of South Africa. I read it in the Constable edition. I have read *God's Step-Children* and consider it a strong, moving, presentation of the reality of the world of which we are a part. You have a very fine gift of writing and should be happy in the privilege to do more and more of it, why aren't you? I have not read the article which you wrote about me but perhaps you will send me a copy. More I wish now and then you would write me. I would like to hear about you and South Africa. Incidentally I wish that you would come to America

again. While the wooden bungalow was burned down,[6] the larger house is intact and very habitable. By the time you arrive here, I will have a new bedroom or two built, one of which you may occupy. If you don't come here, it is entirely possible that one of these days I will come to Johannesburg in which case you could provide me with a bedroom. Now don't grieve, don't give yourself over to thoughts of loneliness and go to work forthwith.

My kindest regards

To Oliver M. Sayler
[CC]

Editing a book entitled Revolt in the Arts, *Sayler had on May 20 invited Dreiser to represent the Novelist in the chapter on Literature and on July 9 had outlined the various topics under which to treat revolt.*

200 West 57th Street
New York, [N.Y.]
July 19, 1930

Dear Mr. Sayler:

I would have answered your request about a chapter in your book, *The Revolt in the Arts,* but the fact is that I am carrying quite all the burdens that I can carry at the moment and besides personally I doubt whether there has ever been or could be a revolt in the arts or whether there ever has or can be any such thing in connection with the arts here in America. I could write one or two typewritten pages on that but not now and if I did it would not be to your purpose.[7] I have the feeling that you would

6 A grass fire begun by Dreiser's caretaker at Mt. Kisco had consumed the house on February 12.

7 In Dreiser's files there is a carbon copy of such a letter to Sayler, dated earlier and apparently withheld in favor of the briefer substitute (the ellipsis marks are Dreiser's):

New York
July 11, 1930

To Oliver M. Sayler

To begin with, I do not believe there is or ever was or that there could ever be a "Revolt in the Arts." There is no such thing as the "Present Revolt in the Arts in America."

not use it. Perhaps another time in some other way I may be of service to you but in this instance you will have to excuse me. Thank you for the compliment implied.

Yours truly

To Thomas J. Mooney
[CC]

On July 5 Warren Billings's appeal for a pardon had been denied by the California Supreme Court; on August 9 Mooney had written Dreiser asking what specifically had Dreiser been doing in his behalf, stating that he had been denied mail privileges, and inquiring about the possibility of securing financial aid in the East.

There exist only political and military (or combined) revolutions. A revolt is a sweeping outburst of all passions, hidden forces, suppressed emotions of a great mass of people. Has anything like that ever happened in the arts? . . . We like to use big words. We say that the stage or the novel or music or the fine arts had been "revolutionized" by certain men or certain happenings. The fact is that arts like fashions come and go in a most perfect continuity, just like the waves of the oceans. The most terrific typhoon cannot make a wave break in an unnatural way. Some waves are milder, some are heavier, higher, shorter, longer,—but they will never split or crack or tear.

When, at the culminating point of a certain fashion, for example the highpoint of the short skirt vogue, (that's quite high, isn't it? especially in the subway) we look back to the highpoint of a certain other fashion, let's say the Crinoline, we are amazed at the "revolutionary changes." But was there any revolutionary change? Not by any means because the change was perfectly gradual, sometimes almost imperceptible from one season to the other. In ten years, the difference becomes quite startling.

So it is with the arts. (All of them). The change is always gradual. But, while fashions are visible to the naked eye in every part of the civilized world, the gradual changes in art are noticed only by the "Chosen Few"—and the chosen few are not really chosen either. And the change is very striking already by the time a whole group of artists, or one famous artist, exposes the result to the public eye.

Most people have a conservative mind, i.e. a mind incapable of accepting new ideas. If there is a revolt, it is the revolt of the public against anything and everything new. But everything grows old. What used to be the most astounding novelty for the public, becomes an everyday spectacle after a while. Something ever *newer* attracts all the antagonism the public are capable of.

The average artist has no more intelligence, not even more individuality, than the average layman. The average man inherited his

Room 405
1819 Broadway
New York, [N.Y.
between August 9 and 27, 1930]

Dear Mooney:

I received your telegram and one from Mary Gallagher [8] just before the decision of the Court in the Billings case was handed down. The next day, I think, the adverse decision appeared in all

---

prehistoric ancestors' instinct of mimicry. (Instinct of fear, really,—the eternal fear of being too conspicuous, and thus easily destructible!) No sooner is a new idea in any of the arts accepted by the public than the average artists all try to imitate the successful achievement. Thus, a so-called new period begins in the history of art. The first artist who had the temerity (or the naïveté) to show the public something new, reached that newness gradually, through the work, the experimentation of several, sometimes many, others. The epigons do not follow the new track before they feel the public want "that kind o' stuff". . . . Where is the revolt in the Arts?

There is no economic revolt either. There are economic changes caused by the social revolutions which entitled more people to take part in what may or may not be called the "Benefits of Civilization." The formerly more or less oppressed classes have enough money now but they haven't got the necessary traditions as yet for understanding, honestly enjoying the products of the artists. On the other hand, the formerly oppressing (or is it Ruling?) classes haven't got the necessary money even in the few cases where they still possess the necessary traditions. The Roman Catholic church, in olden days the greatest patron of the Arts, lost much of its power and wealth too. Thus, the artist has to face grave problems and has to become a businessman in order to survive, instead of remaining the parasite of ducal or kingly courts he used to be. Where is the revolt here?

And morally! Why, there is no change in morality at all. In all ages most people were considered to be immoral by a few self-assumed arbiters. And, in order to assure the safety of their souls, these "immorals" always found exactly the same method: to consider certain members of their own still more immoral. Censorship is an age-old device. An evil it is,—but is it not a necessary evil, after all? In every epoch, oceans grew of the tears spilled over the disastrous changes in morality. *O tempora, o mores!* Is it the fault of the artist, the public or the censor?

I can see no moral (censorship) revolt on this planet of ours. I can see only that a good Laurel & Hardy comedy a week would do us a lot of good.

All this was to begin with.
Now, to end with . . . .
regards.

[8] In charge of the committee to secure Mooney's freedom, through whom communication with Mooney was managed.

of the papers. After reading them I wired the person concerning whom I spoke to you.[9] My telegram was very brief: "What now." The reply was equally brief: "Wait." Since then a digest of the enormous flood of data concerning yourself and Billings has been daily placed on my desk. Even though you personally wished for something more conclusive than that, I do not think that you would be entitled to it for it certainly is of the first importance and I think that the man to whom I spoke realized that also, that the American public and the world at large is entitled to a thorough public threshing-out of this case and I do not need to tell you that it is being threshed out. After it is all over and after an adverse decision, as you seem to think, has been rendered, will be time enough for something more.

You said to me that it is tough to stay in prison for fourteen years. It certainly would be difficult if nothing but silence and indifference went with it. Think of Berkman; [10] he had twenty years of it. In your case, whether you are ever mindful or grateful, you have had all the breaks. I actually think that there are thousands of people in that active, militant world which you do or did represent who would gladly step into your shoes. As I told you, when it is all over and you are free, you are going to look back on this period possibly with regret. Life, excitement, public interest, is certainly worth something. Nevertheless, the job of the moment is to get you out and as I said before, when a decision is rendered will be time enough for anything more.

Very truly yours,

P. S. One of the things that I did on my return here was to see Roy Howard and discuss the advisability of the campaign on his part which subsequently broke and you can thank Roy Howard and no one else for bringing McDonald from Baltimore, for at the time I talked to Howard he told me he was having a nation-wide search made for that missing witness. Regards.

9 See Dreiser to Mooney, June 6, 1930.
10 Alexander Berkman, who served fourteen years of a twenty-two-year sentence, for shooting Henry Clay Frick, chairman and acting head of the Carnegie Steel Company, during the Homestead strike, 1892.

To Charles Fort

[ALS]

Fort's Lo! *was scheduled to be published in 1931 by Claude Kendall in New York.*

[200 West 57th Street]
New York, [N.Y.]
August 27, 1930

Dear Fort:—

I'll even make it Darling Fort. I'm so glad you are alive and that there is another book of yours to read and that I shall one of these days be permitted to read it, and that you have a publisher —I hope one who is worthy of you, and that you are here in New York and that I am going to be able to see you. It is my birthday (today) and I take it as a good omen that I hear from you.

Your publisher wants opinions of your writings. To think that that should be necessary, or even seem so. You—the most fascinating literary figure since Poe. You—who for all I know may be the progenitor of an entirely new world viewpoint: You whose books thrill and astound me as almost no other books have thrilled and astounded me. And you write at once so authoritatively and delightfully. Well, such is Life[.]

But, then, what shall I say? This? Or more than this? Shall I re-emphasize that yours is one of the master minds and temperaments of the world today? It is.

And yet the same old writing paper! Where in God's name do you get it? Have you a storage warehouse full of it? And the same typewriter. And the same habits and in these changeful days the same wife. Now really!

I see you have my house number. The telephone is Circle 2437. Your Bronx Subway brings you to 59th & Broadway. Or, if you come down on the Lexington Ave. line & change to the B.M.T. at 59th St. the B.M.T. brings you to my door. The 57th & Seventh Ave. station is at the foot of this building. But if the

mountain won't move, Mahomet will try & find 2058 Ryer Ave. (Bronx) (Only where is that?) And be glad to. Delighted.

Fairest,

Dearest.

Write me where is 2058 Ryer Ave.

Dreiser

And to your wife—I bow.

To Madeleine Boyd
[CC]

Ernest Boyd's wife, who was an author and literary agent, had written a note of sympathy, November 6, when the Nobel Prize, which both Dreiser and Dreiser's friends had expected Dreiser to receive that year, was awarded to Sinclair Lewis.

200 West 57th Street
New York, [N.Y.]
November 7, 1930

Dear Madeleine:

I appreciate the feeling which lies behind your letter, but I believe you will understand me when I say that I cannot welcome sympathy, because I do not need it. In fact, I would be happy, and even delighted, if I could eliminate the thought of the necessity for any such feeling from my friends and well-wishers everywhere. I cannot imagine the prize lessening or improving the mental standing of any serious writer—writing is, after all, his or her main business.

Thanks for the Sunday dinner invitation, but on that day I am always out in the country, so am forced to decline. But another time, I hope.

1931

To Samuel Hoffenstein
[CC]

Having prepared the script for the moving picture version of An American Tragedy, *Hoffenstein had been assigned by Paramount Publix Corporation to seek Dreiser's "comments, advice, suggestions or criticisms" that the contract with Paramount permitted Dreiser to make. Dreiser had just left New York for a trip through the South when Hoffenstein, February 9, had wired him that he would come to New York. Unable to locate Dreiser immediately, Paramount had formally written on February 13 that they would give him until the 20th to present his views and would proceed with production on the 23rd. On the 23rd, after an exchange of increasingly unfriendly telegrams (February 16-20), Dreiser and Hoffenstein had agreed to confer in New Orleans.*

Jung Hotel
New Orleans, [Louisiana]
February 26, 1931

My dear Hoffenstein:

On my arrival here I found the proposed scenario for *An American Tragedy,* forwarded from New York, and have just read it. To me, it is nothing less than an insult to the book—its scope, actions, emotions and psychology. Under the circumstances, and to avoid saying personally how deeply I feel this, I am leaving New Orleans now without seeing you. You will understand, I am sure.

If, at any time, the studio should permit the construction of a

509

script representative of the book and will seriously agree to work along the lines I know to be most valuable for this purpose, I will be glad to cooperate, and at once, but not before.

Very truly,
Theodore Dreiser

To Jesse L. Lasky
[CC]

Lasky was president of Paramount Publix Corporation.

200 West 57th Street
New York, [N.Y.]
March 10, 1931

Dear Mr. Lasky:

The script of *An American Tragedy* submitted to me for approval I reject because I know that it will make a bad picture, financially and artistically. I cannot make this strong enough. I want this picture to be a success, as much as you and your company do, but it must be obvious to anyone who knows pictures that Sternberg [1] and Hoffenstein have "botched" my novel.

Their greatest fault has been in the characterizations. They have made Clyde an unsympathetic "smart aleck" who cares only for one thing—a girl, any kind of a girl. If, as reported, Philips Holmes is to play this part, then I predict that you will be doing him infinite harm with his movie public. Clyde is a creature of circumstances, not a scheming, sex-starved "drugstore cowboy." They have failed to show this entirely. There is no relentless pursuit, no inescapable web that compels this boy to act as he does. The other characters have been equally neglected.

In addition to that, they have made Clyde's love affair with Roberta a sordid thing. As they picture it, there is nothing

---

1 Josef von Sternberg, the film's director.

idyllic about it, and there should be—there must be. Until Sondra comes into his life, Clyde is content, more or less happy in his love life with Roberta. This the treatment neglects. The whole thing can be summed up by saying that *An American Tragedy* is a progressive drama. This is true of the novel, and it should be of the picture. A certain and given chain of events leads to certain conclusions, which conclusions must be proved.

Sternberg and Hoffenstein are in a rush to reach the drowning, so much so that the boy's antecedents, his early life, etc. are all brushed aside. The drowning then becomes the act of a temporarily crazed youth, instead of the planned culmination of a series of inescapable circumstances, as shown in the novel. And their hurry is for what reason? To give over the major portion of the picture to a trial scene, which is, on the basis of proportionate importance, not so relevant at all! It doesn't warrant that much film or dialogue. The trail scenes, as a matter of fact, are really not important except to show what the successful prosecution of the case means to the district attorney, and even this isn't shown with a "bite." In fact, the courtroom interludes, the "cut" shots, are feeble and ineffective.

And certainly, the end of the picture is not the courtroom, or should not be. The picture must end in the death house, including the incidents of his confession, his meeting with his mother, etc. etc. All of these important dramatic elements have been excluded.

The script lacks imagination, inventiveness, and ingenuity. The elements of suspense, surprise, sympathy, have been entirely overlooked, with a deliberateness that is astounding. I think this is predicated on Sternberg's lack of sympathy for my writing and for the script generally.[2] He is alien to the whole idea, and has probably convinced Hoffenstein of the same line of approach. Certainly a construction such as has been made cannot make any

[2] He had been quoted in the *New York Times*, March 3, 1931, as saying: "George Bernard Shaw is antiquated and old-fashioned. He is operating, thinking, talking and writing in terms of the last century. He emptied himself twenty years ago, and that also applies to many of the so-called literary giants—in particular, Theodore Dreiser."

money nor do the novel justice. It is not even a "good" picture, much less a "great" picture—which it easily can be, and which it warrants because of the expense already involved and the world-wide publicity the picture has already had.

My concrete suggestion is this: I should like say four weeks in which to prepare a script of this picture. For this purpose I should [like] to engage H. S. Kraft, who is already known to you. I don't know what Mr. Kraft would want for his work—that can be arranged. I should also like to have Chester Erskin engaged to direct the picture and Kraft to work with him both on the script and the direction, with my cooperation and supervision. Erskin, I understand, spent his youth in just such a locale as is the *Tragedy's*—knows the people, the types, and also the story—and both of these men have a fine sense of theatre and pictures. I am sure it would be a happy and successful association for everyone concerned.

I am willing to submit the finished script to anyone you designate, confident that the result will be beneficial to all of us and that finally a basis for the successful making of the picture can be gotten under way. As it is, I can have nothing further to do with the picture, and unless radical and advantageous changes are made, will most certainly protest against the use of my name.

To James D. Mooney
[CC]

Mooney, president of the Export Division of the General Motors Corporation, was co-author with Alan C. Reiley, of Onward Industry! The Principles of Organization and Their Significance to Modern Industry *(New York and London, 1931).*

200 West 57th Street
New York, [N.Y.]
March 14, 1931

Dear Mr. Mooney:

I should preface my comment on this interesting book of yours, *Onward Industry*, by stating quite flatly that my solution for the difficulties of the world, and particularly those in America, is Communism. I see that you hold by the feeling that man is a better animal than I think he is, and that understanding and brotherly love, and the good, old, well-planned Constitution ought to solve everything. Feeling as I do about human nature, I question very much whether industry, and particularly the large, aggressive, animal natures which are required to put it over, will ever agree to be so nice to the common man as you think.

Nevertheless, I have this to say about this book of yours: The presentation of it—style, arrangement and all—is excellent. Personally, I feel that it could be condensed somewhat, but, nevertheless, I think that you will be likely to find a market for it as is, particularly just at this time when the general material feeling of America is that capitalism, or the present industrial system, should be maintained. I even believe that this may be acclaimed the proper solution, and that the Communists will be the ones to pay for its appearance, since its program will be lauded and they will be properly castigated for suggesting anything else, but since I know that you believe as you write, this can't possibly hurt your feelings. It looks to me as though you might be going to make some money on it.

If I were proposing a Communistic program, I would really take your book as a guide, but I would go just a little further. For instance, I would urge the integration and uniting of all industries, a monopoly for this purpose—universal service—which I take from your book, only I would let a central government committee of the best minds direct this great work for the benefit of everybody, in order to see that there should be employment, proper housing, food and a lot of other things for

everybody. As you urge, so would I urge, that this method would do away with the injustices and barriers, for instance, a tariff, resulting in differences of wages—that is the point.

Of course, you say that the uniting of industries should preserve the constructive spirit of competition. I think that the unity of industries would do away with competition, but would preserve the constructive spirit none-the-less. You urge that this uniting must be voluntary on the part of the industries. Under my scheme, it would be compulsory, because I don't think that this voluntary proposition which you suggest will ever come about as man is constituted up to this moment. It might be that a lot of the powers in control of industry in America could be gathered around a great table and somebody move them to see what you mean, but again it might not. You say that the purpose of industry must be reformed from money-making to universal service. Your method of reforming will be through your book. If your book doesn't do the trick, would you be willing to consider trying the Communistic method of compelling them to do so? For you insist that this should be done because industries are not in a position now to determine the public policy, and united they would be. Well, under Communism, they would be united, and they would be able to dictate public policy, and probably just as well under Communism as under kindly-minded associated industrial creators.

I present you from your own book a statement which would look just as well in any Communist pamphlet as it would in *Onward Industry:* "The ultimate solution of all labor problems rests on the universal recognition of the cardinal principle that the interests of employer and worker are mutual." They certainly are, and you might add that joined up with them in mutuality are the interests of the government through which they function and the people whom they serve. Only I cannot go on and say, as you do, that the worker must know and co-operate with the business[man], as the A.F. of L. and the Brotherhood of Locomotive Engineers [do], because as I see it, the worker should know and co-operate with everything relating to the gov-

ernment of which he is a part. But you seem to feel in your book that the laborer is now fully protected at law by compensation, hours, wages, etc., and that this constitutes the triumph of our present industrial system. I cannot see that anyone except the union worker is at present protected at law by proper compensation, hours, wages, or anything else. The ordinary citizen is a mere piker compared to the organized union man who gets what he considers satisfactory hours and wages, and ignores everyone else who does not.

In another place in your book, you go on to say that the troubles of industry are no longer of production, but of distribution; markets should be opened and organized to consume the entire world. That is exactly what the Communists say, but they do not want any particular nation to do it. They want to arrange all the nations in such an order that this opening of markets and distribution would be automatic.

I note that many of your judgments are based on morals which form the complete basis for economics, society, psychology, etc., and by moral laws you justify industry several times, but if we look at the world as it is today, I cannot see for the life of me how you can insist that the morals of industry are as fine as you say they are. If I have read the newspapers aright—and I have watched the proceedings of industry with regard not only to its employees, but to the public at large—it seems to me that their morals are pretty close to those of the jungle, and that it is really a case of devil take the hindmost. For certainly you cannot talk too loudly today about bread-lines or anything else, without being told by the police and the press where you get off.

Maybe this book of yours will open the eyes of those strong, powerful organizations to this better scheme, and I cannot but commend one in your position presenting it. Just the same, I think that the further step is a better one. I firmly believe that since the cunning, greed and vanity, etc. of the individual is the amazing and creative thing that it is today and, also, since there is so much of it, that the only thing to do is to limit it in some drastic form, for you will never kill it. Roosevelt, in all the slush

that he troubled to pour forth on a hypnotized world, said one true thing, although I don't think he actually personally believed it. He said that the time is coming when we shall have to shackle cunning as we have shackled greed. Of course, since at that time or since then we have never come anywhere near shackling greed, our chance of shackling cunning is not so hot, and at the present time it looks to me as though it were distinctly cool.

Just the same, this book gives a splendid account of the principles of organization, well thought out and valuable practically, and it connects them more or less well and interestingly with rebellious characters and life in history, and I agree that these principles of organization—excellent as they are—must carry out the economic program outlined above, or the world will pass into Communism.

As you have said to me, you do not think that Communism is necessary. You believe that the good, old American organization as laid down by the Constitution and the fathers thereof is sufficient to put everything to rights. I personally believe that the world needs more organization. The United States needs it, but not along the leave-it-to-the-industry line which you advocate. From an organization point of view, I feel that the book should certainly be helpful to many, and I also think that your economic theories are going to be seized on as a club wherewith to knock out Communism, if that is still possible.

The thing is clearly written, although I insist there is considerable repetition. This might be done away with.

Now if you want to select something from this which you think will benefit the circulation of this volume, you might pick a line or two from this, here and there, and let me see how it looks thus selected. If it does not run counter to my larger program too much, I shall certainly sign on the dotted line.

Yours,

To Jesse L. Lasky
[CC]

Replying to Dreiser's letter of March 10, Lasky had written from New York on the 14th:

Dear Mr. Dreiser:

I have your letter of March 10th with reference to *An American Tragedy.*

I am especially sorry that you did not give your cooperation to Mr. Hoffenstein the script writer assigned to this work whose selection you approved at the time the contracts were signed.

We did everything possible to get in touch with you and were disposed to meet your ideas as to the form of the treatment so far as consistently possible had you given us the opportunity so to do.

For some weeks we endeavored to get in communication with you but were advised that you were out of town, and at your home all information as to your whereabouts was refused. The script was finally delivered to Mr. [Arthur] Pell of the Horace Liveright office to whom we appealed for aid in locating you.

When you finally advised the Studio that you were in New Orleans, Mr. Hoffenstein was immediately dispatched to discuss the script with you. We then received [a] copy of your letter of February 26th addressed to Mr. Hoffenstein declining to discuss the script submitted, and I am told that although you were in New Orleans on that day that Mr. Hoffenstein arrived there, having travelled all the way from Hollywood, you declined to see him.

This left us no alternative but to permit the studio to proceed with the production of their version since the brief criticism contained in your letter of February 26th gave no constructive suggestions, nor idea in what particular the treatment might disagree with your concept of how the story should be told on the screen.

I am stating this at length not in a spirit of controversy, but to remind you of the facts so that you will see that it is far too late to accept your suggestions as to the treatment, writer and director to be selected for the work, without even referring to the qualifications of the gentlemen suggested.

At the time of closing for the talking rights our purpose to

proceed immediately with the production was clearly stated to you and I am at a loss to understand your failure to cooperate by giving us your criticisms of the treatment as we confidently expected you to do.

I am advised that shooting has already commenced on the picture but in spite of that I am telephoning the contents of your letter and airmailing a copy to the studio so that Mr. von Sternberg may have the advantage of your suggestions with respect to the characters as he proceeds.

Very truly yours,
Jesse L. Lasky

200 West 57th Street
New York, [N.Y.]
March 17, 1931

Dear Mr. Lasky:

I have your letter of March 14th. I gather that you feel that the matter should be dismissed without further ado, also that nothing further in connection with this can possibly trouble Paramount-Publix.

Your chief complaint seems to lie in the fact that I was not available for consultation. Actually, in regard to this time business, there is nothing to it at all, as the following résumé will definitely prove:

Here is a picture that for five years has been dormant. It was purchased in 1926, and allowed to rest until 1931, except for using it for bait to entice directors to come with your Company. Now, suddenly, in January, 1931, you buy the talking rights, and after agreeing to allow me to see the script, and sending your own lawyers to tell me about Mr. Hoffenstein and Mr. Sternberg and their enthusiasm for my work, and that both would come here to talk this thing over with me, and after further agreeing verbally and by contract that any suggestions I had to make would be very seriously considered, and that your best endeavors would be used to incorporate them, you now, through a hocus-pocus in regard to time, proceed to shoot the picture at once.

The fact is that I waited here until the first of February with-

out word of any kind. Then finding it absolutely necessary to leave the city, and although I left specific directions with Mr. Pell of Liveright, and in my own studio as to where I could be found, on February 9th there begins a great hoorah as to my absence and the great damage that it is causing.

As a matter of fact, it was on February 9th that the first notice was received that Mr. Hoffenstein wanted to come to New York. On the 10th, he was wired that I was not here. On February 13th, Mr. Pell was advised that Mr. Hoffenstein wanted to see me and on that date he wired me, and on the 14th, I wired Mr. Hoffenstein at your studio in California, so there was no important time elapsed. The long and carefully worded legal notice which Mr. Swartz sent, proves the anxiety for legal haste in the matter.

On the 17th, I wired Mr. Hoffenstein that I was ready to meet him wherever he wished to come.[3] On the 20th of February, he wired me at great length with regard to his injured feelings, and said that he would come if necessary, but only to take such ideas as I had back to Paramount-Publix for consideration.[4] Regardless of this, I wired him to meet me in New Orleans on Thursday, February 23rd,[5] and he arrived there at that time, presumably with the script. On the same day, in the morning, I had received the script from New York, and had had time to read it before he arrived.

Having previously had the pleasure of reading the Eisenstein-Montagu script,[6] as well as a proposed German synopsis of how this should be done in a talkie, and then examining the one that

[3] Dreiser's copy of his wire to Samuel Hoffenstein is dated the 16th, from Ft. Myers, Fla.

[4] Hoffenstein had replied on the 17th regretting that Dreiser had given no notice of his projected trip, because now it would be too late to go over the script. His feelings were not "injured" until Dreiser, on the 18th, had called Hoffenstein's telegram "the usual Hollywood swill and bunk." On the 20th Hoffenstein had agreed to meet Dreiser "to receive your ideas for transmission to studio."

[5] Dreiser, on the 20th, had wired that he would be in New Orleans on Wednesday the 25th, and Hoffenstein had replied, on Monday the 23rd, that he would arrive on Thursday the 26th.

[6] An earlier script prepared by Sergei M. Eisenstein and Ivor Montagu. (For their views, see, in Dreiser's files, Eisenstein to Dreiser, August 21, 1931, and Montagu to Dreiser, August 10, 1931; also S. M. Eisenstein: "An American Tragedy," Close Up, X (June 1933), 109-124.)

Mr. Sternberg had prepared, I was forced to dismiss it because I could not possibly revise any such script as was laid before me. As I wrote Mr. Hoffenstein at the time,[7] and a copy of which letter I enclosed with my letter to you, it was so entirely foreign to the tragedy of the book and even, I may add, to the Eisenstein-Montagu outline, that I was left no recourse but to dismiss it and him entirely. None the less, had he been interested, as stated, he could have wired my New York residence and as quickly as wires could have reached me, I would have given consideration to anything he had suggested.

Not alone that, but the script submitted to me, instead of being the final script, was labelled "First Yellow Script" so that even if I had discussed this script with Mr. Hoffenstein, what could it have availed, seeing that it is positive that you not alone had later versions in your possession, but that you were completely prepared to shoot this picture without informing me of its treatment. If it was the honest endeavor of Mr. Hoffenstein and Mr. Sternberg to improve this script, why did they not come forward in answer to my telegrams with what they thought were improved versions? Your production date on the *American Tragedy* was March 2nd. How do you expect me to believe that you were sincere in your professed and agreed willingness to consider anything that I might have to say when, on Thursday,[8] February 23rd, seven days before you were scheduled to commence shooting, you were sending Mr. Hoffenstein to me to gather such suggestions as I might have to make and which you supposedly welcomed?

In short, the statement contained in your letter, that this leaves no alternative but to permit the studio to proceed with the production of their version, is ridiculous. As I see it, it is nothing more nor less than a studied attempt to sidetrack our various verbal and written agreements, and to rush into production with an unprecedented haste. But just why? To ignore any suggestions that I might have or wish to make. That this speed is unusual

---

7 Dreiser to Hoffenstein, February 26, 1931.
8 Monday was the 23rd. See p. 519, n. 5.

you yourself must know very well, and it will be obvious to anyone in or out of the picture business. I know positively that another picture was to have been made by the two leads now scheduled to appear in the *American Tragedy,* and this picture was sidetracked in this desperate haste to put my novel in quick production and forestall any possible recourse that I might have.

On top of this come Mr. Sternberg's public statements to the press which, as I have already pointed out to you,[9] indicate a spirit so hostile to me, personally, that no honest direction could look to him for a satisfactory result. Personally, I do not sense the mental equipment which permits him to criticize me. So far, if my knowledge is correct, he has produced one successful picture, which chances to carry a star which would make any picture successful. From that, he proceeds, apparently, to the assumption that he personally, in Hollywood, is prepared to arrange and embellish the literary achievements of the world. I doubt it. His achievements so far do not appear to justify his estimate of himself, and if you doubt this, consult the critical comments of his more recent picture, *Dishonored,* in the *New York Times* of March 15th.[10]

Under the circumstances, I can only believe that, as I have previously stated, this is a deliberate attempt to botch the *American Tragedy.* Apart from the book, my study of the Eisenstein-Montagu version convinces me of that. There is no possible comparison between the two. In addition, as you must know, the reports on the original Eisenstein-Montagu script from your own studio readers and officials were much more favorable than the reports these same readers returned on the Hoffenstein-Sternberg script.

Worse, the talking version that you propose cannot possibly

9 Dreiser to Lasky, March 10, 1931.

10 "Miss [Marlene] Dietrich's current picture is for the most part an excellent example of direction with a clever performance by the star. But the story is a clumsy affair and the dialogue is emphatically amateurish. It was written by Josef von Sternberg, who directed the production. He is somewhat out of his element as a writer and like most motion picture directors who turn their own literary aspirations into film form he gives more attention to the cinematic quality of his incidents than to the reflection or portrayal of ordinary human emotions."

fail to give the impression to the millions of people throughout the world who will see this picture, that the novel on which it is based is nothing short of a cheap, tawdry, tabloid confession story which entirely lacks the scope, emotion, action and psychology of the book involved. Here is an inequitable infringement of a vested property.

Furthermore, you must already know that I do not propose to stand idly by and see this done. But before taking such measures as I deem advisable, and in which I am sustained by eminent counsel, I again repeat what I have stated in my previous letter, that I am willing and ready to leave for Hollywood, or meet anyone here, in order that this picture may repeat the artistic and financial success which it has been both as a novel and a play.

In this connection, I call your attention to the opinion of Mr. Otto H. Kahn, who has been acquainted with the matter at hand and who states as follows: "If writers in general would stand up as you have done for the dignity of their work and refuse to bend the knee to the puerilities and sloppinesses of Hollywood, we could expect to get somewhere in having the 'movies' pulled out of their rut." [11]

Since the production of this picture was announced, I have been constantly importuned by Mr. Roy Howard, the *New York Times,* the United Press, the Associated Press and others to answer the ridiculous statements of Sternberg, and this I can and shall do, not only here but in Europe. Such legal action as may be necessary will be joined with this.

Will you advise me finally as to your decision? [12]

11 Kahn to Dreiser, March 12, 1931, after Dreiser had sent him copies of his letters to Hoffenstein (February 26) and Lasky (March 10).
12 The following week Dreiser and H. S. Kraft flew to Hollywood to make detailed suggestions, all of which were approved by B. P. Schulberg, general manager, in a letter of April 1, but none of which appear to have been embodied in the picture itself.

To Morris L. Ernst
[CC]

Ernst was defending the New York Evening Graphic *against a libel suit by the New York Society for the Suppression of Vice, which the paper had alleged received 50 per cent of all fines collected from the prosecutions it instigated. Ernst on March 18 had asked whether Dreiser had had to pay the Society's executive secretary, John S. Sumner, a fee for editing* The "Genius" *to make it acceptable for serial publication, and requested "one of your usual stiff letters telling what you think of the Vice Society." He had concluded: "Am I still welcome at your Thursday evenings, or did my support of Heywood Broun outlaw me?"*

200 West 57th Street
New York, [N.Y.]
March 20, 1931

My dear Ernst:

You are still welcome at my Thursday evenings which occur regularly on Friday at 5.00 p.m. As for your support of Heywood Broun, you might bring along the four or five others who voted for him.[13]

Concerning the Society for the Suppression of Vice, so far as I know you are in error in assuming that serial publication of *The "Genius"* was accomplished only after paying a fee to Sumner. I never heard of his having anything to do with that. The serial form was cut from the book by Mr. Will Lengel, Associate Editor of the *Cosmopolitan Magazine.* The book was suppressed by the John Lane Company after it was threatened by Sumner. That is, he said that if they did not take it off the market, he would seize plates, copies, etc. and thus prevent its sale. They agreed to suppress the book and it was suppressed from 1915

13 Ernst (August 13, 1930) and Alexander Woollcott (August 16, 1930) had each sought Dreiser's support for Heywood Broun in the Congressional election the preceding fall.

until 1922 or 1923,[14] at which time Horace Liveright, being very anxious to take me over, decided to get legal advice and on that legal advice proceeded to publish the book without anything being cut from it, and regardless of what Mr. Sumner thought. Preceding that, though, Mr. Sumner was visited by Mencken who tried to find out from him what would have to come out of the book in order to make it available for publication. He and Mencken together agreed on so many cuts which were obnoxious to me that I finally cancelled the whole proceeding, told Mencken to let the matter rest and went ahead with Liveright as above.

The other suppressions that I have suffered have been by publishers direct. That is, Doubleday suppressed *Sister Carrie* after he had put it in book form and Harper Brothers deliberately threw back on my hands *The Titan* after it had been published, and Messrs. Dodd, Mead, preceding Liveright, told me that they would like to be my publishers and they would handle possibly *The "Genius"* and some other works, providing I would submit to certain cuts which I refused, thereby lengthening my starvation period by quite a little.

Now as to the Vice Society. The worst I can say of it is that it is either lacking in mental or artistic discrimination, or it finds that by attacking and suppressing superior works it is more benefited from a publicity and money point of view than by attacking and suppressing little dealers in purely pornographic matter. We all know the type of pornographic leaflets sold to school children at ten cents apiece, presenting the wonder of the marriage night, also the voluptuous nudes alone in a room in one or another position which are supposed to be very exciting to anybody under fourteen years of age, and insofar as these are concerned, I have no objection to their suppressing this material because as a rule in every school room or corner drug-store of little towns and big ones, there is always some boy or girl who can draw these things very well, and who passes them around for

14 The "suppression" began in 1916 and ended with the Boni & Liveright edition of 1923.

inspection. At least, that was my experience when I was a child and could not afford ten cents for a really literary description.

Personally, I have always looked at simon pure pornography as something which is never reached by the police, preachers or well-intended reformers and moralists. It is too sly.

What probably is desired by both police and vice agents is a "kick" and some publicity, plus a salary. Hence the snooping. That they get a "kick" is obvious, for in doing so, of course, they must legally witness such scenes as well as seize upon for their own private collections such works, etc. as they may find. Consider only the collection possessed by Anthony Comstock at his death, and by him treasured very highly. I think that if somebody raided Sumner, they might find some little collection of his own which would rid us of him for four or five years at least.

As to important literature, or any sane survey of life, there is no more escaping sex or even pornography than there is of escaping your rent or your grocer's bill. It is not only the warp and woof of life as we know it, but obviously the will of the Creator, whether he is divine or supremely evil and contemptible.

The nerve of these people, in seizing on books which chance to contain passages which States like Massachusetts insist are sufficient for prosecution, and suppressing them, always astounds me. It always looks to me as though these activities everywhere spring not only from a desire for publicity, but from an annual salary which can be easily earned in this way, and once a man like Sumner or anybody else of that stripe gets a salary, it becomes a vital business for him to make himself worthy of it, so that it will be continued. How sad he would feel, for instance, if someone who is a better snooper and suppresser than himself should come along and, by rival activities, oust him out of his job. It might even end in his seeking solace in the arms or the pages of these various things which he now condemns. I have seen related actions in the clergy of various denominations.

After reading the summary of the vice law which you were kind enough to send me, and the names of its sponsors and its

enormous privileges, I wish that it could be suppressed at once. God knows, these days, the ministers, district attorneys, moralists, religionists, etc. are hot enough on the trail to cause one to ignore pornography to such an extent that that thing which Roosevelt feared, race suicide, would result. I honestly think that the state legislature should come to the rescue and root those organizations out.

And should this inure to the financial injury of Mr. Sumner, I suggest that he join the Baptist or the Methodist Church, where he will find an ample field for his moral services, and, who knows, he might even be sent to the Congo or China, where he can see immorality en masse. And most prayerfully I desire this for him.

To Harrison Smith
[CC]

After corresponding with Jesse L. Lasky in March, Dreiser had made detailed suggestions for revising the script of An American Tragedy, *and Paramount had agreed to give Dreiser a preview of the completed film. On April 25 Dreiser began to send letters to persons who were interested in literature and the arts generally and who might constitute a review committee. Harrison Smith, a partner in the publishing firm of Jonathan Cape and Harrison Smith, was one of these.*

> 200 West 57th Street
> New York, [N.Y.]
> April 25, 1931

Dear Mr. Smith:

You are possibly aware, through newspapers, of my quarrel with the Paramount-Publix Moving Picture Corporation concerning the proposed talking picture of *An American Tragedy*. I desire to lay before you the nature of the quarrel, because its final outcome or adjustment may, and no doubt will, depend

considerably upon the unbiased critical wisdom which I can call to aid me in passing upon the points at issue.

There is in existence a contract between myself and Paramount-Publix, dated January 2, 1931, whereby for a given sum of money, I assign the talking picture reproduction rights to that organization, and under that contract it has proceeded to film the *Tragedy* and will very shortly offer it to the public at large.

Paragraph 10 of that contract reads as follows:

> The purchaser agrees before production of the first motion picture photoplay by him presented to submit to the seller the manuscript intended to be used as a basis or from which there may be adapted such motion picture photoplay for such comments, advice, suggestions or criticisms that the seller may wish to make with respect thereto and to afford the seller the opportunity of discussing with the scenarist of such motion picture the manuscript thereof, and the purchaser agrees it will use its best endeavors to accept such advice, suggestions, and criticisms that the seller may make insofar as it may, in the judgment of the purchaser, consistently do so.

Apart from this, there is nothing in the entire contract, a copy of which will be forwarded on request, which indicates in any way that the purchaser of the talking rights has the right to change the structure, or what I may better call the ideographic plan of the book so that when shown it will convey to the public a characterization of the work which is not consistent with it nor with my own intellectual and artistic structure as therein manifested.

My ideographic plan for the book before and as I wrote it was as follows:

It was to be a novel which was to set forth in three distinct social, as well as economic phases, the career of a very sensitive yet not too highly mentally equipped boy, who finds his life in its opening phase painfully hampered by poverty and a low so-

cial state and from which, because of his various inherent and motivating desires, he seeks to extricate himself. In his case, love and material comfort, as well as a foolish dream of social superiority are his motivating forces.

Part One of my book was purposely and particularly devoted to setting forth such social miseries as might naturally depress, inhibit and frustrate, and therefore exaggerate, the emotions and desires of a very sensitive and almost sensually exotic boy most poorly equipped for the great life struggle which confronts all youth.

Part Two particularly was planned to show how such a temperament might fortuitously be brought face to face with a much more fortunate world which would intensify all his deepest desires for luxury and love, and to show how, in the usual unequal contest between poverty and ignorance and desire and the world's great toys, he might readily and really through no real willing of his own, find himself defeated and even charged with murder, as was the case of Griffiths in this book.

Part Three of the book was definitely and carefully planned to show how such an inhibited, weak temperament, once in the hands of his dreams and later the law, might be readily forced by an ignorant, conventional and revengeful background of rural souls who would, in their turn, by reason of their lacks and social and religious inhibitions and beliefs, be the last to understand and comprehend the palliatives that might have, but did not, attend the life of such a boy, and therefore judge him far more harshly than would individuals of deeper insight and better mental fortune.

But in constructing the talking picture which is to represent this book and myself as its creator, the director of the Paramount-Publix Motion Picture Corporation, Mr. Josef von Sternberg, together with the advice and consent, apparently of those who provide directors with their authority, decided that, in the first place, economic conditions being what they are, the picture should be reduced from the very serious and extended film planned by Sergei Eisenstein, who was called to America for that

purpose, to an ordinary eight or ten-reel program picture. Next, and possibly in order to do that, it was arranged apparently, I think, between the scenarist and the director that Part One as well as Part Three of the novel should be ignored, and only Part Two, beginning with the arrival of Clyde Griffiths at his wealthy uncle's home in Lycurgus, and ending with his sentence by the Supreme Court Judge who sat in his case after the assumed murder by him of Roberta Alden, should be stressed. The preliminary data which, in the book, shows how he came to wander into such a world, and the subsequent data, Part Three, which makes plain how such a backwoods region as that in which he was tried, would naturally tend to prejudice his opportunities for social understanding and a fair trial, have been discarded.

In other words, the film, as I understand it, now tends to place before the world—and without sufficient data for his understanding,—a more or less over-sexed and worthless boy who, finding himself in a world in which his sensual desires might be indulged fairly easily, concerns himself rather lightly with several girls and finally destroys one in his efforts to further his success with another, more wealthy and more beautiful.

This I maintain, and have maintained with the officers of Paramount-Publix, as well as the people who have so far consulted me in the matter, is by no means a presentation of the problem offered in the book, not even approximately so. Furthermore, the millions and millions who have never read the book and who may or may not have heard of me will, by this process, be offered a distorted as well as a belittling interpretation of a work which is entitled, on its face, to a far more intelligible and broadening conception of the inscrutable ways of life and chance.

As I read the script which has been offered to me as the final plan of the picture, I feel that it might as well have been deliberately calculated to misinterpret not only my character and powers as a novelist, but my mental and artistic approach to life itself. I resent this, and as I personally said to the officers and directors of Paramount-Publix, no such corruption of this work,

under my reading of the contract, can be offered to the public.

Necessarily, I must await the preliminary presentation here in New York in order to be able, along with such critics and authorities as I may persuade to see it with me, to decide whether my judgment in regard to it is right or wrong. If my judgement should prove to be wrong, and the work prove to be an intelligent interpretation of the logic of the book, I shall gladly withdraw my objections and, not only that, add my endorsement of it as a proper interpretation. On the other hand, should it prove as I fear, and my assembled advisors agree with me, I propose to take legal action not only under the phrasing of the contract itself, but under a new principle in equity which I propose to offer to the proper court of jurisdiction in this country.

The purpose of this letter, therefore, is to ask you if, by any chance, you have read the book and, if not, whether you would do me the courtesy to do so, and having done so, whether you would make one in a group which will be asked to view this picture with me on its preliminary presentation here and to say then and there over your own signature to me whether or not in your opinion the picture sufficiently carries out the ideology of the book as to hold me free from any personal or artistic harm before the world.

I am enclosing the proposed list of advisors and will be obliged to you for an early reply.

Very truly yours,

P.S. The date of the preliminary presentation is not yet set, but it will probably take place within a week or ten days.[15]

15 Dreiser's "jury" witnessed the film on June 15 and condemned it. Dreiser sued to enjoin Paramount Publix Corp. from showing it, but lost. (See Dreiser to Louise Campbell, August 5, 1931.)

To David Algar Bailey
[CC]

200 West 57th Street
New York, [N.Y.]
May 18, 1931

Dear Mr. Bailey:

I appreciate thoroughly that the only safeguard to any nationality or any race, for that matter, is a vigorous and reasonably thinking middle class. I know that the rank and file at the bottom cannot think, or they would not be at the bottom so persistently, and I know that the strong and brilliant at the top are not to be controlled by an indigent mass. It takes an intelligent middle mass to balance both.

You talk as though you had some method of bringing this about. If you have, I'd like to know more about it. I have never seen a remedy this side of revolution that appears to work. When the atoms in any pot get too restless, the lid blows off.

My entire plan is to reach such a middle class, if one exists in America, and to stir them to such action (and this is probably a vain dream) as will stop the lid from blowing off.

To H. G. Wells
[TC]

On March 25 Dreiser had mailed Wells, in London, his own copy of Charles Fort's The Book of the Damned, *only to have Wells reply on April 9:*

Dear Dreiser:

I'm having Fort's *Book of the Damned* sent back to you. Fort seems to be one of the most damnable bores who ever cut scraps from out-of-the-way newspapers & thought they were facts. And he writes like a drunkard. *Lo!* has been sent to me & it has gone into

my wastepaper basket. And what do *you* mean by writing about forcing "orthodox science" to do this or that. Science is a continuing exploration & how the devil can it have an orthodoxy? The next thing you'll be writing is "the dogmas of Science"—like some blasted R. C. priest on the defensive. When you tell a Christian you don't believe some yarn he can't prove, he always calls you "dogmatic." Scientific workers are first rate stuff & very ill paid & it isn't for the likes of you and me to heave Forts at them.

God dissolve (& forgive) your Fortean Society[.]

<Yours>
H. G. Wells

200 West 57th Street
New York, [N.Y.]
May 23, 1931

Dear Wells:

At best, your letter hands me a laugh.

In regard to Fort's work, I am still of the opinion that such a body of ideas, notions, reports, hallucinations—anything you will—gathered from whatever sources and arranged as strangely and, certainly I can say in this case, imaginatively, is worth any mind's attention. I think it is arresting just as pure imagination, as Jules Verne's *Twenty Thousand Leagues under the Sea,* or your own *The Island of Dr. Moreau* is arresting. You, the author of *The War of the Worlds* to be so sniffish and snorty over *The Book of the Damned!*

As a matter of fact, as I see it, if you were still in the *War of the Worlds* or the *Doctor Moreau* frame of mind, you might readily see in this data a field for the activities of your own always fascinating pen.

I find this about Fort's books; the few copies of *The Book of the Damned* that were ever printed—a thousand or so—have become actual mental treasures to discriminating readers in many walks. It was I who forced the publication of this book and saw that such copies as were printed were distributed. For years I thought it had fallen absolutely flat, that no one was the least

impressed, but wandering here and there, I encountered over and over people who were enormously interested by this book and the name behind it, and over here where, as you know, all the world's morons dwell, it seems to grow in value. In England, if I can trust your reaction, it will never make any impression.

Still, I think it is material which may, in different ways and at different times, be substantiated. I have a feeling, for instance, when I read a book like Sir James Jeans' *The Universe around Us*, that its enormous calculations have an airy unsubstantiality which may mean anything or nothing, because after all, like yourself and myself, he is using our five senses, elaborated as they may be by implements of various kinds, and I am not sure that these in themselves constitute the sum total of sensitivity or response in nature. I only know that I respond in various ways with the five that I have, but around and beyond me, lie nothing but mysteries which, instruments or no instruments, I have not the slightest ability to solve—nor have I found others who have. And since I have gone through life so far without any particularly valuable solution of anything that has occurred, and know really that behind me in the depths of time have passed billions and billions of people, creatures as confused and mentally defeated as myself, I am ready to at least meditate upon, if not accept, such items of strangeness as are suggested by Fort in his curious explorations among, as you say, "items of newspapers." I notice, though, that a respectable body of his data seems to come from scientific papers, reports and letters written to the Royal Society in England, and the American Academy of Science here, and related bodies elsewhere.

But we won't fight about this. If you ever come over to America again, I want you to look me up. There are a lot of things that can be discussed here at close range which will never be discussed by mail.

To the Association of Southern Women for the Prevention of Lynching
[CC]

200 West 57th Street
New York, [N.Y.]
July 13, 1931

Mesdames:

I have been much interested to read of the progress of your Association in a recent A.P. despatch.[16]

My attitude concerning the estimates and judgment which the law necessitates has always been that the Negro as well as the white person should, before the law, be treated with understanding and liberality, in other words—humanely. Through no fault of their own, a century or two ago, some Negroes were drafted as slaves by the white powers and now that, instead of evoking sympathy, has produced belittlement and hatred. Because Negroes are not, at present, a dominating race, some unthinking members of the white race manifest petty prejudice toward them and their conduct. And, finally, the prejudice-makers have grown to include even the more intelligent leaders who do not stop to analyse the standards and ideas under which they themselves were brought up. Hence, not only laws unduly

---

16   ANTI-LYNCHING GAIN SEEN
Southern Women's Association Cites
Record for Half Year

ATLANTA, Ga. July 5 (AP).—The Association of Southern Women for the Prevention of Lynching in a statement today said that "the first half of 1931 brings much encouragement to increasing numbers of Southern people who have committed themselves to an unceasing fight" against lynching.

Only five lynchings occurred throughout the United States during the first six months of 1931, the association pointed out, compared with thirty for the same period of 1922, "in a similar time of depression."

The statement added that Southern newspapers have played a leading part in the campaign against lynching, and have supported various officials "who by united action have prevented mob execution of forty-nine persons within the Southern States alone."

severe concerning the human relations of Negroes have been made, but these laws in the eyes of the unified Southern population have become so near perfection itself that the people almost justify mob-rule to enforce them.

In the case of the nine Negro boys at Scottsboro, Alabama, two ignorant white girls, workers in a Scottsboro mill, where they were employed only part-time at miserable wages, went to Chattanooga to get a job. Being unsuccessful they hopped a freight gondola for home. They were dressed in overalls. A crowd of white boys were in the car, and they all laughed and joked with the girls who, it is alleged, were well-known prostitutes, until nineteen Negroes—ages 14 to 20—all helpless and ignorant, came along. (Evidence of number of Negroes questioned, but well supported). The Negroes and the white boys got in a fight, and all the white boys and all but nine Negroes fell or were thrown off. The white boys, saying that Negroes were on the train with white girls, wired authorities to stop the train. Anyone who understands the psychology of the Southern people realizes that the news of Negroes alone with white girls is enough to make rape a fact! The train was stopped and two groups of armed deputies captured nine Negro boys and the two girls. The girls denied that the Negroes had committed rape. This crime in Alabama means electrocution. That in itself is to me a horrible travesty on natural human conduct. And these girls, upon capture, presented no signs of assault or violence. Until they were taken to Scottsboro, which was excited with the reported rape, and to sheriffs insisting rape had been committed, the girls remained quiet and made no charges. Finally, they were forced to. Doctors' examinations showed no bruises or evidence of viciousness. There was, however, evidence of coition which, with their consent, is not rape. The Negroes' story is that those indulging in this left the train. Because of the high feeling in the South against relations of any kind between Negro men and white girls, it is very probable that the boys realizing that they might get caught, did hop off.

A conviction in this case was rushed through in 15 days, and

all eight boys (the ninth boy's case a mistrial) were sentenced to die in the electric chair. The state's defense of these chaps, being hurried, was not handled as carefully as more time would have permitted. The other boys as witnesses were lacking. The two girls whose evidence really convicted them disagreed on the testimony. One girl, who said that "all niggers looked alike to her" couldn't identify the Negroes as those who had "raped" her. Evidence of the character of these two girls, who were allegedly prostitutes, was not allowed at the trial. According to Southern law apparently, the boys were much more to blame than the girls, whatever the provocation.

Finally, at the time of the trial, feeling reached such tenseness that the Governor sent troops. Ten thousand people came into town for the trial and swarmed about the courthouse. These people so fiercely believed rape had been committed, and so wanted this vicious so-called justice, founded on their prejudice, that hooting and yelling and rejoicing and applauding not only followed the verdict of death, but this outcome of one trial was being uproariously cheered while the jury for another of these boys was behind closed doors deciding as to their verdict. What would they have done unless there had been a conviction? A lynching, of course! But is it not obvious that these 10,000 people in the yard outside the courthouse, tumultuous in their mob-unity, and with bands of music blaring forth their conception of what was fair and necessary, made the trials of the remaining Negro defendants only slightly above a lynching in the ordinary sense of the word?

The whole Southern attitude toward the Negro has become a national ill. It is unreasoning and immensely unfair. They should begin to consider the case of the Negro from the day of his enforced entry into this country. Instead of that, some Southern newspapers have been insisting that this is a case for mob-rule. Yet such violence as surrounded this entire trial is in violation of the 14th Amendment, guaranteeing due process of law.

The trial judge denied two motions for a new trial. The matter is now before the State Supreme Court, and there are a few

remaining weeks in which new testimony and new witnesses are being gathered to support the appeal for a new trial. If the State Supreme Court denies this motion, then an appeal can be made to the Federal Court—a proper appeal. Personally, I feel strongly that by transferring the case to escape the violence of Southern feeling, a more clear-headed view of the data may be presented. These eight boys must at least have a just trial, even though at this time in Alabama they are suppressed by a law unduly severe and emotionally enforced.

It seems to me that your organization could find no more appropriate field for its activities than this case, and I should be interested to learn whether or not your Association has taken any steps to help prevent the legal murder of these Negro boys.[17]

Very truly yours,

To William L. Green
[CC]

On June 24 Dreiser at the behest of Joseph Pass and William Z. Foster had visited the Pittsburgh mining area where amid the hardships and brutalities of industrial warfare the United Mine Workers of America (American Federation of Labor) and the communistic National Miners' Union were contending for the miners' allegiance. After interviewing a score of miners and confronting uncivil police officers, Dreiser had told the United Press, in a statement datelined June 26, that he was interested "in anything that looks to the disestablishment of the American Federation of Labor, with which the United Mine Workers of America is affiliated . . . because there is ample evidence that it simply is

[17] When (July 30) Mrs. Jesse Daniel Ames, Director of Women's Work, Commission on Interracial Cooperation, explained that the organization's purpose was primarily to rob lynching of the glamor of chivalry and that it could not work effectively if it took official action concerning so spectacular a case as Scottsboro, Dreiser (August 3) acknowledged the necessity and intelligence of the group's procedures.

a closed corporation operated for little groups who get all the money they can for themselves at the expense of all the rest of non-unionized labor. Further, I know for a positive fact there was proposed, and now is being put into effect, a close union between the chief corporations, such as power and utility groups, and the A.F.L. to put a quietus, in so far as possible, on strike and labor troubles, and bring about the general poverty of the rest of the people. The corporations, because of the financial crash, are aware of the fact that without some skeleton form of labor assistance they cannot hold their own. But with an alleged and, so far as labor is concerned, fake association they hope to hold their own. From various sources in New York I learned of the National Miners' Union's invasion of this field and I learned for myself the significance of it. I learned it proposes to do what the A.F.L. never has done and that is open the doors to all classes and conditions of labor, even unskilled workers." Green, president of the A.F.L., had then issued a statement denying the charges and on July 1 written an open letter to Dreiser:

My dear Mr. Dreiser:

The statement which you gave to the press, dated June 26th, is so full of inaccuracies, illogical conclusions and unjustifiable denunciation of the American Federation of Labor that I feel it my duty, as President of the American Federation of Labor, to write you frankly in reply. You have a right to oppose the American Federation of Labor and all its members, if you wish. You have a right to say that you visited the coal regions because, "you were interested in anything that looks to the disestablishment of the American Federation of Labor with which the United Mine Workers of America is affiliated." You have no right to make such unfounded charges against either the American Federation of Labor or the United Mine Workers of America, an affiliated Union, and expect such unfound statements to go unchallenged.

In your statement you said that you had positive knowledge of a proposal to put into effect, "a close union between the chief corporations, such as power and utility groups, and the American Federation of Labor to put a quietus insofar as possible on strike

and labor troubles and bring about general poverty of the rest of the people."

As the President of the American Federation of Labor I would know if any such proposal was made binding the American Federation of Labor to such a plan. I assert positively that no such proposal has been made or considered. You could not have knowledge of such a proposal because I assert that no such understanding exists between the American Federation of Labor and any corporation of any kind. It is difficult to understand how a man with such a reputation as you have gained would engage in making such reckless statements.

You said further, in this article, that the reason you favored the invasion of the National Miners' Union, a Communist organization, into the coal fields was because that organization would do what the American Federation of Labor never did—"open the doors to all classes and conditions of labor, even unskilled workers."

This erroneous statement, alone, is enough to destroy the force, effect and influence of your entire article. It is utterly baseless. It shows conclusively that you either do not understand the character and form of the International Union, United Mine Workers of America, and the American Federation of Labor or if you do then you are influenced by prejudice, passion and feeling—so much so that you recklessly make an untruthful and unfounded statement.

The American Federation of Labor and the International Union, United Mine Workers of America particularly, are as deeply interested in the unskilled workers as they are in the skilled workers. Provisions are made by the laws of the American Federation of Labor for the organization of all unskilled workers. The International Hod Carriers', Building and Common Laborers' Union organizes the hod carriers, the common laborers employed in the streets, on the highways, in excavating work and in every other activity where unskilled labor is employed. Thousands of unskilled colored workers are members of this International Union. The Brotherhood of Maintenance of Way Employes organizes the section men employed upon the railroads of the Country. You cannot deny that these are unskilled workers. The International Union, United Mine Workers of America, accepts into membership all men employed in and around coal mines. They protect the unskilled worker in the enjoyment of all his rights just as carefully as they do the rights of the

most skilled among them. When negotiating wage scales with coal operators the United Mine Workers insist that the wage scale agreed upon apply to the unskilled worker and that he must be accorded the same degree of protection as even the most important key men. If you wish to verify these facts go into the anthracite coal region where a contract for five years exists between the International Union, United Mine Workers of America, and the anthracite Coal Operators.

What are the facts relative to the activity and service of the United Mine Workers of America and the American Federation of Labor among the coal miners of the Nation. For more than thirty years the International Union, United Mine Workers of America has functioned and served the men employed in and around the coal mines of the Nation. They carried on strikes in West Virginia, Kentucky, Ohio, Indiana, Illinois—in fact in every mining center, in an effort to raise the standard of life and living among the men in the mines.

As a result of the struggle of the miners, under the leadership of their Union, and as a result of these strikes collective bargaining was accepted. Coal Operators in many instances were reluctantly forced to recognize the Miners' Union with which agreements were made. The rights of all concerned were clearly defined. Wages were increased and conditions of life and living became more tolerable. Unfortunately about three years ago the coal operators in the bituminous coal fields decided to make war upon the International Union, United Mine Workers of America. All the power and resources of these Coal Operators were used in an effort to crush and destroy the Mine Workers' Union. The unemployment situation which began to develop contributed very largely to the efforts of the Coal Operators to wipe out collective bargaining and destroy the Union.

The United Mine Workers of America and the American Federation of Labor spent many millions of dollars in resisting the attack of the coal corporations. No one ever heard of you or those associated with you going into the coal fields when this struggle was on, investigating the efforts of the United Mine Workers or extending to them a word of sympathy or encouragement.

During these thirty years of collective bargaining, when the Miners' Union was a greater power and influence in Western Pennsylvania and Ohio than it is today the Mine Workers' Union secured

many changes, adjustments and reforms which were of great benefit to the miners. From an economic standpoint they increased wages; they established the eight-hour day in the coal fields; they set up machinery, through wage agreements, for the settlement of disputes and for the adjustment of grievances. Their Union was recognized through Pit Committees and through their elected officers. In a legislative way they secured, through the power and influence of their Union and the American Federation of Labor, legislation providing for proper ventilation and inspection of the mines. They succeeded in securing legislation providing for the creation of Mining Departments in the different states with an adequate inspection force to properly inspect the mines so that violent explosions could be reduced to a minimum. They forced the Coal Companies to permit the Miners to place check-weighmen upon all the coal tipples so that the miner could be protected against short weight and robbery. They forced the coal operators to accept the Mine Run system. You do not know what this means because if you did you would say that the United Mine Workers justified its existence if it never accomplished another thing except to force the Coal Operators to accept the Mine Run system. The Miners know what this means but I assume that you never talked to one of them while you were in Pittsburgh and asked him what it means to the Mine Workers and their families.

This great reform was secured as the result of years of effort and agitation by the Mine Workers' Union. It is the greatest benefit and blessing that ever came to the Miners of the Nation.

The so-called National Miners' Union, which you have espoused, never did anything to assist in securing any of these benefits and blessings for the miners.

There are many other things the Mine Workers' Union did when it was permitted to function. It secured the enactment of legislation in Illinois and Pennsylvania which provided that miners must secure a license certifying that they were qualified to serve as miners before they were permitted to work in the mines. Where the Miners' Union functioned best housing conditions in the mining centers were improved. The abuses of the Company Store and the "Pluck Me" system were wiped out completely where the Miners' Union was powerful enough to achieve this result. Legislation was secured prohibiting the employment of children in the coal mines. This great

reform movement, particularly in the anthracite region, was secured under the leadership of the late John Mitchell when he was President of the International Union, United Mine Workers of America. As a result of the efforts of the Miners thousands of breaker boys were taken out of the anthracite coal breakers and placed in the school room and in the home.

I can recite many other definite, concrete accomplishments of the Miners' Union, all of which clearly refute your argument that the miners care nothing for the unskilled or for the miners themselves.

Now, what about your National Miners' Union. You saw fit to ally yourself with this destructive movement and to give it the stamp of your approval. I am charitable enough to believe you were misled; that you did not know the men that represented it and who were misleading and deceiving the miners. This movement is a Communist movement. It invades the mining communities after the bona fide Miners' Union has been rendered helpless and there mobilizes the discontent which inevitably follows—not in support of a constructive movement but in support of what they term a "world revolution". No responsible person would give such a movement their endorsement.

They have never done a thing for the miners. They never can and they never will. They capitalize the misery of the miners, encourage them to engage in violence, street up-risings, clashings, hoping they will be injured and perhaps killed because through such a process they hope to appeal to the passion and feeling of the public and, as a result, will help along the realization of the "world revolution."

The management of the Scripps-Howard newspapers who published your article would not deal with the representatives of this destructive movement in case they succeeded in promoting strikes among the printers and mechanics employed in the publication of their great chain of newspapers.

One cannot blame the leaders of this Communist movement because they receive their orders from Moscow. The Miners do not know because they are hungry and discontented, the victims of coal corporation oppression. They turn to the first one who offers what seems to be a helping hand. The surprise of it all is that you and those associated with you would be deceived so grossly or are so willful in your action as to give approval, encouragement and help to a destructive movement that has no single achievement to its

credit, which frowns upon collective bargaining and which hopes to seize control of our Government through the misery and woe of deceived miners.

Thinking people will choose between your statement denouncing the American Federation of Labor and its affiliated Organizations and favoring this Communist movement. They will not favor this destructive movement as against the definite, concrete accomplishments of Organized Labor as I have set them forth in this communication which I am sending you.

The American Federation of Labor and the International Union, United Mine Workers of America, will continue to exist and serve the laboring people of the Country. It will live and thrive in spite of opposition from any and all sources. The International Union, United Mine Workers of America, will come back into the coal fields of Pennsylvania, Ohio and West Virginia. It will re-establish itself and it will serve the miners, protecting them and promoting their interests.

I hope you will investigate this whole matter as I have brought it to you. I trust you will, through such an investigation, verify and justify the brief recital I have made of the accomplishments of the International Union, United Mine Workers of America, and of the American Federation of Labor in the coal fields of the United States.

> Sincerely yours,
> [unsigned]
> President,
> American Federation of Labor

After consulting with Foster, Earl Browder, and members of International Labor Defense and Labor Research Association, Dreiser replied:

> 200 West 57th Street
> New York, [N.Y.]
> July 17, 1931

Dear Mr. Green:

Your answer to my charges of June 26th last in connection with the Western Pennsylvania coal strike and the conduct and policy of the American Federation of Labor in connection with

the same and in general, has moved you to charge me with reckless statements and to assure me that I am misled. Your greatest ire appears to center around my statement that I have positive knowledge of a proposal to put into effect a close union between the chief corporations, (for "corporations" read "industrial corporations, their owners and directors") and the American Federation of Labor to put a quietus in so far as possible on strike and labor troubles, and so bring about general poverty to the rest of the people. (For the word "people" read "workers and people," for with poverty for the workers there cannot be any general prosperity—merely specific prosperity for a few.) And with that as a leader as well as a friend of labor and the masses in general, you would hesitate to disagree, I am sure. But suppose, instead of limiting my charge to "knowledge of a proposed close union between the chief corporations and the American Federation of Labor looking to putting a quietus on strike and labor troubles" and so poverty to the rest of the people, I charge that such a union is and has already long been in effect—its results, also.

For if the National Civic Federation, organized in 1900 and which two years later came under the leadership of the notorious Mark Hanna, and of which Morgan, Du Pont, Willard, Guggenheim, Dodge, Speyer and others of the past and present are or before their deaths were members, and of which Samuel Gompers was the first Vice-President, and the purpose of which was to combine the labor leaders of its day under the direction of the employers was not a combination of capital and labor, what could be? The National Civic Federation arranges for meetings of leaders in strikes, and so possibly influences wages. Thus, it dictates economic policy, and the economic trend for many years shows that this policy is not to the benefit of labor. One of the Federation's first moves was to carry on a campaign against the Socialism of that day; later it made an investigation of government ownership, and its reports of this investigation so juggled and obscured the facts as to give the impression that the government was constantly enlarging its management of business. It denounced the failure of the government in operation of telephone and tele-

graph systems; it pointed out the "inefficiency" of government control of railroads. But what other interpretation could be expected from an organization whose prominent members included Frederick P. Fish, President of the American Telephone and Telegraph Company from 1901-1907; Lucius Tuttle, former President of the Boston and Maine Railroad; Frederick D. Underwood, former President of the Erie Railroad?

Besides, is not the present A. F. of L. Vice-President, Matthew Woll, now acting President of the National Civic Federation? And fighting against unemployment insurance, recognition of the Soviet Union (the only economic system which as yet has sought and wisely, I think, to establish society at large on its proper economic, social and political and educational basis) etc. etc.? Compare the Russian labor arrangement and program to yours. And you are supposed to be a friend to as well as a leader of labor.

The truth, as I see it at least, Mr. Green, is that the American Federation of Labor, apart from its continuous aid to capital since 1900, is not so much a failure as a menace to labor in general, its economic, political and social and educational welfare.

It offers no breadth or enlightenment. Under the A. F. of L. leadership and guidance as it is today and has been for years, the worker is in no least way encouraged let alone trained in economic, social and political ideas. And why? Because his leaders have none. I knew Gompers—his ideals and conceptions. They were as narrow and as mass repressive and so destructive as capitalism itself could desire. He saw the worker not as an individual, his family and his possibilities as factors of immense importance to the state—an integral factor of its success, but as the necessary and poorly paid servant of wealth, which, by reason of wealth (not necessarily valuable, mind) was to have the lion's share of everything. And that conception insofar as your organization is concerned, and to this hour, appears to remain in force. Neither you nor your various officers and organizers in the A. F. of L. appear to know how, let alone desire to, teach the worker his place in society and his rights. Rather, if I am any judge of what I read and see, the A. F. of L. would like him to believe in the

basic dogma of Capitalism—his servant position in life—and in such capitalistic compromises as can be negotiated on that basis. Yet in Russia, at which country and rival economic system you sneer, and even pretend to fear, at least the Communists or their leaders provide economic, social and artistic education and betterment. They, not you nor the American Federation of Labor in any of its phases or branches, offer the worker the club, the theatre, the lecture platform, the book, the political arena and all forms of semi-directed social entertainment in the hope of awakening him to a larger and more helpful vision. They believe in his rise and his future, his significance in and to the state, its health, strength, wisdom, happiness. But you—what do you believe in—you and the A. F. of L.? What do you do about it?

Indeed, I truly believe, Mr. Green, that if you were really interested in labor, you would seek to consider this rival economic system in Russia on its merits and what the A. F. of L. could take from it that would be of aid to labor here. But do you? Reread your letter to me.

And in connection with that, I might pause to ask just what has the American Federation of Labor done about the hundreds of schools in America now owned by corporations? Or about child labor, since now in only two-thirds of the states do legislative acts keep children in school even until they are fourteen years old? I know the difficulties of the Federation are considerable here. I know also that money in America desires to control it and in the main does. Yet does your organization turn wisely to your own workers for aid in this great matter, or organize them politically, intellectually and otherwise for the problems they must needs meet? Rather do you not swish along, with no labor party at all, let alone a powerful constructive one? Why you don't even encourage unemployment insurance!

Worse, many of your leaders appear to be either allied by character with capital or are so low as to be just plain out and out grafters and so inducing the same disillusion and faithlessness in the minds of the workers. John Jarrett, President of the Amalgamated Association of Iron, Steel and Tin Workers[,] became an

officer of the American Tin Plate Company. Michael Boyle, business agent of Local 134 and board member of the International Brotherhood of Electrical Workers, in the course of a trial by which he was found guilty of a set of managerial abuses, was discovered to be the recipient of a $20,000 bribe from the Chicago Telephone Company to prohibit strikes during their building program. Robert Brindell, President of the Building Trades Council and the Dock Builders' Union, carried out an agreement to work for the Building Trades Employers' Association if they would shut everybody else out and employ only Brindell men. Brindell's graft was $32,000 from Todd Iron and Robertson, $25,000 from A. Hershkovitz, $17,120 from G. A. Northern Wrecking Company, $25,000 from the Gotham National Bank Building, etc. Hugh F. Robertson paid Brindell $32,000 to prevent strikes during the erection of the Cunard Building and docks. Finally Brindell was sent to the penitentiary for extortion.

But was or is not such leadership avoidable? Is it not really true that if the leaders of labor in America had ever been mentally cognizant of the import or the magnitude of their task that no such low and disgraceful conception of the duties of leadership could have crept in?

In fact, I charge, and this without any hope of contradiction, that from nearly the bginning, the American Federation of Labor, or rather its leaders and officers have deliberately forsaken American labor to the clutches of the cunning as well as selfish financial materialist, his cheap religionist, corrupt politician, lawyer, judge and newspaper for economic as well as social guidance, and to this hour have left him to the results of that policy. Leadership? You and your organization do not know the meaning of the word. Although at one time and another you and your organization have commendably paid for many legal proceedings, the whole policy of the A. F. of L. in the American courts has been a weak defensive which is in itself an indictment. In truth, I cannot find a trace in any court of one case where the A. F. of L. has taken the offensive and sought initially to restrain or enjoin a corporation. Yet in the face of the fact that a corporation is ob-

viously an organized, collective body, occupying to be sure, a position of advantage but with that position none the less thoroughly dependent on labor. And there labor could have taken the offensive, shown its strength, and won its just rights. For certainly, if organized corporate bodies can lay off hundreds of thousands of men at will, casting them on any possible resources or none, thousands of laborers can strike throwing corporate organization on any possible resources or none. Yet just that possibility of action the American Federation of Labor appears not to have tested or fought for. Yet you have money. You speak of three billion dollars spent during the last ten years in the coal fields of Pennsylvania, Ohio, West Virginia, Illinois and Kentucky—furnishing doles and the like. But if so much money could be raised for this purpose, how about money and in quantities for strategy—legal, political, educational, social—which would have put and kept the American laborer not only in heart and conscience by not only teaching him his true economic as well as social position, but his rights as well as his collective power and the use of the same?

But actually what has been your policy? Let us see. I will begin with the United Mine Workers of America, and from them proceed to the whole American Federation of Labor whose entire policy has been for the benefit of select groups of laborers who have consistently co-operated with the capitalists at the expense of labor in general.

Let me illustrate. When in 1919 the nation-wide U. M. W. A. bituminous strike of 70% of the coal miners under the pressure of increased cost of living failed to get more than one half the miners' demands, Illinois miners, refusing to accept this settlement, further continued the strike, but unrecognized by the leaders of the U. M. W. A. and won additional increase. Yet why not an increase for all?

In the winter of 1920-1, the great West Virginia strike was lost through the failure of McDowell and Mercer Counties to support Mingo County, a support which should have been the first thought and will of any true leadership.

Next, in the nation-wide strike of 1922 which was for no wage cuts, what happened? I am dealing with honest leadership now. Immediately the strike was in full swing, enormous force was taken out of the united power of the strikers in general by the U. M. W. A. through its officers sending the miners of Kentucky and Tennessee back to work at the old wage scale before the strikers in other states had won this. But for whose benefit? The Miners? You should know as to that. And later, one Farrington, district president of the U. M. W. A.[,] fanned the report that Lewis, President of the U. M. W. A. at that time and now, and with whom he had many differences, had accepted a $100,000 bribe from Kentucky coal mine owners for this privilege, the while Lewis charged that Farrington, Illinois district president, was party to a contract to allow scab coal miners to work, for which same he received a percentage of the profits. I could cite further irregularities of Farrington, i. e., that he was on the pay-roll of the Peabody Coal Company for $25,000 a year. Also, I might refer to the Lewis vs. Fishwick (of the Illinois district) charges of corruption against each other.

In this 1922 strike, 100,000 non-union miners of the Somerset and Connellsville sections of Pennsylvania struck in unison with the general U. M. W. A. strike of that region. They were per-suaded so to do. The bulk of them worked for the H. C. Frick Company, a subsidiary of the U. S. Steel, and one of the most powerful non-union companies. But once the U. M. W. A. leaders of the region surrounding these non-union workers were able to sign an agreement for their union men, they left these non-union miners to shift for themselves. That meant months of continued strike, without leadership or relief, and finally yellow dog con-tracts.

And yet immediately thereafter, Calvin Coolidge was elected President of the United States, although the A. F. of L. claimed to command about 3,000,000 workers (not counting wives) and although not as voters, still as men. These could and should have been directed according to their own best political and economic interests. They might have prevented Coolidge. But perhaps you

would call voting for Coolidge the best political and economic thing they could do since it made for the economic and so social peace of their employers—the great railroad and steel controlled coal companies of America. Yet as you look at the economic and social condition of America and the world today, do you think it was so wise to give strength and comfort to a few, leaving the rest to suffer as they do now? Consider only the state of the miners in West Virginia, Eastern Ohio, Western Pennsylvania, for whom you are doing nothing—sanctioning war on them, even—and all because they would not return to the A. F. of L. or rather its subsidiary, the U. M. W. A., which deserted them in 1927. And that you call leadership! And standing by labor! God! Yet men elevated to leadership in the U. M. W. A. have been very active in the Republican and Democratic parties which have for years been controlled and manipulated by John D. Rockefeller and others who are the owners of wealth and fighting for that ownership rather than the rights and causes of labor.

Again, though, let me call your attention to the fact that the striking miners in Alabama where the Tennessee Coal, Iron and Railroad Company, another U. S. Steel subsidiary, is very powerful, were compelled, in 1921, to accept arbitration at the hands of a governor opposed to unions. But why? Being leaders of labor and not aids to corporations, could you and your organization not have avoided that?

More, because of their wishy-washy leadership generally, the U. M. W. A. by this time could no longer hold their own anywhere. So true is this that although in 1924 the U. M. W. A. signed a three year agreement with the coal mine operators fixing wages and conditions, the Bethlehem Mines Corporation in the Fairmont section, and the Pittsburgh Coal Company, in Pennsylvania, the very next year, started a wage cut drive to break this agreement! And during 1925 alone, 110 mines in Pennsylvania and 50 in West Virginia ceased to recognize the union. The backbone of the 1927 strike was shattered when agreements were early signed in Illinois, Indiana and other sections with companies which would pay only the old scale. Yet even in this, the old scale

was not given to the machine cutters and machine loaders, who
were compelled to accept day rates, which produced a decreased
average pay. And this, despite your personal avowal, Mr. Green,
of equal protection for all classes of labor. And with the Pennsylvania and Ohio miners of that time left with no support at all.
Your strike failed, and in 1928 the U. M. W. A. ordered district
settlements at lower wages instead of a national agreement at the
old pay as demanded by the striking miners.

But another thing—and most definitely connected with this
pro-capital and practically anti-labor program: During this same
strike, Judge Langham who had $6,ooo in a company concerned,
signed an injunction against meetings near a coal mine near
Rossiter, Penna. But exactly why, I would like to know, did not
the U. M. W. A. take the lead by seeking a prior injunction
against operators' interfering with the workers' Constitutional
rights of free speech and assemblage? [18] They are guaranteed by
our American Constitution, our Supreme Court and the States
which signed under the Constitution. Then why no legal and
more particularly no political fight under these Constitutional
privileges? Why not, for instance, a judge who was *not* at one
and the same time a coal mine owner? Why no impeachment
proceedings against a judge who could so openly flout the law
made to protect the individual in his rights? You say that during
the past ten years the United Mine Workers backed by the American Federation of Labor spent three billions in the coal fields of
Pennsylvania, Ohio, West Virginia, Illinois and Kentucky, aiding
miners, of course. And that is a huge sum. Then why, out of it,
could not enough have been spared to organize a legal battle
which would deter judges of this ilk from interfering with the
plain Constitutional rights of your followers? Rather, through
your Vice-President, Mr. Woll, are you not now busy organizing
an attack on Soviet Russia in order as he says to protect American
business, but the same business you will note that has fought

[18] Foster and Browder were unable to persuade Dreiser that capitalism's courts
were too untrustworthy to be resorted to in a matter as important as the injunction.

every advance of labor here. And whereas as I have said and most certainly the Union of Soviets has sought in every way to increase the power and welfare of labor which should be your business also, the A. F. of L. has continuously lacked the brain and will, if not the money, to fight for the rights of the men whom it is supposed to lead, and by reason of brain and means should.

Even at this very hour, in the fight of the National Mine Workers in Western Pennsylvania, I notice that a Western Pennsylvania judge, and this in the face of the Constitution, the appeal and demand of the State Governor, and of the National Mine Workers fighting for the men there, has had the effrontery to enjoin those strikers from picketing. And with your organization not standing by as it might choose to do in this instance, but rather actively helping that judge and the coal operators by urging the starving miners, neglected by you since 1927, to rejoin the U. M. W. A. and return to work at the old scale! Imagine!

Yet why wasn't a sweeping injunction sought to protect those workers in their peaceful meetings and picket lines? And by you? Why not? Are they not American laborers? And seeking what you pretend all labor should seek? Why fight them when you should be fighting with them on any basis? They are your old men. And why no impeachment proceedings against this judge by the U. M. W. A. or your larger organization, in order to destroy this menace which confronts not only the U. M. W. A. but your workers also? You have the money. Or an attack in the courts on those private police, out there hired and paid for by corporations and who take orders from corporate officials, rather than protect the workers' rights as well as those of the corporation? Is the A. F. of L. without legal as well as intellectual advice? Or can it be that in the activities of this new organization which you so sharply deride, yet which, without money, is doing what you with your billions could not do, you see that heart and the brains to do more for labor than you have ever done? And does that not reasonably justify my call for the disestablishment of the A. F. of L.?

You cry out against the new and rival economic system of the East which is doing so much for uplift of the common man, the

while you here in America do nothing for his general welfare. Rather, as your own fights and wars show, the American capitalist, his trust and bank, have failed labor and will continue to do so. And yet, if I read aright, it is the American capitalist, his bank and his trust, with which your organization has allied itself —a cold and sly support, as I see it. I am sorry to say this, but the facts read all one way to me.

But further to show that the A. F. of L.'s greatest leaders did not have the laborers' cause at heart, let me state that D. C. Kennedy, formerly president of the West Virginia section of the U. M. W. A. became Commissioner for the Kanawha Coal Operators' Association, that John Mitchell, President of the whole union, went from the U. M. W. A. to the National Civic Federation (he left when he died $250,000, mostly in coal, rail and steel securities) and Thomas Lewis, National President of the U. M. W. A. turned and became a coal mine operator of West Virginia and an officer in the New River Coal Operators' Association. In short, they allied themselves with capitalists.

Also that the U. M. W. A. would join and even have joined with the capitalists to the injury of the miners themselves is evidenced by the U. M. W. A.'s very recent agreement with the Pittsburgh Terminal Coal Company. After that corporation would not deal with the National Miners' Union, the U. M. W. A. entered and without consulting the strikers, signed an agreement with the Pittsburgh Terminal Coal Company for miners at less pay than they were receiving before they struck.

But is that *helping* labor or *fighting* labor? And what pitiable labor. You should have gone with me or with President Farrell [19] of the Steel Trust, who also spoke of the condition of the miners and workers in Western Virginia when he was addressing his fellow capitalists of the Steel Trust, and have seen for yourself. There is still time to go, Mr. Green. On my desk is an appeal for food for 90,000 starving miners in West Virginia, and where is

[19] William Elliston Farrell, president of the Easton Car & Construction Co., manufacturers of industrial cars.

your great fund now? Has the A. F. of L. no heart for starving labor unless it is A. F. of L. labor?

But now as to salaries. If I read the data relating to the fiscal conduct of the American Federation of Labor from high to low and back again, it seems to me that what its leaders receive—considering not only the present state of unemployment, but what has not been accomplished for labor—is excessive. From various summaries and documents at this moment before me, I read that you, Mr. Green, as President of the American Federation of Labor, receive $1,000 a month in salary and $667 a month for travelling expenses, a total of $20,000 a year. Besides, as one unfriendly student of your activities troubles to point out, there are additional sums or honorariums for addresses before colleges, rotary clubs, chambers of commerce, the radio, etc. which I mention, but without prejudice. Again, it is stated that your very active Vice-President, Mr. Woll, gets $12,000 and related expenses. Also that John L. Lewis, President of the United Mine Workers is drawing $12,000 annually in salary, and expenses of about $23,000 (and while his mine workers are at the starvation line). Similarly, I gather that presidents of all of your unions average $11,800, that is, whereas the President of the International Ladies Garment Workers and again the President of the Upholsterers receive $7,500 and, I suppose, expenses, annually, those of the Musicians and Stage Employees receive $20,000 each. The President of the Bridge and Structural Iron Workers as well as he of the Teamsters and again of the Operating Engineers each receives $15,000, and expenses. The Presidents of the Elevator Constructors, United Garment Workers and Lathers each receives $12,000.

But these salaries in a working world which is supposed to command a high percentage of idealism and more, to register an enthusiasm which in part at least is based on an intense and understanding sympathy for the plight of the underdog[,] are certainly not low, and, if taken at all—that is, money above the mere necessities of the struggle—should at least show a program and a constructive zeal worthy of the name. And especially here in America, because of the immense division between poverty

and wealth, the devotion to the cause of the underdog should be intense. Yet one hears little but complaints against your organization and from your own members. My mail has been doubled by letters showing why your organization should either be reformed or disbanded, and some very bitter letters, too. But in the last analysis, support is the criterion of leadership, and herewith I append some data as to this which should be of considerable interest. Thus, although the U. M. W. A. in 1920 had 386,-000 bituminous members, by 1929 their support among miners had become so willy-nilly that only 80,000 bituminous members remained. Again, your A. F. of L. figures for 1930, with a total membership of only 2,961,096, list the U. M. W. A. as having 400,000 members in the United States and Canada, but the United States Bureau of Mines reports that while the U. M. W. A. had, in 1920, 467,172 members, in 1929 and this despite your 400,000 claimed, it had a total of only 156,978 bituminous and anthracite members in the U. S. and Canada.

So it would certainly appear that certain weaknesses of leadership as illustrated above had brought about this decline. And more, if I am to believe what I read and hear and myself have personally seen in Western Pennsylvania and West Virginia, the miners must still live in villages of such a filthy nature that the United States Coal Commission found that out of 713 towns examined, only two had a decent water and sewerage system. Again, in these company owned towns (and against which did the A. F. of L. ever lead an aggressive political campaign?) miners have no property rights or protection of the state laws at all. Their lease reads that their house goes with the job and adds that almost no advance notice for eviction need be given. Yet has the U. M. W. A. in its long career done anything really to protect the property rights of miners who live as might feudal slaves? Have your arbitration boards (so regularly resorted to to settle disputes and adjust grievances) or any other U. M. W. A. or A. F. of L. device or achievement abolished these? I saw to the contrary.

Not only that, but the annual average wage for bituminous

miners in 1924 in the U. S. was $1053 and in 1928-9, $996; in 1924 anthracite miners received on an average about $1941 and in 1929 $1594; in Illinois, the only real stronghold of the U. M. W. A. at the time, salaries were in 1924, $1265 and in 1928-9 $1098, for bituminous miners. And this despite the fact that the President of the U. M. W. A. draws $12,000 a year plus expenses, while his assistants receive $750 monthly, all of which comes out of those indecent incomes of miners, which incomes have lessened rather than increased as you stated. And at that pay differs widely for various classes of mine labor.

But this isn't a patch on what they're being paid today under the recent wage-cutting onslaught. And this you must know regardless of anything you may say to the contrary. For despite the $3,000,000,000 you mention as having been spent in the mining fields in the past ten years to protect the coal miners, (one cannot help but question where this enormous amount of money came from as it would mean an annual due of at least $500 per U. M. W. A. member out of their meager annual income) not only the above conditions exist, but death from accidents has steadily increased from 46.1 per 10,000 underground workers in 1916-20 to 83.0 in 1928, and this with your mine inspection program, Mr. Green.

Yet the benefits pointed out by you as having been achieved by the A. F. of L. I will grant, but with just reservations. These are, as you say, the 8-hour day, some child labor legislation, and the run of the mine system of which I learned while I was in Pittsburgh, but which I also learned was regularly being violated there—as much as three days' work being done before one ton of coal was paid for. Think of that, Mr. Green. And at starvation wages.

But in spite of the benefits of the A. F. of L. which you claim, there were, in 1920, 18,500 underground miners and in 1928, 35,500 who were working on the 9 or 10-hour day basis. But let this pass; it is negligible. As you say, most bituminous miners have an 8-hour day underground, although Alabama, the worst offender, shows 60% of its labor on a 9-hour day. Also in 1920,

only about 6,000 boys under 16 were employed in mines which, I grant you is partly, but not entirely by any means, due to A. F. of L. legislation. For you must not forget that improved machinery has also helped to bring about this condition. Also the desire of all middle-class people is for child labor prohibition and they have agitated for the same. It is therefore reasonable to assume that they and their representatives in Congress and elsewhere have supported and most helpfully what the A. F. of L. endorsed, and so helped to bring about this most necessary change. Yet any aggressive leadership on the part of your organization most certainly could have brought national child labor prohibition long before this. And at that it is being violated now. Figures on demand. Yet all along you have had all of three million workers at your command, their ears and their dues, and with any proper social and economic propaganda used among them, do you question that their voices and votes could have stopped this? If you doubt this, I certainly question your ability as a real leader of labor. But have you even tried? I cannot learn so, if you have.

My attack on June 26th, against which your open letter was directed was, however, against the entire American Federation of Labor. My personal aim is its disestablishment because of its policy which (1) furthers selected groups of laborers (2) is not adapted to the betterment of labor as a whole (3) offers no breadth or enlightenment and (4) elevates to leadership only those whose interest is apparently only with capital and who as I have shown have and still do indulge in tremendous personal graft, always so demoralizing to the worker and his needs. I refer you for one thing to the recent trouble in Waiters' Union No. 1 in New York City.

And to show that the American Federation of Labor operates for select groups, I will say (1) that in some cases it limits membership in its unions; secondly, it charges in many cases exorbitant initiation fees, i.e. such prohibitive sums as $100 or $150; next that Negro labor is prohibited either by Constitution or by ritual in eleven international unions under the A. F. of L., and

also that some of these international unions have laws against admitting unnaturalized foreign born. In the printing, building trades, railroad and metal unions, comprising about 90% of the A. F. of L. membership, as I understand it, the skilled men receive their demands frequently at the expense of the unskilled. That is, one craft union is played off against and so weakens another. And although the American Federation of Labor has unions for street cleaners, section hands and road workers, it does not build large and powerful unions of unskilled laborers. Nor does it seek to inspire them with any program for their advancement or social or mental development. Rather, and on the contrary, and as I have asserted, it leaves them to struggle ignorantly and so blindly with the world as best they may, leaving them to the corporation, newspaper, politician, minister, their lawyers, bureaus of propaganda, police and what not. And for what noble purpose? Well, I will tell you, asinine and even insane bank rolls which they cannot even understand, let alone wisely direct— asinine incomes, asinine show, asinine idleness and parade. And you co-operate with the employers of labor who bleed and then shoot them down. That is like fawns cooperating with wolves. But you should not co-operate. You should fight and demand a square deal for those you lead. You know that and so do I.

But what do we see instead? On occasion, their poverty and intellectual state being what it is, and wholly uninfluenced by any social, educational, political and economic programs of enlightenment on the part of the American Federation of Labor, they appear as strike breakers, members of breadlines, agitators for changes in the existing form of government and the like, all of which you personally deplore (note your words as to Communism) the while you do nothing to match that brilliant and economic labor as well as social program that now shines in the East.

In sum, Mr. Green, the American Federation of Labor leadership, as well as its general policy is not adapted to the betterment of labor in this country as a whole, and this in the face of the fact that America is the richest country in the world and that

labor here should enlighten as well as lead. In fact, as I have previously insisted in this letter, labor in the large sense of the word, is not even brushed by your organization. Only about 10% of labor in America is really organized, while in Germany 75% of the workers are organized and in England 65%. More and worse, there is almost no organization in such fundamental industries as iron and steel, rubber, automobiles, oil, electrical manufacturing, etc. For out of 3,000,000 workers in the six most important branches of the metal industry, you and your A. F. of L. have only 136,000 as members. Your Amalgamated Association of Iron, Steel and Tin Workers hasn't any members at all in U. S. Steel. And hence before the big corporations they bow and wilt. Besides, of the workers in the great textile industry, only 5% out of 1,000,000 are organized.

Again, in the printing groups in 1921 and again in 1923, your Pressman's Union gave its men such a wretched deal that they engaged in a strike which was not recognized by their President and who then urged scabs from all of his local unions in the U. S. to come and work at $20 a day and so break this. And more, I know for a fact that your U. M. W. A. now fighting the National Mine Workers Union for place in Western Pennsylvania and elsewhere, formerly hired organizer[s] after organizers who functioned merely in old territory rather than sought to recruit fresh material for the union roll in new fields.

And more and without any rhyme or reason, wisdom or policy, have not you or your organization left the agricultural workers of America out in the cold entirely? Are not they herded like sheep hither and yon, and without plan or encouragement from you? Also, before your organizational campaign in the South in 1929, industry there also had been left almost entirely untouched by labor unions. But why? Your policy, if any, appears to be to establish many small unions as opposed to anything more effective. Thus eleven in the railroad industry, twenty-three in the steel. Also it appears to be against joint and hence strong strikes. For when a whole industry, i. e. coal, is organized in one union, the workers frequently complain, and denounce your A. F. of L.

leadership as being against their interests, i. e. rival unions in Illinois and West Virginia under old A. F. of L. leaders denouncing A. F. of L. policies are set up to really protect labor's interests. The employers pay the union dues directly to the A. F. of L. in order, obviously to frustrate this kind of revolt of the workers against their leadership.

It is such facts as these and others like them which lead me to insist that your organization is actually inimical to American labor and as such should be destroyed.

In short, the policy of Gompers as I understand it now and to which you are heir and with which you appear to be in sympathy, so weakened the union in the great meat packing houses that company unions could be and were established. More the A. F. of L. because of the weakness or bias of which so many complain has permitted over 800 company unions to grow up in America. Yet nothing but demoralized, uninformed labor with no adequate leadership would have stood for that. For these company unions, formed and managed by corporate officials, do not have even the independence of a treasury, in contrast to the limitless corporate wealth for professional services to quell laborers. But any organization of the size and wealth of the A. F. of L. had it wanted to fight this movement, could have achieved some success, I am sure. Yet instead what? Unemployment to the tune of 6,000,000 and now starvation for hundreds of thousands in the richest country in the world. And with our banks and trust companies bursting with hoarded wealth and all our laws and policies shaped and directed for the benefit of the rich man the while the workers, as they have always been in this country, are left at the mercy of antagonistic and as anyone can see today, entirely predatory and so inimical interests, which fight even a modicum of improvement for the worker.

And yet you and Mr. Woll denounce the entirely enlightened and as I see it, highly progressive labor system of Russia. And that too when you are supposed to be a leader and defender of labor.

But this cannot endure. Whether you see it or not, Mr. Green,

the handwriting is on the wall. The rich are too rich, the poor are too poor, and too wholly ignored. Organized society has never been and never can be maintained that way. The day of unrestrained and unenlightened competition as it now exists, with its billionaires and its beggars are over. And you, as President of America's largest federation of labor, should be the first and the loudest to proclaim that truth, and instead of fighting and undermining starving men in Western Pennsylvania, Eastern Ohio, and Northern West Virginia, you should be the first to go there and do whatever your great power would permit you to do to help labor under whatsoever banner it fights.[20]

I am

Very truly yours,
Theodore Dreiser

To Louise Campbell
[ALS]

[200 West 57th Street
New York, N.Y.
August 5, 1931]

Dear Louise:

I've had a hell of [a] summer. Hot. Work. Mental worries. Law suits. Just a day to day drive. Add to that moving. In the place here right now are fourteen trunks which ought to be opened—the contents rearranged—the contents of each new re-arrangement listed—& placed in an [envelope] outside the trunk concerned. How about coming over—sleeping in Helen's room and doing all this work? It shouldn't take much more than four or five days. —And so, hello. I haven't written—but that cuts no ice. I see you as clearly as though you were here. Esherick [21] was here around

[20] Green replied at length on July 23; Dreiser submitted the letter to Browder for comment, but there is no evidence in Dreiser's files that he mailed Green another letter. Subsequently he embodied his arguments and portions of the present letter in *Tragic America* (New York, cop. 1931), ch. XI.

[21] Wharton Esherick, of Paoli, Pa., a sculptor and designer of woodcuts.

July 1 & told me all his plans. Did you see him off. He'll be back—
he said—about Sept. 15. He'll learn a lot—Wait & see.

I lost my suit [22]—but not exactly[.] Actually I made them add
seven scenes—fore & aft—750 feet of screen. They came here &
begged me to endorse it in its new form. I could have called off
the suit and taken the credit but I chose not to do so. And I'm
glad I didn't. The judge's comments are priceless to me.[23]

Can you come over?

T.

TO PIERRE LAVAL
[CC]

*Laval was at the time France's Minister of the Interior. Dreiser
wrote at the request of Emma Goldman.*

200 West 57th Street
New York, [N.Y.]
September 21, 1931

Sir:

During the past several months I have been hearing, from
various sources, of the unremitting persecution to which a resi-

22 Against the Paramount Publix Corp., producers of the film version of
An American Tragedy.

23 Justice Graham Witschief, in denying Dreiser's application for an injunction
against the producer, had been quoted by the *New York Herald Tribune* (August
2) as saying: "Whether the picture substantially presents the book or not depends
on one's point of view. The plaintiff appears to view the book from the standpoint
of the fatalist. Clyde, he says, has the sympathy of the readers because he came to
a tragic end through the vicissitudes of life, most of them wholly beyond his
control and largely because of the psychology developed in his starved boyhood.
In the preparation of the picture the producer must give consideration to the fact
that the great majority of people composing the audience before which the picture
will be presented will be more interested that justice prevail over wrongdoing
than that the inevitability of Clyde's end clearly appear."

dent of your country is being subjected. I refer to Alexandre Berkman. He is, I understand, the object of an order of expulsion issued by you, or by your authority, the basis of his undesirability being alleged Communist activities.

I am informed that the charge which forced him to leave France under this order of expulsion two years ago, was founded on his activity in collecting money for the assistance of political prisoners in the U.S.S.R., and that the condition under which his return was permitted was the cessation of such activities. I am further informed that since his return he has scrupulously refrained from such activities, and from any activities which would connect him in any way with the expression of radical political views, but that he earns his living, such as it is, by editorial work, translation, etc. Nevertheless, I am told that he is granted no more than a three months' permit to remain in France; that at the end of each period he is sought out, served with the order of expulsion, and he and his friends put to infinite trouble and expense to have the permit renewed.

It appears to me that the reactionary attitude displayed by this constant hounding of a person for his political views—views unexpressed, as I am assured—is unworthy of the enlightened intellectual status of France today, and that there undoubtedly exist in your country more potent dangers against which time and what would appear to be bitter effort might be expended than against the desire of one man (regardless of political beliefs privately held) to find in France a place where he might earn a simple and obscure living.

He is old, he is weary. For his one crime—the wounding of H. C. Frick, one of the most savage of our many savage American individualists and money-mad fortune hunters, who warred upon labor throughout his life—he spent eighteen [24] years in the Western Penitentiary of Pennsylvania, and came out broken, his great crime sympathy for the little people of the world whom, after all, he could not aid.

[24] Fourteen is the correct figure.

Let me ask of you understanding as well. Has he not paid enough? And may I not ask of you consideration of his wish, now that he is old, for a place of rest? Cannot France let him have that?

I am
                              Respectfully,

THEODORE DREISER, 1894
(Photo by Morris)

565

Wal Markley, Richard Duffy, Dreiser, Jack Duffy and Horace Markley, 1897

Dreiser, Grant Richards, and Sir Hugh Lane at Monte Carlo, 1912

Dreiser in Russia, 1927

Dreiser in Paris, 1938 (Photo by Harlingue, for Informations Illustrées)

Louis Aragon and Dreiser in Paris, 1938 (Ce Soir)

Dreiser at Mt. Kisco, 1938
(Photo by Robert H. Elias)

Dreiser interviewing Harry Bridges for an article, 1940 (Photo by Clarence Block)

THEODORE DREISER

Aug 23-1938

Dear Mr. President:

While in Barcelona recently I
was invited by Julio Alvarez Del
Vayo, minister of State and Dr.
Juan Negrin, Premier, to dine with
them. On that occasion Rebel and
Loyalist Spain was discussed and
finally I was requested to comment
on the reactions, favorable and
unfavorable of various Elements
in our States to Loyalist Spain.
It was in connection with that that
they presented a problem associated
with both sides which you might
help to solve without publicity and
with nothing but satisfaction to
yourself and many others. Since
they requested me personally to
present this to you I am writing

to ask if you will be willing to
recieve me.

Very Truly Yours
Theodore Dreiser

Mt. Kisco,
New York.

*Letter to President Roosevelt requesting
an interview to discuss the Spanish Civil
War*

1932

To Ring Lardner
[CC]

Lardner had been quoted by the New York World-Telegram *and later* Time *as calling Dreiser "the prince of bad writers." He had written Dreiser on January 2 to disavow the various unfavorable comments attributed to him, and this phrase in particular. "I assure you," he had explained, "I am not in the habit of knocking writers (God help us all), and particularly novelists, whose patience and energy are far beyond any good traits I can claim."*

> Hotel Ansonia
> [Broadway at 73rd Street]
> New York, [N.Y.]
> January 5, 1932

Dear Mr. Lardner:

Courtesy and good will shine through your explanation of the *World-Telegram* and *Time* comments, and I thank you, though you need not have troubled. It is a long while since I have taken umbrage at any comment made either on myself or my work, since, good, bad or indifferent, both are as they are and, as for my work, the best I can do.

Surely only critics are intolerant of those who do the best they can in so trying a world.

None the less, the phrase "the prince of bad writers" cheers me. It is glistering irony that ought to be said if for no more than the saying. I am grateful to you for having called my attention to it.

Cordially and with assurances of my esteem,

To Ralph Holmes
[CC]

Holmes, a Detroit newspaper man who admired Dreiser, had written on December 28, 1931, expressing his general agreement with Tragic America, *his belief that the state should not engage in actual manufacture but should simply control sources, and his feeling that with a radical change in the social structure at hand there was need for "a new political party, a radical revolutionary party, working under leaders with brains enough to effect their changes without violence," the organizer of which ought to be Dreiser himself.*

> Hotel Ansonia
> [Broadway at 73rd Street]
> New York, [N.Y.]
> January 9, 1932

Dear Holmes:

I would like to see a party of ideas, power and discipline change the economic structure of this country peacefully.

I cannot help, however, but emphasize the stone wall of wealth, political intrigue, deceit, prejudice, ignorance and illusion, all with their deadening power, which any such party would meet. Whether they could be overcome, I do not know. I do have the conviction that such a project, if it came from strong Americans, would meet with more success than a program subsidized by foreign money or even influenced directly by any foreign government. The latter would take limitless resources of wealth and effort, as well as organization, and discipline which is truly staggering, whereas something appealing to Americans as their own would move much more easily and swiftly.

I disagree with you fundamentally on economic reorganization. I believe capitalism, with its mighty stock market, so highly manipulated for speculation, with its monopolies depriving citizens of their livelihood, with its waste, and its general cut-throat and by-force methods, is a menace that absolutely must

LETTERS OF THEODORE DREISER 573

not be doctored and dickered with. Since we cannot go back to conditions of the past, or reinstigate or recreate those conditions, the future must be braved. A new method must be evolved, and for that method one must look to Russia. I believe Russian organization should be *studied* in the greatest detail. That may not be a complete success, but all of its faults should be carefully considered. But Russia or no Russia, there is only one thing for America to do, and that is abolish every vestige of capitalism possible. Russia is still trying to do that.

You say that the federal control of sources alone would work as well as my program. Always the people have controlled sources in activities which made monopolists into multi-millionaires, i.e. oil, milk, meat, sugar, etc. The great monopolies are in many cases effected by monopoly of distribution or control of the finished product, rather than of the source.

A change can never be done in halves as, i.e. taking over the means of communication and transportation, because capitalism has the power to boycott, to bankrupt and to prejudice, which power it always uses. No money or power must be left in the hands of any capitalists. As far as the state trying to regulate private enterprise on a royalty basis and regulate valuations, past experience dramatizes the utter futility and impossibility of this. There are a thousand ways capitalists get around it. And consequently, they aren't regulated at all. In any part-way change, they would fight not only against that change, but for all of these "thousand ways of getting around it," i.e., their supposed rights in the courts, etc. The only path is for the government (if a government could ever be elected who would do this) to completely depower capitalists, pay them a few thousand dollars for their billions, and let them go to work under obligation to the State. And betraying that obligation to follow state programs would be treason, and, for major offenses, punishable by death.

Certainly a political party could work on the above program. I believe a party should aim at this complete change for equity and work toward that goal by showing the waste, robbery, lawlessness, legalized force, ignorance and the prejudices of the

church, press, education and radio by which this power is maintained to enforce poverty and serfdom upon the people and voluminous wealth for Wall Street leaders.

TO SARAH GERTRUDE MILLIN
[CC]

Working on her Rhodes: a Life *(London, 1933), she had been speculating about the significance of Rhodes's ambition. "Is it a sign of greatness," she had asked Dreiser on September 9, 1931, "to have big desires?" She had also written a letter on January 8 in which she asked whether he had ever read* The Sons of Mrs. Aab.

> Hotel Ansonia
> [Broadway at 73rd Street]
> New York, [N.Y.]
> January 18, 1932

Dear Sarah:

My neglect of our correspondence has not been intentional, and certainly not desired by me, but I seem to have been involved in such turmoil lately that it has been impossible to keep up with everything. Possibly your newspapers carried some word of my recent work in the Harlan, Kentucky coal fields, with a delegation from the National Committee for the Defense of Political Prisoners, which went down there to investigate the terrible conditions among the striking miners in that district,—and the indictments which followed. You would have even less respect for law in America if you could see the way things are maneuvered here in such situations.

I was extremely sorry to know that you had been ill with influenza, but if you've overcome the insomnia since then, I think you are still on the right side of the ledger. Are you quite better now?

Your work on Cecil Rhodes should be extremely interesting, and I should think that with all those notes you might attain your wish to do a long book.

Possibly it is a sign of greatness to have big desires, but most of my observations lead me to believe that the greatness refers only to the successful individual's overwhelming cunning, combined with egotism and greed, as the world is constituted now, and I can't at all agree that it is only necessary to ask for the big things in order to receive them the same as one would the little. Such a philosophy has never worked out generally, and really could not; I think that your statement that you had discovered Rhodes in some shady finance is the key to that riddle. Curiously enough, much of what I have been writing lately bears on precisely these points, as the enclosures will reveal.

The Sons of Mrs. Aab is absorbingly interesting, and the novel is certainly up to the earlier ones. Your Gideon, with his dull and resentful life, and his one vain grasp at wealth, is a touching figure. And of course, I always appreciate your general pictures of life in your country.

Helen has asked me to send you her kindest regards, and I hope that you may have everything you wish for in the new year.

To Fisher C. Baily
[CC]

Hotel Ansonia
[Broadway at 73rd Street]
New York, [N.Y.]
April 6, 1932

Dear Mr. Baily:

I appreciate your courteous and spirited letter about *Tragic America.*

You are not the first person to ask me to suggest some solution

for the economic mess in which we find ourselves, nor are you the first to suggest that I head such a movement.[1]

Before I go into that deeper, though, I want to reply to some of the questions you ask. There have been two letters from the middle-West, informing me that the public librarians of Cincinnati, Ohio and Elkhart, Indiana have refused to put *Tragic America* on their shelves. Probably there were other such cases; probably there have been and will be more obfuscations of the sort you cite.

As for the Progressives and Socialists, I can only say that any attempt at reform through legislation has shown only dismal failure so far. The Socialists believe, of course, that it is possible to take deliberate and peaceful steps toward social salvation. The Communists are usually met with bitterness if not with bullets, but I am convinced that the reason for that lies in the fact that the American temperament will not accept Communism as technically stated by the Russians. But I believe that Communism as practiced by the Russians, or, at least, some part if not most of it, can certainly be made palatable to the average American if it is properly explained to him and if the title Communism is removed. The thing that has really been holding me back is consideration of this difference in temperament, the number of problems, the kind of program that will get over, and so on.

However, I actually think that the time is here for a preliminary conference of a good number of people as much interested as you are. I certainly know twenty-five or thirty who would gladly come and sit down and discuss just one thing: program. If such a conference were held in Chicago, or St. Louis, or New York, would you be willing to come? I am willing to go almost anywhere, if I can get the right group to meet.

Morris Ernst, a well known attorney of this city, would certainly be one; Arthur Garfield Hays would come, and so would Ralph Holmes of the *Detroit Times* (quite an influential person there)[,] H. H. Klein, a lawyer and statistician of New York,

---

1 Letters similar to this one were written by Dreiser on the same day to Bruce Crawford and Charles E. Yost. See also Dreiser to Ralph Holmes, January 9, 1932.

Ivan Narodny, who represents a group that was once associated with Lenin, here in New York, and there are others[.]

I have talked with individuals in my neighborhood near Mt. Kisco, New York, who were so wrought up by their social miseries that they are ready to organize locals (or at least attempt so to do) of some such thing as this I propose—The American League for National Equity. If we get enough followers, I would be glad to take the leadership.

As a matter of fact, in September, I am going on the lecture platform, making a national tour, and my one subject will be this very thing—the need of drastic change with all the reasons which I can bring to bear to substantiate it.

I am enclosing an advertisement which will show you the reaction, in some quarters, to *Tragic America,* and, to place side by side with it, a copy of a telegram I received from Patrick Kearney.[2] Separately, there will be sent you other material which will interest you and which you will probably want to pass around to friends.

Please let me have your reaction to all this. Again, my thanks for your excellent letter.

Very truly,

To Onorio Ruotolo
[CC]

The sculptor wanted to do a bronze bust of Dreiser for Arthur Pell, who was head and treasurer of Liveright Inc., but had heard that Dreiser was dissatisfied with his art and particularly

[2] Kearney, who had dramatized *An American Tragedy,* had alleged in a telegram, April 5, that he and a friend, Martin Mooney, had been fired by Universal Pictures Corp. because Mooney at Kearney's instigation had addressed the John Reed Club in Los Angeles on the extent to which labor was being exploited at Boulder Dam; he hoped Dreiser would help publicize the matter. On April 6 Dreiser, who accepted Kearney's version of events, sent letters to, among others, the *New York World-Telegram, New York Times,* American Civil Liberties Union, National Committee for the Defense of Political Prisoners. When on April 11 the *Times* printed Dreiser's letter, there ensued correspondence between Dreiser (April 12), and R. H. Cochrane, vice-president of Universal (April 12 and 13).

disliked his 1921 bust of Caruso at the Metropolitan Opera House. He had explained to Dreiser on April 1 that the inadequacies of the Caruso were to be attributed to a young artist's naïvete and exuberance.

> Hotel Ansonia
> [Broadway at 73rd Street]
> New York, [N.Y.]
> April 6, 1932

Dear Ruotolo:

I remember the head which you did of me years ago,[3] and your enthusiasm for the work. For years it stood in Liveright's reception room, and one angle of it seemed satisfactory to me and to people who knew me. As for the other phases of it, they were more or less uniformly rejected by people who knew me best.

God knows there are enough misinterpretative photographs, sketches, paintings, caricatures, as well as sculptures in full and in relief to do me up forever. The trouble with the accursed things is that good, bad or indifferent, they are apparently preserved forever by those who make them, if by no one else, and they crop up to irritate the sitter at the most inopportune times and places.

I did not say that the bust of Caruso offended me. What I did say was that I had listened to Caruso many times, and met him once, and it seemed to me that something more expressive of the blazing emotional content of the man could come forth in bronze or stone. On the other hand, I know the many difficulties of working in clay, and the still greater difficulties of interpreting anybody in paint or clay or anything else. It would not be so hard for me to bring myself to sit for another study, provided it could be agreed beforehand that in case it was not satisfactory to me, it should then and there be destroyed, so that it would not linger around as another misinterpretation.

---

3 1918. See *Ruotolo, Man and Artist,* intro. Frances Winwar (New York, cop. 1949), p. 67.

But the trouble with that proposition is that the artist would say that the sitter was a damned fool, and that he did not know a good interpretation of himself when he saw it, and that it would require all of the generations of thousands of years to really decide who was right, and that is the reason I hate to sit for you or anyone.

I haven't any doubt in the world that, like myself and other people at times, you are able to catch accurately something that impresses you and that you desire to preserve, but all of us, without exception, from the greatest to the lowest, fail at times, and it is these damned failures that cause all the trouble. If you know how this difficulty can be overcome, I wish you would let me know.

To Jonathan Cape
[CC]

Cape and Smith, preparing to publish in the spring of 1933 the English edition of Dorothy Dudley's Forgotten Frontiers, Dreiser and the Land of the Free *(New York, 1932), had on March 30 sent Dreiser galley proofs for comment on any passages that might be offensive to him.*

> Hotel Ansonia
> [Broadway at 73rd Street]
> New York, [N.Y.]
> April 7, 1932

Dear Cape:

I have had three different people read Mrs. Harvey's [4] study of myself. There is really no use in my furnishing you with separate copies of the reports, because I can summarize them in this letter.

---

[4] Dorothy Dudley's married name. See also Dreiser's letter to her, April 7, immediately following.

All three readers agree that the book is beautifully written and very interesting. One critic, whom I shall designate as K.C., thinks that in the early part of the book there is too much detail in regard to the American scene, and that it overshadows your humble servant. I read that particular section and do not agree. It is possible that the American scene could be shortened a little, but it does seem to me that it is more or less essential in the opening of the work. Another critic, Mrs. Campbell, wishes that there were more personal touches, anecdotes, descriptions of my mannerisms, my peculiar and ever-changing philosophy, but with that I do not agree. This work is long enough; from what I can gather, it seems to indicate pretty much what might at least engage another volume.

The third reader considers that there are long stretches of "wearying reading, lighted by some brilliant flashes of summaries, perception and bits of personal interest." This same report states later on that "in her attempt to evaluate the American scene, she goes into too much detail about Masters, Frost, Sandburg, etc." Mrs. Campbell, on the galleys which I sent you, marked one chapter particularly offensive, as she said, in its over-discussion of Masters, Frost and Sandburg. Boyd [5] would better look at this rather carefully.

There is one thing that I want to emphasize, and that is this: There are extracts from Mencken's letters to me. In order to facilitate Mrs. Harvey in getting a general impression of my early years, I allowed her to examine personal letters to me from various people, Mencken, Masters—quite a few, but with the understanding that they were personal and private and that no excerpts should be made without the consent of the writers. It appears that this has not been done. I certainly do not want her to quote Mencken's confidences to me, particularly one which reads, "that old bitch, N. P. D." [6] And there is another statement referring to "that ass, Brander Matthews" and a whole lot of

5 Ernest Boyd, literary critic and adviser to the firm.
6 Mrs. N. P. Dawson, a book reviewer who had attacked *The "Genius"* as well as Dreiser's other works. (See Dreiser to Harold Hersey, November 18, 1915.)

excerpts which I have marked. They are, God knows, remarkable enough, and make mighty interesting reading, were it not for the fact that they will, with the greatest certainty, bring more criticism on me and, in this case, it is not justified, and I feel that as the publisher of this book, you should protect me in this matter.

From what I gather from all three readers, there is nothing else to which I can object. K.C. insists that there is some awkward writing, meanings in places that are not quite clear, and she has marked these places. Mrs. Campbell thinks there are too many extracts from my various books. I do not think this is important since they all agree that the thing reads exceptionally well as it is.

I wonder if you would be good enough to let me see the advertising which you are preparing. I ask this because, in a letter to me, Mrs. Harvey complains that some of the announcements in the Cape and Smith Spring catalog were, to her, nauseating, and not true to her meaning. She also objects to what she calls "Sandburg's statement only half quoted, which ruined it."

I am satisfied that the book can be properly presented without too much rough stuff, and I guess you are of the same opinion.

To Dorothy Dudley Harvey
[CC]

Hotel Ansonia
[Broadway at 73rd Street]
New York, [N.Y.]
April 7, 1932

Dear Dorothy:

Very recently, Jonathan Cape, who is over here, brought me galley proofs of your study of me, of which both he and his new partner,[7] he said, thought very highly, but he was anxious to get

[7] Harrison Smith, who in partnership with Robert Haas published the American edition in 1932.

my opinion and that of some of my critical friends because, he said, both he and his partner feared some of the material might be offensive not only to myself but to Mencken and Masters.

Apart from my own reading of most of the book, I had it read by three estimable critics whose judgment I think you would value along with mine. All three agreed with Cape and his partner that the book is brilliantly written and full of interesting material and that it is likely to attract attention and sell. All three objected to this and that and, so that you may know exactly what they objected to, I am sending you a duplicate of my letter to Mr. Cape.[8]

In that letter, you will read what I have to say about the letters from Masters, Mencken and so on, and your excerpts from the same. What I say there in regard to no direct quotations without their consent is my memory of my agreement with you, but, apart from that, I cannot feel that it is fair to any of those who have written me privately, nor that it is good policy to set them forth in a book published other than by myself. I have not the slightest objection to your saying that I allowed you to read them, and that from reading them you gathered certain impressions, but without Mencken's or Masters' consent, you cannot possibly have them say things which will create quarrels for them and unkind remarks as regards my good taste in such matters. I feel that you will be willing to cut them out, and I am writing you now to ask if you will not do this, and inform Cape and his partner, by return mail.

In regard to what you say about my lack of interest, it sprang from enormous pressure on me just then in connection with many things—*Dawn, Tragic America,* the Russian Ballet [9] and such—all of which were more or less in hand at one and the same time. I don't think you can accuse me of any lack of real interest, though, when the material with which I provided you shows up so extensively and so well.

8 April 7, immediately preceding.
9 Dreiser had early in 1929 been trying to raise funds to subsidize an American tour for the ballet company he had seen at the Bolshoi Opera House in Moscow during the winter of 1927-28.

Further than this, I find no glaring errors of fact or supposition, and insofar as supposition is concerned, I would not want to interfere with that anyway. If you feel certain things to be true about me, it is certainly your privilege to feel that way and to say so. My answer to most that has been said about me is likely to appear in the history of myself which I hope to continue.

By the way, *An American Tragedy*, presented by Piscator,[10] the dramatist and producer, and with a very fine cast including Joseph Schildkraut, and actors and actresses selected from the Reinhardt group, is to open on April 16th, both in Berlin and Vienna. If, by any chance, you could go to either place and see the performance, I would be delighted to hear what you have to say about it. I have been asked to go over, but I cannot possibly make it, as my present intention is to move much nearer the Mexican border than I am now.

In regard to my interest in economics, I have this to say. I have always been interested in economics and the social set-up in this country and all countries—humanity in general. I think that the text of my books shows that from the first to the last. My reason for troubling with the economic phase here is because conditions as they are now are certain to be addled and to make ridiculous literary achievements of almost all kinds other than economic. There is a social unbalance here which would not permit of any sane picture that did not clearly reflect social unbalance. However, at the same time that I am interesting myself in our social conditions, I am concluding the last volume of the Trilogy which, I am sure, most of my critics will pounce on as decidedly unsocial and even ridiculous as coming from a man who wants social equity. Nevertheless, I am writing it just that way.[11]

Thank Katherine for her interest, and tell her I treasure the negro painting she gave me past almost any other that I have. It is so colorful and so richly human.

[10] Erwin Piscator.

[11] *The Stoic*, concluding volume of Dreiser's "Trilogy of Desire," was nearly completed before he died in 1945 and was published in 1947.

To Simon and Schuster
[CC]

The publishers had sent John Cowper Powys's forthcoming book in hopes of securing quotable comment.

Hotel Ansonia
[Broadway at 73rd Street]
New York, [N.Y.]
April 9, 1932

Gentlemen:

Having read *A Glastonbury Romance,* I could, as you know, write my customary essay on Jack as a novelist, critic, philosopher and astonishing and arresting personality. However, I have done it so often I feel that it is really not necessary.

This particular tome of his is really nothing more than the gorgeous play of Jack's mind over a world of his own devising. He places it in Glastonbury, England; as a matter of fact, except for the name, its exact location is in his own skull. Wonderful, to be sure.

I have never tired of sitting on the side-lines and observing the procession of his characters marching by, and marvelling at the playful and ironic and almost anachronistic scrutiny which he brings to bear on them. Positively, and as usual, he and the book are astounding.

He says that he stems from Scott. If Scott ever encountered Jack or read any of his books, he would rush to the nearest telegraph office and disown him. They have about as much in common as Mephistopheles and the Angel Gabriel, and yet if Scott would endure it, I am absolutely positive that Jack would take him by the arm and indulge in the friendliest social and philosophic discussion imaginable. But Scott would not stand it.

I see that some complain because this book is 400,000 words long, and they think it is too long. I have also heard that it is 600,-

ooo words long. I wish to record that if Jack wrote a book 900,000 words long, I would still find it interesting from the first page to the last.

To Louise Campbell
[ALS]

[Hotel Ansonia
Broadway at 73rd Street
New York, N.Y.
April 15, 1932]

Dear Louise:

I know I should have answered at once but you should see this place. I am sick of running a bureau & of being a clearing house for nothing. My dream is to get out—this month if possible—close Miss Light's office [12]—get her a desk at Liveright's & close out my room here. Me for a simple hut in [the] west where I can write & save expenses. Everything seems to be going under.

I am sending you Monday [13] the first 15 Chapters of *The Stoic* to read. When that comes back I'll send you some money. I thought your criticisms of Mrs. Harvey's book very good & told Cape so.[14] Mrs. H— has arrived from Paris & is now rowing with Cape because he gave her text to Ernest Boyd to revise. She objects to his cuts & criticisms but not to yours.

I'm sorry about your mother. Lord life is a slow sandpapering process. We all get worn down. Sometimes I admire Helen [15] as much as anyone. She keeps up a strong front & looks toward a simple form of existence under a new government. She likes flowers & dogs & the country & so I think she may come out ok. As for me!!?

Come over.
Love from T.D

12 Evelyn Light was his secretary.
13 April 18.
14 See Dreiser to Jonathan Cape, April 7, 1932.
15 Helen Richardson.

I would have sent parts of *The Stoic* before but the changes were constant & the going hard[.] I'm getting into form though for better sailing I hope[.]

TO DALLAS McKOWN
[CC]

For some months Dreiser had been hoping to establish an organization similar to the National Committee for the Defense of Political Prisoners but free of Communist Party evangelizers. When in the spring of 1932 McKown and a friend had proposed to organize the Intellectual Workers League, dedicated to achieving "clarification of viewpoint of the American intellectual workers toward the economic crisis" so that sides would be soon chosen, Dreiser had given his encouragement, even declining subsequently to support a similar group headed by Edmund Wilson, Lewis Mumford, Waldo Frank, John Dos Passos, and Sherwood Anderson, lest he weaken I.W.L.'s struggle. McKown had on May 3 sent Dreiser an extended account of objectives.

> Reply to:
> Room 709
> 1860 Broadway
> New York, [N.Y.] [16]
> June 9, 1932

Dear Mr. McKown:

You will understand the reasons for the long delay in replying to your letter of May 3rd, which I now desire to take up with you.

As you know, it has long been my desire to organize into an ultimately effective group the American workers, professional people, etc. who may be designated by the broad term "intellectuals." You know as well that I am not a member of the Com-

[16] Dreiser was at the time in San Antonio, Tex.

munist Party, that the Party would not accept me as a member, and that, while I have found Communism functioning admirably in the U.S.S.R., I am not at all convinced that its exact method there could effectively be transferred to the self-governing of the people of the United States, or accepted by them. I have made it plain in numerous articles and in *Tragic America* that my sympathies lie with some equitable system which would be acceptable here, and the accomplishment of which I believe can and must be effected by the efforts of the group named above in sympathetic co-ordination with the mass of workers.

It will not be surprising to you, therefore, to learn that my objections to the plan as set forth in your letter of May 3rd rest mainly on the League's apparent mental if not actual Communist affiliation.

On page 4 of your letter are set forth three of the activities already undertaken by the League, and each one is definitely tied up with and assistant to Communist activities. I have, as you know, spent considerable time and writing effort on the Scottsboro case, and my objection to the League's activities therein has nothing whatever to do with an attempt by anyone to assist some Negro boys who are so obviously being led to a legal lynching, but it does lie very definitely in the fact that this case, already vastly publicized by the various Communist organizations, still remains only *one* instance of the enormous inequity with which we are faced. The same objection applies to the second instance—that of supplying funds, etc. to the Harlan miners.

In the third instance, the *Daily Worker* is mentioned. I cannot agree with you (and the League's support of that paper to the exclusion of any other would indicate your acceptance of it as an effective medium for your group) that the *Daily Worker* will ever be embraced by Americans—particularly the group in which I am now interested—as a leading representative of the press. I regard the *Progressive,* for instance, as a much better newspaper and as a much more appropriate and satisfactory channel—one of many others—through which to spread the sort of information and to provide the guidance which is needed.

I note, too, that you say that the Chairman of the Committee on Policy is a member of the Communist Party. From that fact alone, I feel sure that, consciously or unconsciously, the destiny of the League would be definitely guided according to Communist principles. As you know, I have often requested assistance from the Communist Party, asked their advice and used it, or not, according to what I judged the necessity of the situation. And that is the method which I believe should be adopted by the League.

These paragraphs, and without the necessity of going into further details of your letter, will give you the trend of our differences. To sum it up, I can say this: I do not believe that the American workers, and by this I mean the mass, and not the group in which I am interested for this movement, are sufficiently advanced to understand or appreciate the highly involved, intellectual and idealistic terms by which Communism seems to find it necessary to explain itself and its program. If they were able to, the Communist Party here would not occupy the minor place that it now does. I think that they would welcome an equitable system if it could be explained to them in simple terms which they could understand.

It is apparent to me that you do believe that this mass of workers understands and welcomes Communism as it is set forth by the Communists, when you say that, on the one hand, the League is assisting in the matters of Scottsboro, Harlan and the *Daily Worker* and, on the other, that the League "joined the May Day Parade in New York to show its logical, natural affiliation with the workers and their cause."

It must be obvious, to anyone who has witnessed the almost fantastic refusal of American labor in general to countenance what it considers (as narrowly, as mistakenly as you please, but the fact remains) any radical teachings or tendencies, that the workers do not regard Communism as their cause and that the League's activities comprise a desire, rather than a fulfillment.

If the League is content to consider these points, and, after so

doing, to accept them as part of its program so that this attitude would inform its activities to the exclusion of the present Communist trend, I shall be pleased to hear from you further.

Very truly,

To Louise Campbell
[ALS]

San Antonio, Texas
June 10, 1932

Dear Louise:

Forgive me for clearing out on short notice and for the long silence. I've been working—and hard. Starting on Chapter XXXIII [17] this morning which proves it. Because she hasn't had so much else to do I've been sending Miss Light the hand written copies & having her make three. One comes back to me for corrections & two stay there[.] I've been intending to go over my set & correct them but so far haven't done anything but write— and think it best. Once I get forty chapters done I intend to have certain corrections or rather additions I have made to the 15 you edited plus the remaining 25—(all typed[)]—sent to Kyllmann in London [18] for revisions—that is checking for English names, places, language,—their way of saying things. After these come back my plan is to send the forty to you for examination, editing, etc. The remaining forty (if there are that many) will be handled in the same way.

How are you. And your mother. I had to get out of N.Y. Couldn't get a thing done. Besides expenses were eating me alive. Here I spend about 20 a week. In El Paso where I am going tomorrow I will not do much worse. If I do I'll come here. Helen is up at Mt. K.[19] Wharton [20] was over there. And Poor [21] and some

17 Of *The Stoic.*
18 O. Kyllmann, of Constable & Co., Ltd., Dreiser's English publishers.
19 Helen Richardson had remained in Mt. Kisco.
20 Wharton Esherick.
21 Henry Varnum Poor, painter and ceramist.

others. I'm sticking here instead of going back there because I need a change of mind as well as place. But as soon as this book is in shape I am going back of course. My El Paso address will be General Delivery but you'd better (after June 16th) address care Miss Light. I wire her any change & she forwards all stuff. Sorry I've been so negligent—but work—18 chapters in five weeks has kept me going. Please write & give me the news. I owe you money—but how much. I think I ought to fix a lump sum for the book. But I still think you cut a little too close. I don't want my style to become too crisp or snappy. It has an involute character which to a degree should remain[.]

Love. Regards to everybody[.]
D

Next week East Lynne—(I mean El Paso)[.]

TO LOUISE CAMPBELL

[ALS]

> [Iroki
> Old Bedford Road
> R.F.D. 3
> Mt. Kisco, New York
> July 19, 1932]

Dear Louise:

Thanks for your note. I'm glad you like the story.[22] I do. When it's all done it should be gone over again for cuts like we did the *Tragedy*. More trouble in my camp. Liveright Inc[.] is busted. No money. They are breaking their contract with me which means 7/8th of my annual income. Now I have to start out & find another Publisher. Also some way to live. That means Horn & Hardart's I guess. But with time I get down to bed rock—say $50 a week maybe. The good old days. Meanwhile I'll find some way

---

22 *The Stoic.*

to pay you. . . . .[23] Pell is no publisher. Neither is Smith.[24] Their fall list is pathetic. And now is no time to sell books. 5,000 is considered a sale!

Will have more stuff shortly. Yes I worked hard.

You don't need a janitor do you?

D

To Louise Campbell

[ALS]

[Iroki
Old Bedford Road
R.F.D. 3
Mt. Kisco, New York]
July 23, [1932]

Dear Louise:

Thanks for the chapters 1 to 17 inc. Wish you would let me know exact number of Chapters [those] you have now would make. I have four more ready but am mixed as to the total number to date[.] But you can straighten me out by telling me what you have. . . . .[25] Sorry about your brother-in-law. I can understand it though if he was as one-track minded as you say. It's tough but I don't think we need to die exactly[.] Will have to learn to do with a little. . . . . Personally I am being assailed with bitter letters from my relatives & those whom I have been assisting. *I should have seen this coming & duly warned them.* As a matter of fact I did—but they don't remember. I'm suddenly cut out of a guarantee of 1200 a month to nothing. Out of that went 200 to Mrs. Dreiser. 80.00 to Mame & Rome. 100 to Emma

---

[23] Dreiser's punctuation.

[24] Arthur Pell was to succeed to the presidency of the reorganized Liveright Publishing Co., while Thomas R. Smith continued as chief editor.

[25] The ellipsis–like marks are Dreiser's throughout this letter.

& Sylvia.[26] 75.00 to Helen.[27] Taxes on property aggregating 50.00 a month, salaries to Miss Light, Pell, office rent, car maintenance, clothing, food[,] what not[.] I've knocked out one car. Closed up the office, cut Miss Light's salary & cut all the others but I'm nowhere in sight of how to keep it all up—even so. My stocks & bonds went to all but nothing[.] I have interest aggregating $6000. Now it totals 210.00 per year. And income tax. Well, I won't have that. When I get this book done I hope to use it to make a new deal. I'm going pretty good & when all shaped up [it] ought to be really dramatic. . . . But publishers are very low. Covici-Friede are busted. Brentano's too. Doubleday[,] Page nearly failed but cut everything for a few lines they have. Just where to go for a real advance is beyond me. I'm fishing but no word yet. Meantime writing—9 to 5. It's the best bit. I live[,] eat & sleep here now—daily. As for you I'll send you 50.00 at the end of next week—more later. Pray for better days.

By the way in that chapter where Cowperwood and Berenice visit the Cathedrals I think I wandered a little on the last three paragraphs or so relating to Berenice. It's too purely romantic. Should be romantically appreciative but with realistic if not esthetic reservations. Perhaps you could tone down a sentence or so here & there & let me see it.

Incidentally don't let dullness or turgidity escape. If you're afraid to cut mark for me to look at.

Love,
T.D

You know I'm sure Liveright is miles from being solvent[.] How they can go on is beyond me.

26 Dreiser's sisters (Mary Frances, Emma Wilhelmina, and Cecilia) and brother (Marcus Romanus).
27 Helen Richardson.

To Louise Campbell
[ALS]

> [Iroki
> Old Bedford Road
> R.F.D. 3]
> Mt. Kisco, New York
> [July 31, 1932]

Dear Louise:

Chapter 1 as revised came & I feel it may do. Will tell you later. The book goes along. I am on 54. Up to that is typed but not revised. When I have 10 I'll revise & send them on. It's going to be long—this final draft. But when it's all done I think it can be gone over & condensed. Feel so. If so it will have a lot of go & color & drama. . . . .[28] Can't tell you how I've slaved over this— usually 9 to 5—often 9 to 7. Several times 9 to midnight. If I get it done I can do a lot with it because it completes the trilogy. One question: Should I or should you make a brief synopsis of Vols. 1 & 2 & put them in the front of this one by way of introduction. Or would that hurt the sale of this book as a separate thing? Pell is mailing you a check for $50.00. Later on I'll send you some more.

Isn't that tough about those bonus men.[29] Now you begin to see the money crowd in full action. Next comes cold-blooded dictatorship & the guns for the small fish. Wait a little while[.]

D

[28] Dreiser's punctuation.

[29] At the order of President Hoover, troops with tanks, guns, and tear-gas bombs had been sent to rout out of Washington some 10,000 destitute veterans of World War I who had marched on the capital to agitate for a bonus.

TO VICTOR SMIRNOV
[CC]

The president of the Amkino Corporation in New York had sought Dreiser's endorsement of the The House of Death, *a Soviet moving picture depicting "the tragedy of Dostoyevsky's life"; i.e., his journey "from the ideas of Communism, to the sugary compromising Slavophil-Christian philosophy, to those libels on socialisms—his novels of the type of his* Evil Spirits." *The statement prepared for Dreiser's signature concluded: "The proletariat and the working class intelligentsia honor the memory of those who raised their voices in defense of the downtrodden and the offended, but among those names, dear to them, we do not find the name of Dostoyevsky, although his life is a vivid example by which we can learn how impermissable, how criminal it is to be inconsistent."*

Room 610
1860 Broadway
New York, [N.Y.]
August 5, 1932

Dear Mr. Smirnov:

As you know, I liked the moving picture of Dostoyevsky's political career very much. Personally, I was surprised to see portrayed that either his political sufferings or the natural turn of his disposition had led him to the acceptance of the philosophy of Christ as the single solution for the political, social, and other ills of man. My present personal knowledge of the details of Dostoyevsky's life does not warrant me in either crediting or discrediting the data in the film.

My reading of *Crime and Punishment, The Brothers Karamazov,* and *The Idiot* leaves me with the deduction, in regard to him, that his observation of life led to no fixed political, social or religious deductions of any kind. He seems in the main, to me, at least, to have reported the idiosyncracies of man, and this rather anomalous condition in which we find ourselves, without bias and without a personal social plan.

So great is his gift as an artist, so supreme his analysis of the vagaries of our human dispositions, that I find it impossible to criticize him for other lacks, however great. It is entirely within the province of the Soviet Government to point out that his philosophy does not accord with its economic and social views, but to denounce him for failure to accept these, or for presuming to offer a plan which, as I see it, has neither political nor social worth, is without value to the Soviet system, and absolutely outside my mood and wish.

He is a Russian, he is a great artist; his temperament, twisted by torture or not, does enormous honor to the race from which it springs. Whatever the reason, it cannot in my judgment, be safely belittled.

Therefore, I cannot sign or endorse this particular introduction.[30]

Very truly,

To George Jean Nathan
[CC]

On May 27 Ray Long and Richard R. Smith, Inc., had agreed to publish the American Spectator, *to be edited by George Jean Nathan, Ernest Boyd, Eugene O'Neill, James Branch Cabell, and Dreiser. Stock would be issued, the publisher to have 50 per cent and the editors 50 per cent. On June 17 Nathan and Boyd had informed Dreiser that the details had all been worked out and the first number would be dated November 1; they hoped "you will be able to let us have something for the first issue which will be, of course, in your characteristic vein but omitting all social and political references, inasmuch as we have decided that the review will ignore that side of things."*

---

[30] A carbon copy of an undated, apparently later letter, acknowledged by Smirnov on August 18, indicates that Dreiser finally did write a letter on behalf of the picture, but it was a letter praising its cinematic art in contrast to "the absolute failure of the motion picture as an art form in America and most other countries." Nothing was said of Dostoyevsky's having betrayed the proletariat.

[Iroki
Old Bedford Road
R.F.D. 3]
Mt. Kisco, [New York]
August 7, 1932

Dear George:

Further and final consideration of the *American Spectator* plan leads me to conclude not to ally myself with it in any way—editorially, financially, officially, or as a preferred and so publicized advisor or contributor. My reasons are several.

Chief among them of course is the fact that the original plan for all this, merely roughly suggested by you to me before I left for New Mexico and you for Europe, and which later was to be much more carefully worked out and discussed before any more of any kind was made, was never so worked out or discussed, and without further word of any kind.

Around July 1st, in El Paso, I received a letter from Boyd saying he was, in your absence, in charge of the business of getting out the first issue and asking for a promised article from me. Our correspondence is on file of course. Also he specified the policy which had apparently already been decided upon. But by whom? As I wrote him, I had no understanding that the plans for the *American Spectator* had been settled and asked for details. There was no reply to my letter.

But on the papers announcing my return to New York I received a second note from Ernest asking me to call him and let him explain the situation. On doing so his explanation was that you had told him that all the details had been settled with me before I left. Since I knew nothing of this, as I told him, I extracted from him that Long and Smith, Publishers, had been induced to act as publishers for 50% of the stock of the new venture. In other words to take over the practical management of the business. And that the remaining fifty was to be divided in some way between those who were its editors—yourself, himself, myself, Cabell. But in exactly what way he did not appear to know. Neither did he mention that Sinclair Lewis was to be one

of the editors, a bit of news which has just reached me. And I must point out, his name could not have been joined with mine anyhow. Long since, as you know, he has recorded himself definitely in regard to me.[31] And in consequence I reserve the right to reject association of his name with mine.

Next, as you said to me Friday, I am to suggest what I think to be a fair division of the editorial 50% of the stock, assuming that I were to be a part of the editorial ownership and direction. Yet as you know I can not fairly venture to do that. For primarily the idea is yours. It was you who thought it all out and then arranged with Boyd, Lewis, Cabell, Long and Smith, as their acceptance of the same shows. And that acceptance covers not only the editorial but the financial set ups and policies, two things in regard to which I personally am still in the dark.

Personally I do not see why Long and Smith should have been given 50%, particularly with such a group to give name and distinction to them. A 33 1/3%, at most 40% would have been plenty. As for the technical and practical phases of the editorship, those should fall to yourself and Boyd and with most admirable results. For both of you have genius for that.

As for policy, however, and regardless of reward in any form, which is by no means my present concern, I see no way in which I personally can share to my satisfaction in the editorial direction. First, because I cannot possibly give the time necessary for that; and secondly, since five or six editorial heads are involved and I cannot see any personal place for my own private and very definite views, not in connection with what I might write, (I can control that) but of what I think such a paper should stand for. For with five others to combat, the multiplicity of views to placate, I feel that my own views would lead to not only a waste of time but very likely hard feeling, and worst of all, a seeming endorsement on my part of viewpoints and conclusions with which I personally could not have anything in common. It is an avenue

[31] On March 19, 1931, Lewis had publicly accused Dreiser of plagiarizing "three thousand words from my wife's book on Russia" (Dorothy Thompson's *The New Russia*), a charge to which Dreiser had responded by slapping Lewis's face. Lewis never became one of the *Spectator's* editors.

or door that seems to lead to self-misrepresentation and so self-stultification. And time has at last convinced me that my personal views are not easily harmonized with those of others.

At best, I am a lone editor or a lone contributor, whose views should stand singular and alone. And joining with four or five others with whom I could not always hope to cooperate would merely create an illusion of direction and endorsement which would have no reality and which I could only resent. And as you know, I have had my share of that in many directions. I have therefore decided that in so far as possible I will guard against it in the future. And so I hereby withdraw in every shape and manner.

George—this may sound like a hard and quarreling letter. It is not. I have merely invoked formality in order to emphasize what appears to me to be the fair and friendly reality of it all. I cannot move off on any left leg with you. And since this *American Spectator* has already slipped beyond any real influence that I might have or wish to exercise, I cannot write differently.

So please give out to all that I am in no way connected with the *Spectator,* editorially, financially, or as selected or preferred contributor or advisor. That I will sell whatever I can to you or your editors, at one cent a word or whatever the price is, goes without saying. I will.

And I hope that this in no way affects a plan or a friendship that I have for this long time sincerely valued.[32]

32 Despite his objections, Dreiser helped edit the *Spectator* for more than a year. On September 11 he delivered a note to Nathan and Boyd entitled "My Program for the *American Spectator*":

My idea of a balanced issue would be:
1. A poem—lyric, free verse, or prose.
2. Scientific presentation of something—preferably an examination of an important scientific fact or an interesting speculation.
3. Philosophic discussion of an abstraction after the manner of Santayana, Spencer, James, or whomsoever (not over 1000 words)
4. Critical or picturesque study of a literary or artistic personality (painter, novelist, poet, actor, dancer, singer, musician or composer)
5. Brief but colorful picture of the special state of a community, tribe, sect, caste, anywhere on the face of the earth.
6. A bit of adventure (important) by one who has done the adven-

To Louise Campbell
[ALS]

[?New York, N.Y.
August 8, 1932]

Dear Louise:

You have refrained from comment on this 3rd vol. which strikes me as ominous. In editing up to 45 I have rearranged & cut not a little. As I wrote you Chapters 1 & 3 were combined—with most of 3 constituting the opening & a condensed version of the last 1/3 of no. 1—the close[.] Chapters 29—30 & 31 have been condensed & rearranged. Most of the Sheik stuff with Aileen —together with the Clown dinner are out. The last half of 43— (Aileen & C.[33] again & Pryor's Cove[)]] has been reduced to a few references—in order to speed things up. But even so I would like a severe critical sand-papering in order to shake me into closer work. Not can you—but will you oblige[?]

                                                              D
I hope you're better[.]

_____

turing—Byrd, Lindbergh, Post and Gatty, Amelia Earhart, Stefansson, or whomsoever.

7. A defense of someone or something either by the accused or a partisan of the thing attacked.
8. A picture of the difficulties, pleasure, profits, amusement, annoyances, reward, etc. of some profession by one in it—priest, lawyer, doctor, engineer, scientist, educator, administrator, banker, industrialist, or what you will.
9. A presentation of something by a technician.
10. A skit or playlet ridiculing some phase of something in the State or Nation or world—religious, political, artistic, athletic, dramatic, social, intellectual, etc.
11. A worth-while protest against some definite ill—savage and uncompromising.
12. A short story.
13. A discussion of a single important play.
14. Ditto a really important book. (just one)
15. One or more genre commentaries by world celebrities anywhere—such as Hauptmann, Mussolini, the Pope, Stalin, Greta Garbo, Shaw, or one of the reigning Chinese Generals.

Dreiser's collaboration virtually ceased with his letter to Nathan, October 7, 1933 (*q.v.*) but he did not formally resign until January 4, 1934.

33 Frank Cowperwood.

To George Douglas
[ALS–TEH]

Early in September, Dreiser began very actively to solicit both suggestions and manuscripts for the American Spectator *from anyone, famous or unknown, in the United States or elsewhere, who might produce sketches of "human interest."*

[Iroki
Old Bedford Road]
R.F.D. 3
Mt. Kisco, New York [34]
September 14, 1932

Dear George:

Hail!—wherever you are. This is a personal presentation of something that should interest you. As you see it is called A Literary Newspaper.[35] A better description would be "an open forum for aesthetic temperaments." It seems to me it is your paper par excellence for it is intended to be the medium for personalities such as yours. As a matter of fact kicking around among your old literary and human meditations on this and that must be a hundred that would slip into this medium perfectly. And you will be—mentally—among people of your own calibre. For to speak accurately this is an international and not a purely national paper and will go far and wide. I am personally calling on individuals in India, China, Russia, Australia and South Africa for things about which I know they can speak with sincerity and feeling. Among all of whom I have been thinking I most desire to hear from you. And don't forget that conventional acceptances play no part in the material of this paper. It is the unconventional & the very plain spoken that is desired—And as it is written so it will be printed. Will you let me see something.

Now as to the practical policy. It is—at first to be a monthly— and printed on plain newspaper stock. Later a weekly. No article

---

[34] Although writing on *American Spectator* stationery, Dreiser specified Mt. Kisco as his address at the foot of his letter.

[35] The phrase is the subtitle of the *American Spectator*.

can be more than 2500 words nor less than 500. At first the price paid will be 1 cent a word—later 5 cents. No single editor can order or accept anything. The *editors* do that. But any editor can do what I am doing and present the result with his endorsement. In your case you are known to Boyd, Nathan, O'Neill & myself. I don't know about Cabell. At any rate this will be a united invitation after the next conference. Let me hear from you. And all my best wishes.

Dreiser

To Howard Scott
[CC]

Scott, a friend of Dreiser's who had been working in the Department of Industrial Engineering at Columbia University, was organizer and director of Technocracy, Inc.

[Iroki]
Old Bedford Road
R.F.D. 3
Mt. Kisco, New York
September 17, 1932

Dear Scott:

On September 2nd, I read in the *New York Times* a condensation, whether accurate or not, of your remarks (in a lecture given at Johnsonburg, N. J.) on technology in its relation to the state. It spoke of charts covering a ten-year study of the impact of technology on human society, and stated that you denied that any of the suggested financial or monetary reforms, economic planning, etc. which are currently proposed, could deal with the production machinery which has developed and which reduces the necessity for individual labor. It quoted you as saying that the old price system was a hang-over of the past, and that the three hundred thousand technically trained men in the United States would have to become the arbiters of the social system of tomorrow.

In the same paper, I believe, was printed quotations from a lecture by Professor Miles Walker of Manchester, England, in which he called for an experimental state of 100,000 people to be conducted and directed by technicians, principally in the engineering field.

Around August 31st, there was a statement by Sir Alfred Ewing of England, who insisted that the human race as it now stands is ethically unprepared for the inventions which it has made, and that it is likely to be wrecked by its own achievements. All of these things interested me a great deal, but of all of them your probably badly quoted comments interested me most. I recall various talks with you concerning technology in general which always seemed to me to suggest the amazing possibilities for the state of the human race in general if only they could be understood and applied.

Recently, as you see by this sheet of paper,[36] I connected myself with an intellectual venture which looks to me to be promising. It is headed "A Literary Newspaper." I am perfectly willing to leave that title because of its usually propitious effect on the average intellectual, although to me it is a misnomer. The paper, as long as I have anything to do with it, will be far more far-reaching and humanly significant.

It is not out yet, and won't be for some little time. Its purpose, really, is to gather not only critical but genuinely illuminating data about life, and the possibilities of the human race in essay form. When I say essay form, however, I am speaking of articles of no greater length than 2500 words, but, in that length, it seems to me and to the others connected with this venture, that it is possible for a person who is sufficiently drilled in the data which interests him most to communicate the most important points of his program or his criticism, whatever it is.

For this particular paper, I am wondering if you will not be willing to condense into 2,000 words, and into very simple language, your views of modern technology and its usefulness in building a new kind of state. In this particular medium, and

---

[36] With the *American Spectator's* letterhead.

along with the varied and world-scattered personalities who are certain to appear there, it should have great weight. I personally would so much like to see it there. I must explain, however, that I, personally, cannot order an article. No one of the five editors can do that. It is the editors who really accept and publish a good paper. Any one of the five, however, is free to do just what I am doing—solicit and, if possible, by urging, bring about the creation of an article which will have real force.

The reward, to begin with, is practically nothing—one cent a word, but the medium is something very different and, naturally, very valuable. In your case, I have already spoken to Nathan and Boyd, both of whom you know, I believe. Boyd told me that he was going to write you, and to try to explain what it was that I wanted, and how glad the *Spectator* would be to have it. However, he and Nathan are terribly busy shaping up the first issue, and, for fear that he slips up on the time or the explanation of what it is I am after, I am writing you personally. If you have received a letter from Boyd, or still do, you may look upon it as subsidiary to mine, and if you do decide to interest yourself in this idea, I would like you to send your paper to me, because I am the one who is most interested in the idea, and who wishes to see it most effectively done.

Having written all this, I want to say "Hello!" Also to add how glad I am that your technical energies are bearing fruit, for I cannot but feel that such ideas as you have set forth are bound to have weight.

I don't know where you are living now, but I reside in Mt. Kisco, and my telephone number is Mt. Kisco 5414.[37] If you are anywhere in my neighborhood, or if you ever pass this way, I wish you would give me a ring, because I should like to have a talk with you about conditions in general, and, more particularly, about material that might find its way into a thing like the *Spectator*.

Anyhow, regards and best wishes.

[37] A typing error: on September 19 Dreiser's secretary wrote Scott that it should have been 5415.

To George Jean Nathan
[CC]

[Iroki
Old Bedford Road
R.F.D. 3]
Mt. Kisco, New York
September 19, 1932

Dear George:

I want to tell you how valuable I feel the meaning of Friday evening [38] to be.

In every worth-while enterprise, to say nothing of a distinguished one, there must always be, as you know, unintentional disarrangements of action, thought, and, consequently, results. Unfortunately, maybe, you will always find me aggressive and insistent, probably irritatingly so, but the target and the goal is that evanescent thing, perfection.

One thing I want to say, and it springs not only out of that evening, but all else that has gone before in this instance, is this: There is that about your courageous, diplomatic, optimistic approach and efforts in connection with this really big thing which gratifies me enormously, and evokes my sincere respect. I think you are due a bouquet, and this is it.

In the case of Ernest,[39] I feel constantly an often wordless but really priceless aesthetic value there which can and will do as much with this venture as anything else that will be done by anybody to give charm and strength to this paper. To me, his aesthetic approach is like a flag in the wind, indicative of an important and so necessary ideal. Some good came of this thing, I know.

More important and most important, if it can possibly be arranged, and that quickly, is to bring to New York, for conference, both Cabell and O'Neill. Regardless of the merit of their

38 Probably September 16, concerning the *American Spectator*.
39 Ernest Boyd.

names, you know and I know that mere names at a masthead, unless joined with active co-operation, mean nothing. I cannot sufficiently emphasize how meaningful I hold this to be. If I could persuade it into immediate being, I would do so. If I could brutally command it, the order would go forth now.

As it is, with five equal temperaments trying to harmonize themselves, the best I can do is to urge you to use your personal persuasiveness and force to bring it about. Will you do this? You know me.

To Bruce Crawford
[CC]

Room 610
1860 Broadway
New York, [N.Y.]
September 22, 1932

Dear Crawford:

I recall your telling me that you sought to get this phase of that village you described into the *Virginia Review,* but that they had cut it out.

As you described it to me riding east from Kentucky,[40] you put in personal character touches and sex color that somehow seem to be wanting in this ms. As I see it, it is not sufficiently vivid, and for that reason I am not passing it on, because I know that you would not want me to.

Just the same, I am satisfied that not one but a number of phases of the rural and small town life that you encounter must be interesting, colorful and valuable. I fancy, for instance, that a brief and telling skit of 1200 or 1500 words could be gotten up about the small plotting that goes on among small town politicians for position and place, the petty achievements, etc. Couldn't you picture that to the life?

[40] Crawford, the editor of *Crawford's Weekly* (Norton, Virginia) had accompanied Dreiser during the investigation of the Harlan and Bell County (Kentucky) coal mines, November 1931.

Again, I am sure, from bits you told me, that if you were to head something "Religion in Jake's Corners" you would ring the bell and delightfully, because I recall your telling me of the various religionists, including one girl who went from house to house asking for permission to enter and pray, and your own comments.

These and other things like them, done without much introduction of any kind, the very briefest possible, and holding fast to the actual conduct of these individuals, moved by whatever they chance to be moved by, would be thrilling.

Won't you try it, and that quickly, because if there is one thing the *Spectator* is going to need it is just that type of thing and principally for relief from the more serious considerations of so many things that it will necessarily have to consider.

Personally, and insofar as this crisis and social change are concerned, I have put the oars in the boat and am floating. I now see some things which I did not see anywhere near as clearly when we were together in Kentucky, and one is the enormous significance of the machine in any equitable form of society, and the need of the technician as a part of a newer kind of state.

Well, the technician, the chemist, the physicist, the mathematician, the inventor and the economic student and expert are not quite the same as the factory hand or the farmer, and while my sympathy for the worker and the farmer is exactly as it was before, the introduction of the working formula which is to remedy their troubles is not quite clear. I am thinking about it, and one thing I am thinking is that the intelligent worker and farmer and white collar man should be most thoroughly informed as to what technology could be made to mean, and then, with some sense of that knowledge, be urged to do something about it. More of this later.

But won't you turn your hand to this other thing, and let me know?

Regards.

To Sergei Dinamov
[CC]

Room 610
1860 Broadway
New York, [N.Y.]
September 22, 1932

Dear Sergei:

There are two things that you can do for me in connection with the *Spectator,* and both are important. One is this:

If possible, I would like a five-or six- or seven-hundred word signed statement from Stalin on anything that he chooses to talk about. For instance, if he would like to deny that he lives richly and is guarded by machine guns, and explain that the truth is that he lives very simply and is not guarded—if he would write six or seven hundred words on a thing like that, it would be really priceless for this paper.

The other thing is this: From you or such people as you could influence, I would like some little sketches not on the theory and practice of Communism or anything relating to it, or whether the five-year plan is working or not working, nor about the completion of any great work, but what I really want is some human interest sketches, little pictures of how the farmer or the worker actually lives, but without Communist dogma being lugged in in any form whatsoever. "A Day with a Communist Laborer" would be almost an ideal title, and would be much more illuminating and valuable in this paper than any God's quantity of propaganda, however brilliantly done.

Another brief sketch could relate to the Russian medical system as it now functions. I mean not so much the clinic as the visiting doctor—the man who goes when the person is too sick to come, and what he achieves.

Furthermore, I would like someone to present in light and, if possible, gay and very human colors the way the Russian educational system is applied, for instance, to the people in the extreme

north of Siberia—the wandering tribes that inhabit that region.

It has been described to me before and indicates absolute genius on the part of the Russian educational department. Just the same, if someone who has actually worked with these people or with the   [41] or the Mongolians in the new Mongolian state would bother to sketch these things it would be intensely valuable to me and to this paper because in it it would carry more weight than almost anywhere else that you can think of.

Therefore, any little essay that you write or can pick up from any source whatever I would like to have. One thing on which I would like to have fifteen hundred words would be [the] foreign author in Russia and exactly where he gets off which is, as I know, nowhere, but you can tell this better than I can.

If you do all of this and promptly, I will send you a couple of white shirts, or a bunch of American magazines or some book of your choice.

Regards—and reply promptly.

To Harrison Smith
[CC]

Smith and Haas were the publishers of Dorothy Dudley [Harvey]'s Forgotten Frontiers, Dreiser and the Land of the Free.

Room 610
1860 Broadway
New York, [N.Y.]
September 22, 1932

Dear Harrison Smith:

Thanks for the book and your comments on it. Mrs. Harvey, of course, submitted it to me in proof form, and I noted only a very few things which I thought she might like to change or

41 Left blank on Dreiser's carbon copy.

leave out, but otherwise did nothing because I like the book very much.[42]

In fact, and regardless of my own part in it—which seems a rather large thing to disregard in this instance—it is a very interesting reaction to and interpretation of the American scene. However, I do not feel that I should be quoted in any way in connection with the book, particularly since my views and my reactions are quite fully presented in the book itself.

Ernest Boyd was telling me only the other day that he edited it for Cape, and that in order to make sure of the willingness of some of the authors of letters quoted to have them so quoted, he addressed Masters, Mencken and others, and found that all but Masters was willing to have his opinions registered, but stated that on account of Masters he had been compelled to eliminate a very considerable quantity of matter.

I have the original set of proofs of this book and can, some day when I have time, determine for myself exactly how much had to be removed.

I am sorry, though, that he did not trouble to call my attention to it before, because if I had known I could have pointed out that while the letters themselves—Masters objecting—could not be quoted, nevertheless the substance of them could be set forth without legal interference and that, of course, would have been the intelligent thing to do.

I do not know even now that it has not been done in this way, and if it has, all I can say is that I am very glad it was so solved. I have never been able to understand Masters' change of heart nor his objection to having his once very definite opinions clearly set forth. All I can say now is that I wish you and the book the best luck in the world.

Very truly,

[42] See Dreiser to Jonathan Cape and to Dorothy Dudley Harvey, April 7, 1932.

To Charles E. Yost
[CC]

Yost was editor of the Fayette Review, *Fayette, Ohio.*

Room 610
1860 Broadway
New York, [N.Y.]
September 22, 1932

Dear Yost:

In the first place, here is a letter that I was going to address to you and am now enclosing it.

In the next place, I have not lost interest in Communism or the social problem in any way, but I now see some things which I did not see anywhere near as clearly when I was, say, in the middle of that Kentucky business.[43] One thing of this sort is the enormous significance of the machine in any equitable form of society, and the need of the technician as a part of a newer kind of state.

Well, the technician, the chemist, the physicist, the mathematician, the inventor and the economics student and expert are not quite the same as the factory hand or the farmer, and while my sympathy for the worker and the farmer is exactly as it was before, the introduction of the working formula which is to remedy their troubles is not quite clear. I am thinking about it, and one thing I am thinking is that the intelligent worker and farmer and white collar man should be most thoroughly informed as to what technology could be made to mean, and then, with some sense of that knowledge, be urged to do something about it. More of this later.

Apart from that, all this talk of yours of not being able to do something for the *Spectator* is nonsense, and you know it. With your long contact with and experience of the small town citizen, physician, politician, religionist, farmer and laborer in general

---

[43] His investigation of mine conditions in Harlan and Bell Counties, November 1931.

you should be able, if you will only attempt it, to formulate a type of colorful study that would present these different species at close range. Personally, I think a sympathetic if slightly ironic study of the small town religionist or politician or moderately equipped worker in any line would be fascinating and very probably beautiful and most readable.

As errant and hopeless of almost everything as I personally am, I have never actually lost the feeling that the mild and simple religionist is as much entitled to his prayers and his fears and his petty little church and the comfort that he gets out of it as I am to my speakeasy and my raucous company of ironists. Of course, I do not like to see him become too powerful and, Mohammed-wise, start out to make trouble for other people as he has and still does in this country, but, in another sense, there is a picturesque and amusing apology to be made for him, just as there are sympathetic studies to be made of the numbskull farmer, worker and white collar man who is led by the nose by politicians and made to deride and sneer and spit on the other people who would like to do something for them.

Taken at these angles, these individuals should prove material for you and for the *Spectator*. Can I encourage you to try? May I hope that you will get on the job and do it? The first issue is not out yet, and is not likely to be for a little while yet, but when it does appear, you will receive a copy.

Please let me know whether I have accomplished anything and oblige[.]

To Constance M. Griffin
[CC]

Mrs. Griffin was collecting material for her Henry Blake Fuller, a Critical Biography *(Philadelphia, 1939).*

Iroki
[Old Bedford Road]
R.F.D. 3
Mt. Kisco, New York
October 10, 1932

Dear Mrs. Griffin:

It is true that *With the Procession* by Henry Blake Fuller is the first piece of American realism I encountered.[44] It must have been published in 1885 or 1886, because, if my recollection serves me well, it was in 1886 that I first saw notices of it and somewhat later that I found a copy in the Chicago Library.[45]

I did not know Fuller at all well.[46] I first saw him in January or February of 1913, when I was working on data for *The Titan*. He introduced himself and we discussed American literature in general. This was in one of the halls of the Library. After that, although one or two letters were exchanged, I saw him but once, and that in the one-armed restaurant in Nassau Street, where we were accidentally lined side by side at the pie counter. There were some more comments on American life and related tid bits.

I hold the novel *With the Procession* in high esteem. It is one of the first and, even at this date, one of the best of examples of American realism.

Very truly,

[44] Dreiser had described Fuller as "the man who led the van of realism in America." (Introduction to Frank Norris: *McTeague* (Garden City, N. Y., 1928), p. viii. See also his comments in "The Great American Novel," *American Spectator*, I (December 1932), 1.)

[45] *With the Procession* was published in 1895.

[46] See Dreiser to Henry Blake Fuller, November 7, 1911.

To Arthur Davison Ficke
[CC]

Iroki
[Old Bedford Road]
R.F.D. 3
Mt. Kisco, New York
October 14, 1932

Dear Ficke:

Here is a letter from Nathan, and your ms.[47] and the poems. I wish you would consider these points he makes and if you see the way clear to revising the essay, let me know. At the moment, I cannot think of who you might substitute for Sappho and Ellen Terry. Although Nathan said he was going to try to think of possible substitutes, I notice he has not done so. I am writing him to come across with some ideas, but perhaps enough will occur to you. If so, will you revise the essay and let us have it back because I think it is a fine idea for the *Spectator*.

In regard to the poetry, I like "Caroline," "A Horse," "The Snake," and "The Fawn" very much, but the point is that everybody connected with the paper feels that for the first six months or so, until we find ourselves, we will not try to introduce poetry. Later, the paper being larger, we will probably take it up, but in addition to this particular skit of yours, I would like you to make some other suggestions, because by corresponding in regard to an idea, we may work out something that would be really ideal for the purpose of the paper and very satisfactory from an authorship point of view for you.

Are you good at skits? Could you, for instance, undertake a humorous skit in regard to the League of Nations on the basis of the characters being First Big Nation, Second Big Nation, Third Big Nation, Fourth Big Nation, and then four or five Little Nations with complaints, and show how the game works for the

[47] "The Value of Non-virtue to the Woman Artist," *American Spectator,* I (January 1933), 2.

little fellow and the big fellow? In it somewhere might be Official Observer of Unnamed Nation, as a side kick or something of the Biggest Nations.

Anyhow, write me further about this, and accept my regards and best wishes.

To Evelyn Scott
[CC]

> [*The American Spectator*
> 12 East 41st Street
> New York, N.Y.]
> October 28, 1932

Dear Evelyn:

I am not going to take time in this letter to argue about our perpetual quarrel. We fight, or rather you do, but it is all surface stuff. You know what I think of your work and I know what you think of mine—maybe.

The point is this: I want you to write at least three different articles for the *American Spectator*. I am going to suggest two, but you can throw these suggestions in the waste basket and suggest three or as many as you please of your own, but as quickly as possible, because I want you to be in the paper. One of my suggestions is that you make one of your caustic studies of the American woman novelist. Seeing that you are one yourself, you will know exactly what to do about it. Another is that I would like a comparative social study of England and America as it not only meets the eye but the daily life of an American like yourself or an individual who is not English but finds himself or herself facing the English social world. There are probably things that you admire about the English, and many things that you quarrel with, just as there are some things in America that you admire and some things that you quarrel with.[48]

---

[48] See her "Gentlemanly Englishmen—and Americans," *American Spectator*, I (February 1933), 1, 3; and "Voyager's Return," ibid., I (September 1933), 5.

Neither of these articles should run over 1500 words. It is not that we would not print articles of three, four, or five thousand words if we had the space. As a matter of fact, in due course we probably will, but right now pressure is extreme for the shorter form.

In so far as radical orthodoxy is concerned, that is out. In this paper, you are allowed to say what you actually think. The last thing we want to do is to edit either the individuality or the conclusions of any person who is invited, as you are, to contribute to this paper. It is not a right-wing periodical.

As for my Communism, it is a very liberal thing. I am not an exact Marxian by any means, and while I was in Russia, I was constantly threatened with being thrown out for my bourgeois, capitalistic point of view. My quarrel is not so much with doctrines as conditions. Just now, conditions are extremely badly balanced, and I would like to see them more evenly levelled.

As for your welcome here and your desirability, you are just the person that not only I but Nathan, Boyd, O'Neill, in fact all of us, want.

Please get busy and send me, by return mail, your suggestions. I'll reply promptly. I may even cable. If, without bothering to write, you want to sit down and pen something and send it to me, I wish you would, because it is a hundred-to-one chance that it will be acceptable, whatever it is.

Will you use this address, instead of the Mt. Kisco one, please?

To Ernest Boyd and George Jean Nathan
[CC]

Iroki
[Old Bedford Road]
R.F.D. 3
Mt. Kisco, New York
October 31, 1932

Boyd,
Nathan.

In connection with Cabell's article, Woodward's article, Ernest's first article, "Aesthete's Progress," and again in my own, "The Great American Novel," [49] there is either a listing of literary failures of comparatively recent as well as current days, or, as in Boyd's and Woodward's, a denunciation of the pseudo-aesthete, while in Cabell's, there is a dismissal of all American writers, including Boyd, yourself, myself, for want of style.

The point in all this, as I see it, is a preoccupation with the writer and his style, or lack of it, or mental twist of some kind, which will be well enough if distributed over a period of time, but to countenance a burst of this in the opening issues of the paper seems to me unsatisfactory. Obviously, letters and art must occupy a reasonable place in the program, but the more general activities of life from which these particular preoccupations take their rise should receive first consideration.

I am opposed to any one number having articles relatively alike, and particularly in the literary critical field. In the next number, it seems to me that my article and Cabell's run side by side. They would be better in separate issues.

T. D.

[49] Branch Cabell: "Prose of a Pallbearer," *American Spectator,* I (December 1932), 2-3; W. E. Woodward: "Babbitt, 1932 Model," ibid., I (January 1933), 1-2; Ernest Boyd: "Aesthete's Progress," ibid., I (November 1932), 1; Theodore Dreiser: "The Great American Novel," ibid., I (December 1932), 1-2.

To James D. Mooney
[CC]

Replying to Dreiser's request for a contribution to the Spectator, *Mooney on November 30 had offered "a completely drafted article on Russia and the Soviet form and philosophy of government."*

[?*The American Spectator*
12 East 41st Street
New York, N.Y.]
December 16, 1932

Dear Mooney:

I suppose you want this original. As I told you, I think it is very right and very interesting as far as it goes, but I still maintain that in Russia there is not only the theory of equitable participation by every member of the state in all of the benefits of the state, but, in so far as the fallibility of human nature will permit, an attempt to give the same organic expression.

Whether the present organization and its intelligence is sufficient to achieve this may be open to question and even to disproof, but unquestionably the officers of the machinery of state as it stands now desire to cause it to function equitably. At least, I think so. More, the problems and processes of equitable function are studied not only by the officials, but, because of their encouragement, by the people who are not only invited but compelled to aid in the equitable results of such study.

Your contention that here in America we have the same idea is, in a sense, true. That is, I believe that the American people at large are inclined to think or at least feel this way, and unquestionably the fathers of America—Washington, Jefferson and others since—have wished and worked for this idea of equitable distribution, but certainly the capitalistic system which is now in the saddle and will not get down is faced in the opposite direction. As you say, they prefer to sit tight and let the thing drift to see if, in the end, they will not still be in the saddle with the same capitalistic machinery functioning as it now functions. Since they

control and drive the American people in their direction at least so far, it is not quite fair to dismiss any reference to the admirable ideology of Russia while implying that since their economic structure is relatively the same as ours, that ours works the same way. It does not and will not until those who now ride in the direction of individualism are content to face about and ride in the direction of equitable balance,—the very kind of balance that you are so wisely working for.

The fact is that you and I, intellectually and economically, are not a sixteenth of an inch apart. How to reach the goal which we both look toward is probably more of a matter of diplomacy than of method. Since any mention of Marx or a red flag or Communism frightens the horse and throws the rider, it is probably that a white flag, and the words equity and balance will have to be substituted and even at that, you will have to come up on the blind side of the horse so as not to be kicked.

We should talk further about this, because I think we might get somewhere.

Regards.

To Diego Rivera
[CC]

[?*The American Spectator*
12 East 41st Street
New York, N.Y.]
December 30, 1932

Dear Rivera:

Well, how are you? I have been admiring the paintings you so generously contributed to Mike's place at 146 E. 61st Street. As a matter of fact, I have been trying to get at least one of them out of him, so far without any luck, but I have hopes.

In regard to Mexico, I certainly agree with you that not only many but most people, in writing about it, have made their facts fit their theories or literary or financial interests, and I think that

anything that would forcefully contradict that nonsense would be valuable; also that it would have double and treble its ordinary value if you did it.

Also, I think there is something to Mexican art in its true light as a social expression, and would like to see that, but, more than that, since Mexico now writes itself so large in the economic and social thought of our time, I wish, if you can, that you would make some other suggestions which would throw some little light on the characteristics of the Mexicans as a people, their real condition, their social and economic intelligence if they can be said to have any and, if not, the nature of their mental lacks in these fields.

I remember your telling me about the existence of the Mayans, their knowledge and architecture undisturbed up to this hour. I don't know whether that fact has been broadly advertised or not. If it has not, then a discussion of it by you would certainly be valuable for this paper.

As you know, though, I am just one of five editors and material that comes here even when invited sometimes provokes a stormy discussion and even bitterness of feeling, but that merely shows how alive and intellectually sensitive this particular organ is. Personally, I feel keenly that these things, if done by you in a light and discursive way, should appeal intensely to all of us. The spirit that I mean is that which animates the paintings in Mike's place.

In addition, you must remember that the length of an article for us cannot run over 1500 words and that the rate of payment is one cent a word—a sum which will scarcely keep you in ink, but so it is. Let me know your reactions.

If I return to California as I expect to, I will stop off at Detroit and have a conversation with you, as I judge that by now you speak English, although I will say that the Judge on the trip over to England made a marvelous interpreter.[50]

Regards and best wishes.

[50] A reference to Dreiser's trip on the *S.S. Mauretania,* October 1927 (see Dreiser to Franklin and Beatrice Booth, October 26, 1927).

1933

To Ralph Fabri
[CC]

The Hungarian artist, a friend of Dreiser's in New York, had translated and sent Dreiser a review of Dreiser's work by Dr. Karl Sebestyén, a former instructor in Latin and Hungarian literature at the Royal State Gymnasium, Budapest, and now a critic on the staff of Pester Lloyd, *a German-language daily, Budapest.*

> The American Spectator
> 12 East 41st Street
> New York, [N.Y.]
> January 20, 1933

Dear Fabri:

I like the résumé or summary of *Newspaper Days,* which is the American title of the book Dr. Sebestyén refers to. It seems intelligent, fairly comprehensive and equitable. You ask whether I have anything to say about it. Is anything more really necessary? For, all said and done, there is the book, to be examined by who wills so to do. I recall Dr. Sebestyén and found him very interesting.

As for the Hungarians not liking *Tragic America,* I did not know that it was published over there. It must be the German version. It does not matter. The book is a résumé of facts, not hearsay, and contains no social or political bias other than that generated by ample and palpable inequity now and for a long time past operative in America.

I feel that the immense gulf between wealth and poverty in America and throughout the world should be narrowed. I feel that government should truly emphasize and, in so far as hu-

manly possible, effect the welfare of all of the people—not that of a given class. I am for the mental and physical and social advancement of all men everywhere, if that is possible. And my hope as well as my faith is that it is possible. I am against vaulting pride and showy waste, and inequitable and unintelligent power vested in any group or individual. I feel that the voices of all of the people should be heard, and their needs, in so far as possible, met. No one enslaved and no one, except by the natural and moneyless admiration of the world unduly elevated.

If that is a sound and fair reason for being criticized or hated then I am content to be so criticized and hated.

Regards. And thanks for the translation.
[Dreiser] [1]

To William Randolph Hearst
[CC]

The American Spectator
12 East 41st Street
New York, [N.Y.]
January 24, 1933

Dear Mr. Hearst:

Friends of Mooney have appealed to me as follows:

"There is a matter of the utmost importance we wish to take up with you. You will remember that some years ago when you approached William Randolph Hearst, you were able to induce him to take some interest in the case. It is apparent that the effort to bring Tom to trial again is likely to be successful. The attached clippings will be self-explanatory. Fremont Older [2] has just informed us that Judge Ward [3] stated he would probably proceed

---

[1] Signature taken from handwritten copy, January 18, 1933.

[2] Editor of the *San Francisco Bulletin* in 1917 and among the first to insist upon Mooney's innocence.

[3] Louis H. Ward, the judge before whom the case would be brought.

with the trial. We are rather dubious about this matter, but feel that if sufficient pressure were brought to bear upon Ward and District Attorney Brady,[4] the chances that Tom would be tried again would be more than even. The most powerful influence with both Brady and Ward is William Randolph Hearst. Opinion here is unanimous that if Hearst would make it known that he wanted Mooney tried again, and that if he would instruct the *San Francisco Examiner* to editorially so state, we would be on the road toward victory. We understand that Hearst at the present time is immersed in countless projects and is facing a financial crisis. It will undoubtedly be difficult to gain his attention. Without a doubt, you are the only one who could do this. February 11th is approaching and whatever is done in regard to Hearst must be done very shortly. We know how busy you are, but we feel that, realizing the importance of this matter, if at all possible you will do what you can to help us. We feel that if you would put the matter before Hearst that you would succeed in inducing him to help Tom. We are asking no one else to approach Hearst on this matter, knowing there is no one who is likely to obtain satisfactory results as you are.

"Will you please let us know as soon as possible what you will do on this matter? Fremont Older especially urged us to communicate with you, in addition to Tom."

At the time I was in San Francisco, and after I had examined Callicotte [5] in the Civic Auditorium, I, in company with several individuals interested in the release of Mooney, visited District Attorney Brady, and presented to him the possibilities of a new trial. He stated to me, Lincoln Steffens, and Leo Gallagher [6] that certainly he was for a new trial for Tom Mooney, that personally he wished him released, that he would be glad to examine Callicotte and, furthermore, press the remaining indictment

4 Matthew Brady.

5 Paul Callicotte, an Oregon mountain guide, had confessed late in 1932 to having planted the famous suitcase. On November 6, 1932, a mass meeting in the San Francisco Exposition Auditorium had heard his story. It was at this time that Dreiser had questioned him.

6 Attorney for International Labor Defense.

against Mooney in the particular court in which Judge Ward presides, all this in the hope that if the case were decided favorably to Mooney, Governor Rolph [7] and whatever other anti-Mooney elements were involved would be not so much moved but compelled to sanction his release.

With that statement in my possession and in my mind, I, together with Lincoln Steffens, approached Judge Ward, not with the thought of influencing him personally, which would not be in line with my mental approach to this or any other debated question, but to discover whether, if District Attorney Brady moved to try Mooney on this indictment, he judicially saw his way clear to try this case. He immediately announced that he would not sanction any preliminary discussion of a possible move on the part of Brady, but that if Brady moved to try Mooney on this indictment, and it seemed reasonable so to try him, he would be glad so to do, and would most certainly favor whatever was equitable.

I recall my visit to your splendid estate at San Simeon, and I recall your assurance that whatever you could do for Mooney you would do. Is it possible that you could do anything in this case, and, if so, with my guarantee that your communication is confidential and not to be divulged, would you be kind enough to let me know?

Very truly,

To Vernon C. Sherwin
[CC]

The Florida writer's grim story of a lynching, "Souvenir," origi-nally sent to Dreiser, was printed in the March 1933 American Spectator *(I, 1).*

[7] James Rolph, Jr.

[?*The American Spectator*
12 East 41st Street
New York, N.Y.]
February 16, 1933

Dear Sherwin:

As you probably know by now, your story is in the current issue—first place, most space.

There is some talk here of the *Times* interviewing me in regard to it, and I will be glad to talk about it and about you and the rising generation of writers in the South. The appearance of such things as "Souvenir," Heyward's *Porgy*, *In Abraham's Bosom* and other of Paul Green's plays, Faulkner's *Sanctuary*, and a number of sane, vigorous Southern thinkers in other fields—journalistic, scientific, technical—whom I have personally encountered, all these make me feel that the old traditions of the South are about to die and be replaced by the sanity that now governs in your case and in that of so many others.

If you have a picture of yourself, you would better forward it at once by air mail, as the *Times* may wish to use it.

How does it feel to be famous at the age of eighteen?

Regards.

To Esther McCoy
[TLS]

She had written Dreiser, January 27[?], complaining about confusion and inefficiency in the Los Angeles office of the National Committee for the Defense of Political Prisoners, where she was working.

The American Spectator
12 East 41st Street
New York, [N.Y.]
February 17, 1933

Dear Esther:

I have been out of town for the last three weeks, and so have had no opportunity to answer your letter, but I assure you that it has peculiar and valuable interest for me. It illustrates what has so often been proved to me in connection with Communist organizations and efforts, that is, that there is very little organization and very little effort. In other words, just what you say—theorizing and sometimes money-wasting, but with no results worth speaking of.

When I introduced you to Ornitz,[8] it was, as I explained to you at the time, because he had told me what he wished to do, and how much the particular movement he had in mind needed some one person or several who would help to put it over, but even at that, I had no idea that the situation was as higgledy-piggledy as you present it.

I wish I had your permission, though, to make copies of your comments on the situation there. I could send them to some of the leaders of the party here. I think it would be of value.[9] As a matter of fact, in all my browsing around among Communists, trying to do things with and for them, the only effective organization I ever encountered was in San Francisco, where, due to one or two genuinely-in-earnest and capable young men, really wonders were accomplished not only in connection with the Mooney case, but in connection with other things that really were important out there. If they had such people in Chicago, Los Angeles and some other American cities, I believe the essen-

8 Samuel Ornitz, one of those who had accompanied Dreiser to the Kentucky coal fields and whom, after the Mooney mass meeting of November 6, 1932, Dreiser had tried to help to organize sentiment against William F. Hynes's anti-red police squad in Los Angeles, where Hynes headed the Intelligence Bureau.

9 After receiving a second letter (February 23 [?]) from her, Dreiser sent her criticism (without mentioning her name) to Ornitz, Browder, and the head of International Labor Defense.

tial values of Communism would grow in public favor. As it is, they are getting nowhere.

Let me hear from you further in regard to developments there. Of course, I am not going to Los Angeles unless some very significant arrangements are made.

Do I understand and clearly that Hynes is now publicly disposed of,[10] and also, what is the character of the new man and of his activities? Will you let me know as to this?

T.D

To Lamar Rutherford Lipscomb
[CC]

The American Spectator
12 East 41st Street
New York, [N.Y.]
February 27, 1933

Dear Mrs. Lipscomb:

Thank you for your note and the clipping and your solicitude for my literary welfare. I have never been much given to criticism either in the field of letters or elsewhere. Life, as you know, is stubbornly selective. Each may carry his wares to market—be they what they may. That some are sought and some not; some cherished and some not, is part of an awesome and betimes tragic spectacle which I observe with interest, awe and sometimes pain— the pain that springs from knowledge of the defeat of any honest effort.

I am cordially
[Theodore Dreiser] [11]

10 Hynes had offered his resignation, because of marital difficulties, but it had not been accepted.

11 Signature taken from handwritten copy, February 19, 1933.

To Ernest Boyd

[CC]

On March 29 Dreiser had sent Boyd and Nathan an excerpt from a letter written to him, March 16, by Henry Pratt Fairchild: "It is easy to understand how your Board might feel that the topic I suggested was hackneyed. (Incentive under a more equitable form of government.) It is, indeed, one of the matters that are always discussed whenever socialism is mentioned. It is just because of the stereotyped and erroneous attitudes that most people take on the question that it seemed to me worth while to present a logical statement in the light of modern conditions." Boyd had replied at the foot of the letter: "Dear Dreiser—Bernard Shaw— in addition to a few thousand other Socialists—did this job in 1887 when he wrote 'Socialism & Superior Brains.' It is the stalest of all Socialist debates."

[*The American Spectator*
12 East 41st Street
New York, N.Y.]
March 31, 1933

Dear Boyd:

Your comment on the Henry Pratt Fairchild suggestion in regard to incentive under a more equitable form of government is typical of what I have been commenting on for months.

To Nathan, any topic that has been once done in the entire fifty years of his daily criticism is done forever. With you it is exactly the same. Anything that you saw done, as in this instance, in 1887, is old in 1933. The assumption is dumb. So dumb that it makes me laugh even though I am sore at finding it in this office.

T. D.

To George Jean Nathan
[CC]

[*The American Spectator*
12 East 41st Street
New York, N.Y.]
April 17, 1933

Dear Nathan:

I have read "Sex Life in Hollywood" by Kearney,[12] and like it. Actually I see little wrong with it except where he gives the impression that he is apart from and above all this. Why declare himself either way? Just leave it out.

A thing that is entirely uninformed is his opening statement that the legends of wild orgies, dope parties, current about ten years ago have no foundation in fact. This is pure ignorance. Kearney was not there. I happened to be there at the time and know details and can give details aplenty, but one is sufficient: The party in the St. Francis Hotel thrown by Fatty Arbuckle which caused the death of the young actress whose name I forget, but the orgy phases of which are a part of the criminal records of San Francisco.[13]

These things were as common as pig tracks, beginning at the end of any day on which a director or producer decided to throw one. All the attractive girls that could be commandeered were called off the lot, brought into the party, and work ceased insofar as they were concerned until the party was over and they were in shape to go to work again. To ignore this truth is just nonsense. Either leave it out or state the facts.

Otherwise, I think the article, edited, would be valuable, and I cannot see, since it is so, how it happens to fall below our editorial dignity, particularly after the Barbary Coast [14] and some others.

T. D.

12 Patrick Kearney.
13 Arbuckle's trials for manslaughter, 1921-22, ending in acquittal.
14 Herbert Asbury: "Pretty Waiter Girls," I (January 1933), 3, and "A Forgotten American Christian," I (April 1933), 1-2.

To Max Eastman
[CC]

Eastman, trying to find "a number of distinguished Americans of revolutionary mood" to assist him, had on April 23 sent Dreiser "an appeal for help to imprisoned Bolsheviks who were loyal to Trotsky's anti-bureaucratic and international revolutionary program."

The American Spectator
12 East 41st Street
New York, [N.Y.]
April 26, 1933

Dear Eastman:

I would answer your question about those Russian prisoners at once, except that I am so much interested in the present difficulties in Russia and in Russia's general fate, that I am not prepared, without very serious consideration, to throw a monkeywrench such as this could prove to be, into their machinery.

It seems to me, whether badly managed or well managed, that it is at least a set-up which should be preserved and fought for. If that means serious and, in some cases, seemingly cruel sacrifices, it is, as we say, just too bad.

But, after all, if, by any process whatsoever, this, or any other, Russia is seriously crippled or destroyed, no good will come from this great effort anyway.

I am not saying that I will not do as you ask, but I will require additional time for consideration.

To Max Eastman
[CC]

When Dreiser had written Eastman on April 26, he had also written Peter A. Bogdanov, chairman of the Amtorg Trading Corporation, with offices in New York, asking his advice. Bog-

danov, sympathetic with the U.S.S.R., had pointed out in his reply, May 3, that Dreiser's signature would be "interpreted as your looking with favor upon the movement of a man who has been expelled from his country for anti-Soviet activities and as your standing with him on the same political platform. This would be a great disappointment to your friends the world over."

The American Spectator
12 East 41st Street
New York, [N.Y.]
May 26, 1933

Dear Eastman:

I have meditated almost prayerfully on this Trotsky business. I sympathize very much with the position of his adherents, but it is a question of choice. Whatever the nature of the present dictatorship in Russia—unjust, or what you will—the victory of Russia is all-important. I hold with Lincoln: Never swap horses while crossing a stream.

Until this present war entanglement is adjusted, if there is any possibility of its being adjusted, and until the Japanese danger is at least clarified, I would not want to do anything that would in any way injure the position of Russia. And, heaven helping me, I will not.

Cordially,

To John Dos Passos
[CC]

Dos Passos had promised to call on Dreiser before sailing for Cap d'Antibes, but, he had explained on April 24, he had been ill with rheumatic fever and in a hurry to leave and therefore could not stop in. He wondered what the Spectator wanted, and would like to talk over "U.S. politics."

[?*The American Spectator*
12 East 41st Street
New York, N.Y.]
June 14, 1933

Dear Dos Passos:

Thanks for your letter. I was really very sorry not to have talked with you because, apart from the *Spectator,* I wanted to talk over things in America. The old direct Communist line seems to be breaking up, and I have a feeling that there is possible a reformation of groups along a new line; that was what I wanted to talk about.

In regard to the *Spectator,* I feel very keenly that you should be in it, and I'll tell you why. The paper has a strong pull with intellectuals of a very varied character all over the United States. Nathan, Boyd and Cabell, if not O'Neill, are more or less intransigents, but with clear orientation toward the aesthetic, the ironic, the purely clever.

My desire has always been to inject into the paper a spirit of social criticism and also valid arguments in favor of mass dictatorship, and, to quite an extent, I have succeeded with it.[15] The value of this is that social criticism and argument for change in this paper reaches mentally valuable people who are not as readily swayed by the more direct arguments of the Left.

Nevertheless, what I want from you is not direct social argument in the way of essays or editorial indictments, but rather the thing that you do best of all, and that carries the most weight, and that is presentations of specific instances of extreme social injustice as it relates to the individual—the kind of study, for instance, that you published some time ago in the *Masses*: the study of the young I.W.W. who was so brutally murdered by the henchmen of the current industrialists in the Northwest. That was a beautiful thing. I would like not one but several variations of that idea from you if you can possibly give them to me.

---

[15] Dreiser also desired, as he had explained to Llewellyn Powys on April 20, to get into the paper "idealistic, philosophic, poetic material." Indeed, to Powys he had earlier (April 12) complained that "in this office there is a Broadway complex against anything wise, poetic and altogether lovely."

You understand, of course, the financial situation in regard to the *Spectator*. It is only ten cents a copy, and costs all that it earns. For that reason, the rate is one cent a word for the insiders who do all the work as well as the outsiders who contribute. It really is a very generous and, except for the publicity involved, unrewarded effort to brace up American critical standards.

I am really very sorry that you are so badly off in the matter of health, but I hope that this letter finds you better and that you are going to swing back into your normal vigor. If you do, and return here, I hope that you get in touch with me for the reason first mentioned. If, while you are lying in the sun on the sands over there you can think out something for this publication, do so, and send it on. To wise you up in regard to it, I am sending the last three issues, which please be on the lookout for, as they will also go care of Murphy.[16]

Regards.

To Max Eastman
[CC]

[?*The American Spectator*
12 East 41st Street
New York, N.Y.]
June 14, 1933

Dear Eastman:

A copy of the *Spectator* with Yvette's article [17] is being sent you.

I cannot quite understand why you don't examine this paper more carefully, and see the value of contributing to it. It certainly reaches a large body of the semi-right as well as semi-left and middle-of-the-road intellectuals of this country and, all told,

16 Gerald Murphy at Villa America.
17 Yvette Szekely: "The Hungarian Yen for America," I (May 1933), 2.

this constitutes a very widespread and influential audience that should be addressed.

Because of the very limited size of the paper, we cannot use articles of much more than 1500 words in length, but our experience has proven that this very limitation produces a conciseness and force which larger essays lack, and some startlingly valuable points are being made within these limits and even less.

In writing this, I speak only for myself, because getting into the *Spectator* actually means getting past the editors, not just one editor. However, where a thing appeals to any one of us very much, it is likely either to appeal to the others or at least to produce a battle which frequently results in its admission. Thus, one enthusiast is occasionally able to down four lukewarm opponents.

If you are interested, give me a suggestion or two which I can discuss with the others, and that will help a little in side-stepping something that could not possibly get in.

I hope you are as vigorous and enthusiastic as ever. Rivera was telling me that you and himself and some others constitute a particular Communist group which walks apart from the seventy-eight other divisions of this organization in America. What I cannot understand is why there are so many groups and why they waste so much time critically belaboring each other and ridiculing each other for their interpretation of Marx, when the world situation and particularly the American situation requires a united front against a very obvious problem. Just why is this, and why, in God's name, can it not be remedied?

I would like to take a few lessons in how to bring the various warring factions together, if anybody were lecturing on that particular subject.

By the way, what is the Labor Temple, and what, if anything, does it mean to the lay individual?

Regards.

To John Slavens
[CC]

Commenting on the letter from Sherwood Anderson to Dreiser printed in the American Spectator, I *(June 1933), 1, in which Anderson says he has found no signs of a coming revolution, Slavens had written the* Spectator's *editors that the universal law of industrial evolution, working through capitalism, was driving the people to revolutionary communism. The letter had been given to Dreiser to answer.*

[?*The American Spectator*
12 East 41st Street
New York, N.Y.]
June 29, 1933

Dear Mr. Slavens:

In the first place, since you are so emphatic and subtle, you should be writing something for the *Spectator.*

In the next place, I am as much of a mechanist and fatalist, whether deistic or not, as you are. I have always held that the creative force was entirely artistic and either consciously directive or, mechanistically speaking, unconsciously directive, if anybody can imagine such a thing about all that seems so conscious. I also hold that a force beyond the control of men directs their actions and their so-called progress, if progress it be.

I do not believe that writers, reformers or any other individual forces change or affect greatly the creative process. I do think that they sometimes affect and color the temporary thoughts and emotions of masses who have already been created. At any rate, they picture it rather charmingly.

When I asked Sherwood Anderson if he saw signs of a revolution, I was just asking if he noted what so many others were proclaiming. All of the things that you explain to me, of course I knew, but whether the creative force is driving the discredited

industrial and financial system into the Communist camp's arms will have to be determined. You may be a little ahead of God in interpreting what is coming.

Cordially,

To Arthur Davison Ficke and
Gladys Brown Ficke
[ALS–YU]

Dreiser had been visiting the Fickes at Hardhack, in Hillsdale, New York.

Hotel Ansonia
Broadway at 73rd Street
New York, [N.Y.
July 14, 1933]

Dear Ficke and Mrs. Ficke:

What I took with me from Hardhack was *loveliness*—one of the most delightful memories I have garnered in years. Heaving sunlit fields warm with sunheat. An old house permeated with genuine sweetness. Wisdom, hospitality, courtesy, diplomacy. I think of mint juleps and the depths of life and space staggeringly suggested by diatoms. And naked bathing in rain and sunlight; and dreams and their sure evanescence[.] Both of you must come to Mt. Kisco and Helen and I will try to make you as *at home* as we were with you. Gratefully

Dreiser

Catch Jack [18] alone in the fields. Throw a bag over him, truss him up and deliver him to me.

[18] John Cowper Powys, who like the Fickes was living in Hillsdale, N. Y.

To Wiley Post

[CC]

Post during July 15-22 had made the first solo flight around the world.

> Hotel Ansonia
> [Broadway at 73rd Street]
> New York, [N.Y.]
> July 29, 1933

Dear Mr. Post:

After all you have received, there would be little point in my sending you one more word of congratulation on your remarkable flight, although I followed it with intense interest.

I want to say to you something more concrete and, I hope, more valuable, and that is to urge you to make the very wisest choices among all the offers which are probably now being presented to you, or to seek such as will ultimately prove the most profitable.

If you allow yourself and your flight to be exploited indiscriminately for the present moment of your popularity alone, you may miss out on opportunities which would provide you with the means to continue your work.

I say this because, with your ability, you deserve to obtain the utmost assistance and security, and you are now in a position to demand such contacts as will assure success for your future projects.

> Very truly,

To Arthur Davison Ficke

[ALS–YU]

Ficke had written two letters on August 8 thanking Dreiser and Helen for a party and had composed a poetic fantasy addressed to "The Heathen tribes beyond the Law" expressing his feelings for Dreiser.

[August 12, 1933]

Dear Ficke:

Your letters and your poems are beautiful. I find a delightful thing—that I am at rest in your company. And why? I can tell you why. Your seemingly changeless poetic response to life,— lovely though sombre or gay moods or emotions that appear to me to bubble or sweep upwards to expression—as water rises over grass and moss in a dell or, over the hard rocks and hot sands of a desert: Aspirations and dreams that face courageously the futility and death of aspirations and dreams; Spirit that, centered in loneliness and futility can still smile[.]

We shall look forward to another day and another group or not as you wish. Regards to Gladys. When I come again I will pose for her[.]

Dreiser

To Arthur Davison Ficke
[TLS–YU]

The American Spectator
12 East 41st Street
New York, [N.Y.]
August 18, 1933

Dear Ficke:

I feel that these two papers of yours on tuberculosis are very important. The first one, "The Psychology of Tuberculosis," is wise, clear and helpful. It should be sold to some magazine of large circulation—the *Saturday Evening Post, Collier's*—or at least to some quality magazine.

In connection with it, I note that you recommend serious books (Marcus Aurelius, Jack Powys, Thoreau, etc.). You should

make it clear that these are not for the mass of consumptives. The dub could not read them. Better for him would be moving pictures (if only television were at hand!)[,] the radio, interesting posters or wall pictures, some cheap paper, such as you would not endure in your toilet. Certainly a circulating library or news-paper rack should be at hand. No doubt some find religion of aid—that heaviest of all drugs.

If your paper cannot be sold to *S.E.P.* or *Collier's,* why not *Atlantic, Harper's, Mercury, Pictorial Review, Woman's Home Companion* (circulation 2,500,000, I believe). I wish it were not so long. I would like The Editors of the *Spectator* to consider it. But 1500 to 2000 words is *long* for us.

The second paper, "Notes from 1 to 36," is to me a master-piece. Truly it is beautiful—so human, so honest, so irascible, so kindly. I am holding it for Nathan and Boyd, but not actually showing it until you write me that I may do so. I love it so that I would pay two cents a word myself. If you don't mind, I want to have a copy made for myself (unless you sell it to the *Specta-tor,* in which case I can keep a copy). I cannot imagine, you see, their voting no.[19] But if so, it should go to *Atlantic, Mercury* or some class magazine. Truly, I love every line of it.

How are you? Now that I read these two papers and see what you have faced multiplied by your own peculiar sensitiveness, I feel as though I should like to do something—reward you in some way. But just how? Besides, to be able to write two such commentaries on your past miseries is almost reward enough. They are so sane, calm, helpful, even to those as well as myself. (Physically, I mean.)

I wrote you about your poem to me. I'm glad you think so well of *Moods.*[20] Quite all things therein have bubbled up from the dark depths within myself. Write and tell me about the notes.

19 It was printed: "Notes from the Diary of a Tuberculosis Patient," *American Spectator,* II (November 1934), 12-13.

20 Ficke had written on August 10: "I have been reading your *Moods* tonight. It shakes me from head to heels. I doubt whether even you know how great a book it is. To me, it seems terrific. Yes, very terrible."

Also whether by any chance you will be able to make a second visit to Iroki. I would like so much to have you and Gladys there without any others.

Dreiser

Regards to Jack.[21]
Gladys [22] understands, of course.

To Franklin D. Roosevelt
[CCTel]

Henry Ford had refused to sign the certificate of compliance with the National Recovery Administration's automotive code, which guaranteed employees the right to bargain collectively and set up a policing agency—the National Automobile Chamber of Commerce, to which Ford did not belong—that would have the power to inspect books. On the eve of the code's effective date, Ford was vacationing and silently leaving the next move to the President.

Mt. Kisco, New York
[September 5, 1933]

You are facing the outworn exponents of a defunct autocratic industrial system of whom Henry Ford is one. Owing more to the land that has prospered them than the land owes them they still seek to dictate not the details of their business but the policy of the nation that makes them possible[.] Some public adulation of business success has caused them to look on themselves as not merely tradesmen but statesmen. Dispel that illusion[.] Order this swollen Ford to appear before you in Washington. Use your official powers in full and dictatorially for its effect on the American people. The legal technicalities can be brushed away afterwards. You are the president of all of the people of the United States, almost unanimously they rested in you authority to ex-

21 John Cowper Powys, who lived nearby.
22 Mrs. Ficke.

press their will and to do as their needs necessitate. Really generously you have snatched from dishonor, reprisal and obloquy these so-called captains of industry who have not only sweated wealth out of America, but like prodigals and ingrates have wasted it over the world[.] Tolerate defiance from not one. With the authority of all of the people of the United States which is yours say to him what he is to do. If he defies you take from him the sanctions which the American people through its official servants have granted him. Close his factories and sales room[s] and demand before permission for their reopening is granted that he apologize through you to the American people[.] You cannot do less[.] He dare not[.]

Theodore Dreiser

To George Vaughan
[CC]

Vaughan, professor of law at the University of Arkansas, had on June 26 written to ask whether Dreiser thought there was soon to be an extensive spiritual awakening.

The American Spectator
12 East 41st Street
New York, [N.Y.]
September 13, 1933

Dear Mr. Vaughan:

It is a little late, but still I am answering your letter of June 26th, in regard to a spiritual awakening.

As far as I am concerned, and speaking of a spiritual awakening, you may sweep away all reference to organized religion. I have no interest in that, other than as it sometimes gives a very material symbol to an important esoteric idea which the mass is never capable of comprehending.

The Vedanta philosophy, particularly the last portion, the *Upanishads*, asserts, as did Mary Baker Eddy, who borrowed her idea from that source, that the ultimate spirit or self is in all material things as well as in the totality of space, in other words, is space, but that it in itself does not reflect the imperfections or degradations of the material world which we see. With that I disagree. Whatever may be said for illusions, and there is a great deal to be said for non-science or non-truth, there is still a body of moods and actions in the material phase of life which must be accounted for on some grounds, either on the ground of the dual nature of the great spirit, or on the ground of a devil warring with equal strength against pure mind.

Certainly I think there is likely to be a revival of the esoteric mood. It has occurred from time to time, and may occur again. But that does not alter the fact that, in my humble opinion, after the spiritual revival has occurred and endured for a sufficient period, the non-spiritual or material drift will recur.

The ultimate power or force, whether single or divided, does not appear to me to be still, as the theory of Nirvana would suggest, but to be subject to change. It ticks like a clock, now forward, now back.

To Eric M. Knight
[CC]

[*The American Spectator*
12 East 41st Street
New York, N.Y.]
September 15, 1933

Dear Mr. Knight:

Boyd has been in Europe, and we have had some difficulty in getting this article of yours examined. Now that he is back, the general decision is that the idea of a hot attack is all right, but that it should be even stronger than this.

Nathan objects to including D. W. Griffiths as a great creative director, and certainly I am rather inclined to agree with him. Also, except for *Morocco,* I do not see where von Sternberg ever made out a case for himself. I thought highly of that, but of nothing else.

Furthermore, this neglects some really brilliant foreign cinematic illustrations: *Under the Roofs of Paris,* for instance; *The Mona Lisa; An Hour with Chekhov; The City of Song,* German; *Twenty-six Commissars,* Russian.

Never doubt that I believe that the cinema is a new and powerful art form. I have always thought so, and have seen proofs of it from the very beginning. Consider *The Cabinet of Dr. Caligari.* The crime is that, as you say, the movie community harps on just one string, and will not consider the enormous realistic possibilities of things in America, let alone those in other lands.

If this were really much stronger, it could be a little longer, and I feel fairly well satisfied that it would get by. Thank you for letting me look at it.

To George Jean Nathan
[CC]

[Iroki
Old Bedford Road
R.F.D. 3
Mt. Kisco, New York]
October 7, 1933

Dear Nathan:

Steadily, since I agreed to become one of the editors of the *Spectator,* there has developed an issue which I think is far more definite and of greater import to me than it is to you. I would address this letter generally to Boyd, Anderson,[23] Cabell and O'Neill if it would make any difference, but it would not. The

23 Sherwood Anderson had lately joined the editorial board.

issue is between yourself and myself and, unless it is remedied, you can look forward to speedy dissociation of myself from this group.

Fundamentally, Mencken stated the case to me in regard to you in 1926. It was that from the beginning there had been a fundamental difference between your points of view; that all you could contemplate was the frothy intellectual and social interests of the stage, the Four Hundred, the Bohemian and mentally dilettante worlds, whereas he personally was for serious contemplation of science, medicine, education, literature and what not. The issue, as you know for yourself, proved fatal. I was a little dubious as to his stand at the time, and so said, because always I felt that opposed to his solid philosophic, economic, sociologic, scientific and historic interests, your lighter touch was important and, for general literary as well as magazine purposes, made for a more charming and, to my way of thinking, almost equally valuable publication, the old *Smart Set*. He disagreed with me and, of course, since he pursued his intellectual course so ponderously, the *Mercury* failed, and, to a certain extent, I think, rightly.

On the other hand, I am satisfied that if the present course in regard to the *Spectator* is followed without modification and, I am vain enough to announce, if my serious predilections in regard to what it should represent are ignored, while it will not necessarily fail, it will pass into something with which I do not care to be related.

We will pass to specific instances. There was once an article in the office entitled "Physicists Come to Earth." It was to me a very interesting geodetic survey of the relation of physics to physical geography and, regardless of what you, or Mr. Boyd or anyone else might think, it was a fit paper for this particular publication. It was neglected on the ground that it was heavy, or this or that, and instead of the man being encouraged to whip it into shape, it disappeared.

What has been said in regard to science is equally true of economics and government, in so far as the Soviet regime is con-

cerned. Two of the most appealing and important articles I have ever read in regard to Russia came into this office. I am referring to "The Russian Prostitute" and "The Russian Municipal Court"; powerful, antithetic revelations and reflections on the capitalistic approach toward these same matters. While the second was rejected out of hand, the first has lain dormant apparently for the reason that it would not look well with the Broadway items about the stage and English and French books.[24]

Another instance relates to the article that dismissed the International Court of Nations as something dishonest, partisan and futile. Although to my way of thinking, there was nothing wrong with the article, actually all that was wrong with it was the mental point of view of yourself and Boyd, and, frankly, I think principally of yourself, since Boyd does not seem to be able to achieve a definite position where you and your theories as to magazine-making are concerned. As usual, the article was returned on the ground that, by the time we could come to market with it, the interest in the matter would be over.

A similar problem arose between us in regard to the article about the female warden in charge of the insane in a Northern Ohio detention hospital or asylum, the sadly curious anachronisms and irony of the deficient. In so far as I could see in your case, this was anathema. The excuse, of course, was that it was not sufficiently well done. That is the usual cry and, to me, a cheap one, since, in the main, it is distinctly not honest, and I personally am weary of hearing it, and infuriated by the fact that not only is data of that character ignored and thrown out, but that no effort to discover anything that is suitably written is made on the part of anyone but myself. I may be wrong, but it is my feeling that any material of this character that should arrive in the office and be read by you would be quietly discarded and no comment made, on the ground, very likely, that I would be for it. I object to that attitude; I object to this censorship on your part of the manuscript mail, and this objection has come to the point where, unless the manuscript mail is surveyed by Miss

[24] By Esa J. Gennet. It was printed in the January 1934 number (II, 2).

Light for me and reported on, I will sever my connection immediately. I want to know what is presented to this magazine, and on what ground it is rejected.

The latest instance, of course, is the Ben De Casseres piece in regard to Shan-kar. According to the comment attached to the article and returned to Miss Light, the article was junk. It so happens that having inspired the article, and presented the essential aesthetic and philosophic structure on which it was to be reared, I now find certain definite mental processes of mine being commented on as junk. Everyone is entitled to his reactions, his convictions. The data in regard to Shan-kar even in this article is not junk, you, Mr. Boyd, Mr. Anderson or whomsoever you please to the contrary notwithstanding. At the same time, however, that you refer to super-aestheticism and a modified measure of poetic mysticism as junk, you have the temerity to address me in regard to such unutterable trash as the article on columnists which, with modifications, you and Boyd could endorse for the *Spectator*.[25] And this is equally true of "Perberty." [26]

There is an additional phase, and that relates, as I have said before, to the Catholic Church. You personally are invariably so free to comment on the Protestant Church, the follies of its ministers, its adherents, and so on. However, the moment it comes to the Catholic Church, in so far as I see, there is no honest intellectual approach to the question. You are never enthusiastic about anything in relation to even a comment on the Catholic Church. Either you have apologies or you raise dull and technical or dishonest objections to any comment of this character whatsoever. This was true before the arrival of Catherine McNelis [27] who is, I understand, a Catholic, and because of her, it is probable that it will not only continue, but be reinforced. The data which I presented in regard to the Catholic Church, its money policy, its contribution policy, is of the utmost importance. To publish it would substantiate the decency and the

[25] Possibly "Editing the Editorials," I (October 1933), 2.

[26] Lillian Hellman Kober: "Perberty in Hollywood," II (January 1934), 4.

[27] She became president of *The American Spectator, Inc.*, succeeding the publisher Richard R. Smith, with the October 1933 number.

courage of the editors of the *Spectator*. But seemingly because it relates to the Catholic and not the Methodist Church, there is profound silence. You not only raise every possible objection, but mentally and emotionally are indifferent, and commercially, I am satisfied, totally opposed. This attitude toward the Catholic Church and its policies in this country must cease if I am to continue my relations.

From the beginning, as I have said before, in connection with John Cowper Powys, Llewelyn Powys, Evelyn Scott, and now De Casseres, this problem of the esoteric and the aesthetic in connection with the *Spectator* has been a source not only of contention but of inadequate understanding. I maintain that neither you nor Boyd are in a mental position to contemplate this matter intelligently. Confronted by the mystical, esoteric and the speculative in regard to life, its origins, its anomalies and anachronisms, you are either intellectually unequipped or temperamentally opposed to serious consideration of this field. And the worst of it is that you are satisfied that a magazine which would venture to present the astounding speculations and creative mentations of a man like Charles Fort, for instance, would be ridiculous and useless.

With this, I disagree, of course, because and easily I find myself able to confute you by reference to the mystical realm of music. Here, where the mind is free to interpret the emotional responses of the spirit of musical genius, you are at ease to endorse and even to introduce into the pages of the *Spectator*, aesthetic nonsense in regard to music. I am referring to the dismissal by an incompetent of the works of Debussy, Wagner, Strauss and some others as musical nonsense.[28] Furthermore, the veriest nincompoop can step up and discuss music in the *Spectator*, voice theories and deductions as ridiculous as you please, without a word of comment from you or Boyd or any other, and for the very excellent reason, I take it, that neither you nor Boyd truly comprehend music, either its mystical or its humanly emotional references, and probably not even its technique. However, since

[28] Edward Robinson: "The Composers Turn Buffoons," II (November 1933), 3.

it has a public of its own, it becomes passable, and o.k. in the pages of the *Spectator*. But when it comes to the matter of original mentations or emotional reaction to mysteries in the field of science, or the arts, etc. where no important public following is in evidence, you find yourself shouting, "Junk!"

Personally, I may as well announce that in so far as I am concerned, that position and that attitude is not to be further endured by me. My sole reason for allying myself with the *Spectator* was that I felt it was to be really and truly a door for the original and the creative in all fields of thought and endeavor, not merely a book and theatre review of a medium which would rejoice the hearts of the columnists and the editors of second-class American papers. I cannot be accused of not being willing and even eager to provide a note of gaiety and even levity to this paper, but solely as a foil to really distinguished, serious mentation. In that, I have been bitterly disappointed. We have now reached the point where I am satisfied that my wishes in this respect are hopeless, or nearly so.

Therefore, I now say frankly that we will either come to an understanding as to the proper program of this paper, and its intelligent prosecution and enforcement not by me but by you and Boyd, Anderson and whoever is connected with it, or I personally will resign. I refuse further to be a figurehead for something which misrepresents me entirely. Accordingly, unless within the next three weeks we can come to some definite understanding, and some definite theory with regard to making this paper what I think it should be, I shall publicly announce my resignation and you and Anderson and the others may run it as you please.

In fairness, I wish to add that my notice to my associates in regard to my resignation will carry either a copy of this or the same with slight modifications.[29]

P.S. I will, of course, return to the treasury the shares allotted me.

29 He sent Nathan formal notice of his decision to resign, January 4, 1934. See also Dreiser to George Douglas, January 9, 1934.

To Hutchins Hapgood

[CC]

In the September 1933 number of the Spectator, *covering almost the entire first page, there had appeared "Editorial Conference," a transcription of a discussion among Nathan, Cabell, O'Neill, Boyd, and Dreiser concerning the Jews, an alternately serious and flippant conversation in which Dreiser had paid tribute to the poetry of the Old Testament but had complained of shrewd merchants, Nathan had belittled their music, and after O'Neill had proposed a homeland in Africa, Boyd had proposed that the United States give the Jews the State of Kansas. To all this Hapgood had objected in a letter to the editors, October 4:*

Gentlemen—

When I read the Jewish symposium, in the *American Spectator,* I had a feeling that it was to be regretted. But at first I passed it by with the idea that it was only a sort of editorial amusement—the way editors get together over a cocktail and a little half-serious talk.

But when I talked to a Jewish friend of mine, a painter, who had never been troubled by the Jewish question, and who had led the life of an artist, who had no felt nationality; and when I saw that he had suddenly and violently discovered that he belonged to the Jewish race, partly because of the Hitler epidemic and partly because of the article in the *American Spectator,* that article seemed not as innocent in its results as I had hoped.

The editors of the *Spectator* are no longer young, and no doubt are a part of the liberal past. Their values are the values of our traditional culture. It is difficult to think that these values are dispersed, almost overnight, by the shock of the recent nationalism that has overtaken the world. It is to be hoped that the Symposium is but a temporary and rather thoughtless gesture; for at a time when the peace and sanity of the world is troubled and threatened, we need all the convinced liberals that we can muster. True liberals are not reactionary to any forward movement. Norman Thomas

for example although a Socialist, is also a liberal. It is probable that by this time some of the Russian Communists are liberals, without ceasing to be Communists. But a liberal, if he remains a true liberal, can never act against the fundamental morality of a slowly worked out emancipation of the individual from racial, nationalistic and religious prejudices.

The legitimate struggle today is between groups divided on economic policy and interests. Other points of struggle—national, racial and religious—are throwbacks and barbaric remnants, and so obscuring and harmful.

At a time like this, we liberals cannot afford to approach the immediate passions of the time in any spirit that is not serious. We should consider that it would take very little added emphasis on the side of national and race feeling, as a basis for special privilege on a large scale, to plunge the world into a more destructive war and depression than that from which we are struggling to recover.

If we remain true to our liberal faith, we shall, I am convinced, and at no distant day, have cause to congratulate ourselves that we did not yield to a moment of nationalistic madness. Not to yield thus tests not only our liberalism, but also the independence of our individual judgment as opposed to majority pressure.

Hutchins Hapgood

[?*The American Spectator*
12 East 41st Street
New York, N.Y.]
October 10, 1933

Dear Hapgood:

Your letter to The Editors of the *American Spectator,* although answered by Boyd, has been turned over to me.

Liberality has always had a dubious standing in my mental court. It is so easy to be liberal when there is nothing to be illiberal about, but, on the other hand, it is so easy to pose a few problems to the liberals which will cause him no end of trouble.

Let us say that it is necessary to sustain a liberal attitude toward sectarianism. Well, a mild form of religious sectarianism

would not work much harm and might be liberally treated. Supposing your liberalism were faced by a rising tide of Mohammedism in the United States as it is actually faced by a rising tide of Catholicism and before it all, not only a little, but all of what you deemed true liberalism would be certain to go down. What about liberalism in that instance?

Or, let us take, for instance, the rising tide of color. I like the Negro as much as anyone in the world. I believe he is honest, I think he is industrious and I think he has gifts which, particularly in the matters of vitality, humor, if not romance, the white race lacks. It is entirely possible that a blend is not only possible but desirable and even unescapable. But if the people of England—I am not speaking of South Africa, which does not concern me very much, or Australia, or any of her outlying provinces— if the people of England, I say, were faced by a rising tide of color, how do you suppose the English liberal would feel about it and, if he opposed it, would there be any justification for it? It would be interesting to know. His temperament and the institutions which are the result of it reflect one very interesting state of historic life. The occupation of England by Negroes would certainly result in an entirely different state of affairs. Should the one, without argument, and for the sake of liberality, be abandoned for the other? It makes an interesting problem.

Let us take the divine right of kings, and its final smash. According to your theory of liberalism, the divine right of kings should never have been disturbed and, by the same token, should be flourishing in whatever philosophic or tyrannical form it might have assumed, until this hour. It was really overthrown by illiberalism, as the divine right individualist saw it. It would be interesting to know what liberalism would say to that.

In the same line, you can take the Jewish question. Liberalism, in the case of the Jew, means internationalism. He is to wander where he pleases and retain, as he does, his religion and race-characteristics without change. In America, Jewish temples are multiplying about as rapidly as Catholic Churches and, thank

God, they are a little more artistic. The Jews, despite all argument to the contrary, are multiplying in number. It is admitted now that there are at least 2,400,000 in New York City. In other cities, they bear the same ratio to the population. They do not, in spite of all discussion of the matter, enter upon farming, they are rarely mechanics, they are not the day laborer of the world—pick and shovel—they are by preference, lawyers, bankers, merchants, money lenders and brokers and middlemen. If you listen to Jews discuss Jews, you will find that they are money-minded, very pagan, very sharp in practice and, usually, in so far as the rest is concerned, they have the single objective of plenty of money out of which they build a fairly material surrounding.

The profession of the law is today seriously considering, in such states as Pennsylvania, New Jersey, Oregon, limiting the number of Jewish lawyers and, as they see it, for a very definite reason. The Jews lack, if I read the Pennsylvania Bar Association correctly, the fine integrity which at least is endorsed and, to a degree, followed by the lawyers of other nationalities. At least, that is the charge. Left to sheer liberalism as you interpret it, they could possess America by sheer numbers, their cohesion, their race tastes and, as in the case of the Negro in South Africa, really overrun the land.

Well, if liberalism means that you are to accept that change without thought, without opposition, bow to whatever is coming without trying to stay it or keep what you have, well and good. There is no reason for anybody saying anything. But if that is not to be done, then some consideration by at least someone must be given to what befalls a given state and also whether anything can be done to maintain one type of civilization, or life, or racial life, as against another type of civilization or racial life. If the liberal says that is *not* the thing to do, there are many who would still consider themselves fairly liberal who say it would have been better to preserve Greece against the Romans or barbarians than to stand by and see it overrun by Rome and, actually, even later by Barbarians. If these are fair examples of true liberalism, I

decline to endorse it, and I think it is a fair criticism because I believe that ideals are not garden weeds. They do not just take care of themselves; they are inspirational and have to be maintained by enthusiasm and by sacrifice. It is the same way with social organization; it has to be maintained against these invasions, or there will be no organization. If the liberals say not to bother, but to let this other organization come in if it would, well and good, only that does not seem to be reasonable and certainly not admirable nor desirable.

In this particular symposium, I did not say anything which should cause an intelligent Jew to quarrel with my position. I simply said that I saw no reason why a race as gifted, as definite, as religious in its predilections should not be willing to occupy a country of its own, and what is wrong with that argument, I still fail to see. The Jew insists that when he invades Italy or France or America or what you will, he becomes a native of that country—a full-blooded native of that country. You know yourself, if you know anything, that that is not true. He has been in Germany now for all of a thousand years, if not longer, and he is still a Jew. He has been in America all of two hundred years, and he has not faded into a pure American by any means, and he will not. As I said before, he maintains his religious dogmas, and his racial sympathies, race characteristics and race cohesion as against all the types or nationalities surrounding him whereso-ever.

For that reason, I maintain that it is the hour in which laissez-faire liberalism might be willing to step aside at least to the extent of suggesting to or even advising the Jew to undertake a land of his own. I say this because I am for nationalism as opposed to internationalism. I think that differences in nations in the world will always exist, and that it is interesting and better that there should be differences, if for no more than the matter of entertainment and of developing new characteristics through the various mediums which differences invariably give rise to.

So what?

P. S. It just occurs to me that the Jewish artist who was made so conscious of his Judaism is very likely the same artist who expressed the opinions which I quoted.[30] I am not sure, but I think so. If it is so, it is very interesting.[31]

To Sherwood Anderson
[CC]

[*The American Spectator*
12 East 41st Street
New York, N.Y.]
October 17, 1933

Dear Anderson:

After you left me, I called up George Bye [32] and talked to him about you, and he is very much interested. I gave him your house address and telephone number, and I think he is going to call you up, but if he does not, you call him, because I know he is very busy and a little forgetful, but he will be glad to see you and he told me that he thought he could do something for you and for himself through dealing with you. So, good luck!

I read the story "I Get So I Can't Go On" and like it very much. The other one, "Harry Breaks Through," which I read up in the country and which I am sending on to Nathan and Boyd, I think would really get by if it could be made just a little

---

[30] In the symposium Dreiser had quoted a letter from a friend who believed that "the Jews are a peculiarly and specially tempered people, who are not interested to construct an all-round nation, but prefer to share in and take advantage, if possible, of selected aspects and gifts of other nations. . . . [Their inclination to drift] constitutes a Jewish fate which is not to be overcome by either agreement among themselves as a nation, or any agreements with the world in general permitting their liberty of wandering. And because of this, we Jews must be prepared to suffer the things which such a peculiarly minded and motivated people might be expected to suffer. . . ."

[31] To an answer from Hapgood on October 18 Dreiser replied on December 28, 1933 (*q.v.*). Most of the Dreiser-Hapgood correspondence was printed in Hutchins Hapgood: "Is Dreiser Anti-Semitic?," *Nation*, CXL (April 17, 1935), 436-438.

[32] George T. Bye was one of Dreiser's literary agents.

more poignant. All the points are there, but it strikes me now as a little baldly narrated, but, with a touch of poignancy, it will be as good as the other; maybe better. If so, I vote yes.[33]

What is this Penguin Club stunt? It looks to me as though it were a scheme to get business for the Lido Beach Club House in winter, when they cannot get business in any other way: If it is not that, what really is it? [34]

Regards.

To Roy Howard
[CC]

[*The American Spectator*
12 East 41st Street
New York, N.Y.]
October 17, 1933

Dear Roy:

Sherwood Anderson was up to my place talking about things he would like to do.

He is so naturally and sympathetically in touch with the American small town working and farming class of Americans all over the country, that I thought you might be interested to get hold of him for a few articles or perhaps a roving tour.

I believe that a series of papers by him in the *World-Telegram* [35] in regard to the middle, lower, and bottom class condi-

[33] Neither appeared in the *American Spectator*: See "I Get So I Can't Go On," *Story*, III (December 1933), 55-62, and "Harry Breaks Through," *New Caravan*, ed. Alfred Kreymborg, Lewis Mumford, and Paul Rosenfeld (New York, 1936), pp. 84-89.

[34] Dreiser's copy indicates that this last paragraph was to be deleted. It refers to a brochure inviting Dreiser to become a founder member of The Penguin Club and thereby enjoy golf and fishing privileges at the Lido Club, Lido Beach, Long Island, and various kinds of hunting at exclusive lodges in the Poconos and the Carolinas.

[35] The Scripps-Howard chain's New York newspaper.

tions would be very effective, and arrest attention, as his reactions are so intelligent and fair and kindly, and he has no really radical convictions.

I told him to get in touch with you and, if he does, I believe it would profit you a very great deal to talk to him.

TO GEORGE JEAN NATHAN, ERNEST BOYD, AND SHERWOOD ANDERSON
[CC–New]

> *The American Spectator*
> 12 East 41st Street
> New York, [N.Y.]
> October 17, 1933

Nathan/Boyd/Anderson:

In regard to the dictatorship conference, I feel that it did not really establish a text or a theory of structure. What I was trying to say in connection with the dictatorship data that was in my mind was this—that there appear to be three kinds of dictatorship; first, that springing out of the ills of the people themselves; the first Spanish Rivera dictatorship having been inspired by fear of the proletariat who were genuinely furious because of the ills put upon them, and the second Spanish dictatorship of Azaña sprang naturally from the opposition of the proletariat to Rivera's checkrein.

In the early Brazilian revolts and dictatorships which disposed of the Emperor Dom Pedro (really a dictator president) the inspiration was similar ills, or impositions which the mass could not endure. There have been other illustrations, France, Russia, Cuba.

The second idea of dictatorship is that inspired and effected by our late American capitalistic regime which desired to seize on special material supplies in given countries: copper and nitrates, for instance, in Chile; copper in Peru; beef, grain and hides in the Argentine; coffee in Brazil, and related things. The

trick here was to overthrow any government, however satisfactory to the people of the country, in order to replace it with one ready to do the bidding of the bankers. Usually this new government consisted of an Army dictator and such advisors as might be suggested by the banks. And it would then accept a loan from one of the great American banks and thereafter control the country in favor of the bank or the corporation which loaned the money, and which was desirous of operating the industries, whatever they were, with cheap, local labor.

The third form of dictatorship sprang out of the great war, and was really of two forms. First, the type of dictatorship which was inspired by the major powers, England, France and the United States, in order to prevent seizure and control by Communists. Of that sort were the dictatorships of Pilsudski in Poland, Horthy in Hungary, Bratianu in Rumania.

The other type of dictatorship, but springing from the same source, was really genuinely patriotic, as in the case of Masaryk in Czechoslovakia, who wanted to preserve his country from radicalism and, at the same time, put it on a mental and commercial basis which would be really suitable to the intelligence and talents of the people of his country. Venizelos of Greece was another illustration of this type of dictator. Of course, he was deposed and driven out by a more kingly order, but he is certainly to be cited side by side with Masaryk, even though he lost. Also in this classification should go (for Mexico) Madero, Obregón and Calles.

By some process or other, these divisions should be made perfectly clear and, personally, I feel that the discussion should lean toward the Obregón, Madero, Calles, Masaryk, Venizelos, Azaña type, and proceed to castigate the American and royalist types of dictatorship, which are reactionary.

When the thing is typed out, all should aid in shaping it up. I will try to supply some conversation which may, if desired, be distributed among the various editors.

T.D.

To George Jean Nathan
[TL]

The American Spectator
12 East 41st Street
New York, [N.Y.]
December 13, 1933

Nathan:

With regard to Lina Goldschmidt, I think the suggestion she made "About What Do People Laugh in Moscow" is a good one. The Slav sense of humor is very different from the Western European or American sense of humor, and if it were analysed it would be a good thing for the paper.[36]

I like the fourth one, too: "Is There Romanticism on the Russian Stage?" I certainly think that should be analysed in the light of the very realistic Communist program. Ideologically and philosophically, I think the government belittles it, but the Russian temperament is at once mournful and romantic, and how this point works out in connection with their program, if she could indicate that, would be valuable to us.[37]

T.D.

To Hutchins Hapgood
[CC]

Replying to Dreiser's letter of October 10, Hapgood on October 18 had accused Dreiser "not only of anti-Semitism but of intense nationalism in general": For that letter could have been written

---

[36] After this paragraph Nathan jotted: "*Excellent*: Let her go ahead with it. G. J. N."

[37] In regard to this paragraph, Nathan wrote at the foot of the letter: "I fear this has already been covered by Oliver Sayler and Lee Simonson in the recent Sunday papers. However, if she has some new points, I'll string along with you. G.J.N." Beside this Dreiser commented: "These two can't write worth a damn[.] Dreiser."

by a member of the Ku Klux Klan or a representative of Hitler. Hapgood had insisted that, contrary to Dreiser's assertion, the majority of Jews were laborers, inasmuch as they constituted most of the needleworkers and workers in sweatshops in New York City. Meanness and sharp practice, he had pointed out, were not peculiar to nations or races, but were individual characteristics. In addition, the tendency was not for Jews to retain their religion and racial characteristics but to drop them, having kept their distinctiveness largely because of ghettos and other forms of segregation practiced by non-Jews. By implying that he would like the Jews removed from the United States, Dreiser was contributing to their racial and national consciousness. Hapgood had concluded:

You go back on our cherished civilization, on what has been painfully attained during hundreds of years. A part of our culture is the recognition of the evil of religious and racial intolerance and persecution, and no man who is a part of our civilization can safely ignore it, otherwise he is either ignorant or an agent provocateur, and therefore a danger to the peace of the community, for, in a time like this it is easy to stir up trouble. And for you, who ought to be a leader in our civilization, to take this barbarous attitude, is to me inexplicable on any decent ground. Ignorance, as I have said, is the only tolerable excuse, and even that is hardly tolerable. . . .

> *The American Spectator*
> 12 East 41st Street
> New York, [N.Y.]
> December 28, 1933

Dear Hapgood:

Two months ago, I had your reply to my letter, and would have answered it except for pressure of other matters which, in my case, is great. I hasten to do so now not because, as you seem to indicate in your latest, that I fear publicity for my letter. After all these years, I feel you do not know me. I underwrite all of **my** opinions as well as convictions, and now stand by what I **wrote** as written. The single purpose of this letter is to take up

some of your counter-charges and arguments, and see what they amount to.

One of them is that I exaggerate the number of Jews in the United States. I do not think so. It is true that the census for 1927 shows the total Jewish population in the United States as 4,288,000 as against a total population of 118,000,000, but the accuracy of this can certainly be questioned, particularly in the face of the fact that so many Jews deliberately pass as Americans, using American names and, to a degree, this would be further qualified because of the number of half-Jews and quarter-Jews who, none the less, because of their Jewish blood, adhere racially and religiously with Jewry. I notice that the *World Almanac* gives the Jewish population of New York City in 1927 as 1,765,000 and that of Chicago as 325,000. Anyone who has observed New York, Chicago, Cleveland or Los Angeles on a Jewish holiday or, more particularly, on their religious fast and feast days, would know that these figures are ridiculous. New York is practically deserted. You would think that all but one-third of the people had retired to their homes and, in Chicago, the impression is that at least one third of the life, if not more, had departed from the city, which would certainly bring the Jewish population there to over a million. Besides, these figures are 1927 as against 1934.

Another of your deductions from my letter is that I would like to have the Jews removed from America. I said nothing about removing them, and I actually think that Germany, in assaulting, torturing and robbing them, and driving them forth without means or a land of their own to go to, acted not only without social justice, but without wisdom. A decent way, if they felt that they could not live with them, would have been to negotiate with them, and the powers of the world for land and social opportunities of an equal character elsewhere. In fact, a great opportunity for statesman-like posing of a difficult national as well as international problem, if it was one, was lost by not entering into negotiations with the German Jews as a people, and then and there posing the problems seemingly so irritating to the German people. What with the wisdom and genius of the

Jews on the one hand, and German as well as the associated statesmanship of the other nations on the other—for foreign aid could and should have been secured—a peaceful and, what is more, very likely an illuminating and generally beneficial solution of the difficulties might have been reached. As it is, Germany now stands indicted of barbarism, and that indictment will not be easily set aside. Certainly it could have done no harm to publicly and internationally thrash out this age-old quarrel between the Jews and the people with whom they have found themselves associated. For I hold that either they are to be accepted and joined up peacefully and fraternally with all nations everywhere, or they are not. And if not, then most certainly they should have been provided not only with an important and suitable territory of their own in which to display their social genius, but with the means to transfer themselves. Otherwise no decency. And if that is related to "removing" them in the sense that you use the word in connection with my letter, then you are welcome to that use of it—but none other.

What really should be done, if the various nations now quarreling with the Jew and his internationalism wish to be fair, is for them to call an international conference with all Jewry and therein thrash out all the problems now seemingly worrying so many of them as well as the Jews and by wise counsel on the part of all reach as acceptable a program as possible. I see no other honest or fair way to deal with the Jews. And they, scattered and quarreled with in so many places and nations, should be the first to welcome it.

As for dismissing the problem of the Negro and the Mohammedans as too remote for any useful discussion—you may recall that we unjustly enslaved the Negro after bringing him here, and then fought a war to free him and, to this hour, have not truly freed him. And yet with some thirteen million of him under a general social ban, you call that remote. It seems to me very immediate, and one of the things that some day or other will have to be faced by a white world—whether by intermarriage or repatriation or, as you vaguely put it, "by thought and cultural ex-

perience" (a phrase, by the way, which means absolutely nothing to me, since it may mean anywhere from a day to a billion years of time and thought and cultural experience) I cannot say.

As for Catholicism (not "the Catholics" as you incorrectly put it) it represents a problem in mental liberation and at this hour is up and straining for solution in Spain, Mexico—indeed in every country where there is thought as to the wisdom of opposing disestablished dogma with ascertained knowledge. Yet you say of that, "It can only be handled by thought and cultural experience." Well, maybe, but over how many millions of years? The Russians, in so far as the eastern equivalent of Catholicism is concerned, swept it away, and rightly, as I see it, and in favor of ascertained knowledge as against "revealed truth." In Germany, there is a compromise in favor of keeping the masses ignorant. Here, we dawdle, as we dawdle with all problems until angered by delay or chains or legal fictions which we cannot peacefully dispel, we resort to the arbitrament of arms. It is the fool's way. Better an open and free discussion—a public and free re-examination of the intentions as well as the intellectual proclivities and tendencies of this nation as it now is rather than a piddling and dawdling reference of it to future thought and cultural experience. We are fairly at the crossroads now. And now is the time for us to choose our mental direction. As I see it disestablished dogma should bow before ascertained knowledge. And only ascertained knowledge should be taught the child by the state. If Catholicism disagrees with that, its schools should be closed and its children educated by the state.

In connection with this, and my discussion of the Jews, you assert that "the most marked thing about the Jews is that they drop their religion in the second generation after reaching America, and that they would be willing to drop their race if the non-Jews allow them to do so." Primarily, I would like to have the opinions of ten different Jews in various walks of life, religious, legal, commercial, artistic, labor, and the like, and see how heartily, if at all, they would agree with you. I have noted the growth

of architecturally aesthetic Jewish Synagogues, America over. I note the current call for the re-establishment of the Saturday Jewish Sabbath. I note the appearance of New York and Chicago at such times as the Jews enter upon their religious observances of the Passover and related race and religious days, and I am not ready to believe what you say. I think you are blinking realities because you greatly admire and strongly sympathize with a brilliant and gifted people. My own observation as to the Jew's tendencies in this respect is different. More, I greatly respect their race and religious solidarity even though you personally proceed to dismiss the Jewish race as a myth. I quote you: "the 'race,' whatever that may be." Imagine! Then there are no Semites and hence no anti-Semites. Be reasonable. In the next sentence, you say, "certainly the Jews would have been much more nearly assimilated were it not for the fact that for a great many years they were penned up together in ghettos and were the object of fanatical outrages which, of course, helped still more to keep them together." Perfectly true. But if there are no Jews—if "the 'race,' whatever that may mean" does not exist, as your line seems to indicate, then against what nation or race, if any, were the outrages committed?

You call me barbarous and anti-Semitic—even "Jew-hating and Jew-baiting." As you please, but I am supposedly barbarous and anti-Semitic because in the face of all of the attacks upon the Jews, their crucifixion in Germany and elsewhere, I rise to assert that these very gifted and highly integrated and self-protective people are, whatever their distinguished equipment, mistaken in attempting to establish themselves as Jews, with their religion, race characteristics, race solidarity and all, in the bosom, not of any one country or people, but rather in the lands and nations of almost every country the world over, the while they assert that they are not Jews but Germans, Frenchmen, Englishmen, Americans, Russians, Poles, Hollanders, Italians, Hungarians, Turks, Rumanians, what you will. It is not reasonable. It is not the way —especially since, being as gifted as they are, they so rapidly rise

to power and affluence wherever they go. To say the least, it is provocative of comment and in all too many cases of jealousy, the jealousy of the not-so-clever and gifted of those who are so much more clever and truly gifted in so many ways. And, though I be counted barbarous and anti-Semitic and what you will, I now rise to assert that, having grown in wealth and numbers and ability and distinction the world over, it is time for them, as well as wisdom, to realize that they are, after all, a dispersed and, in many ways, annoyed race or put upon nation, and that, as such— and anti-Semitism being what it is today, culture and liberality to the contrary notwithstanding—they should now take steps to assemble and consider their state and their future. There are lands as well as nations—international statesmanship being what it is at this hour—which should be willing and able to furnish them forth not only with an entirely adequate country, but with the loans and equipment necessary to start them upon an independent and, as I see it, certain-to-be successful and even glorious career as a nation. And to that I should think—the Zionist movement being what it is—they should be willing and even anxious to subscribe.

But, not wanting that, some anti-nationalistic, if not anti-social feeling or mood animating them, why not a program of race or nation blending here in America—the type or kind of race or nation blending that has been in progress here since America was founded, and between the English, French, Germans, Italians, Poles, Hungarians, Russians, Swedes, Chinese and others. They have all come as members of separate races and nations, yet slowly and surely they have been absorbed in that strange and perhaps worthless people, the dub American. As Shaw urged only recently—why not every Jewish male forced to marry a Gentile female, and every Jewish female a Gentile male? Would not that solve this very vexing question of how the Jew is to be disposed of among the various races and nations of the world?

But if not that, then perhaps the Jews will rise and say what they think should be done to allay this very obvious international

bitterness. And I, for one, should like to know what their answer would be.

P. S. I am attaching a more readable copy of my first letter,[38] with one correction, as you will note. The word was, incorrectly, "liberal" in the original.[39]

[38] For future publication. See Dreiser to Hapgood, October 10, 1933, n. 31.
[39] The second sentence of the second paragraph originally read: "It is so easy to be liberal when there is nothing to be liberal about. . . ."

1934

To George Douglas
[TLS–TEH]

Hotel Ansonia
[Broadway at 73rd Street]
New York, [N.Y.]
January 9, 1934

Dear Douglas:

Thanks for the clippings and notes about Montrose.[1] It is very kind of you and very important. If the damage is very great, I will probably relinquish my payments at once on one of the pieces of property and let it go if I find out that the trouble is too extensive.

I am also obliged to you very much for the article on "The God Standard."[2] It is a very brilliant bit, and one over which Nathan and Boyd are enthusiastic. Personally, in regard to the *Spectator*, I have information for you. I have resigned my connection with it, and my reasons for doing so are several.

For your personal eye only, I am enclosing a copy of a letter which I wrote Nathan on October 7th of last year. It is just to be read by you and returned to me.

After this letter, we reached certain agreements with regard to different things. One was that there was to be no more of this silly reference to the Protestant preachers and their crimes when any reference to the Catholic Church was shunted out. Another

[1] In California, where Dreiser had some property concerning which Douglas had sent him requested information.

[2] Published in the *American Spectator*, II (March 1934), 4, under the pseudonym John Adam Smith; Douglas was unable to use his own name, because employed as he was on the editorial staff of Hearst's *Los Angeles Examiner*, his personal views might have proved an embarrassment to him.

thing which has since come up in this connection is an apparently pro-Catholic influence in the shape of one of the publishers, Catherine McNelis, which has come into the paper and, incidentally, the advertising [3] seemed to be turning into something which has to be considered editorially. I fear those influences greatly. The mere thought of them annoys me, and still later advice that O'Neill is turning toward Catholicism makes me feel that the sooner I am out of it editorially, the better.

Actually, I have no objection to contributing to the paper at any time any more than anybody else as long as I can say clearly what I please, but I do not want to appear to be responsible for an intellectual approach which is not all that I would like it to be.

When I brought in Anderson, and talked to you about the paper,[4] I was pretty warm with the feeling that perhaps by having Anderson and yourself here I could swing the paper into defiant or intellectually left trends, or, at least, a socially radical point of view.

Recently, also, there has been the feeling in my mind that Nathan and Boyd were reaching the conviction that the paper, after all, would be best and most successful if it represented them and their particular standards, and with that I do not agree.

So, because of all this, and because of a rather promising situation with relation to the moving pictures, I decided to drop out, and have so done. Practically, I think I am wise, because the thing, in correspondence and time and this and that must have cost me several thousand dollars a year, and with no possible return in view and no particular support from the people inside.

I do not want you to take from this that I feel that you should not continue to write for the *Spectator* or connect yourself with it in any way that you see fit, because I think the connection may well prove advantageous and further your connections here in New York, and I know that they would be delighted to have your

3 The *Spectator* had been able to avoid the use of advertising through its first nine numbers, but with the August 1933 number the magazine had begun to rely on it.

4 Dreiser had hoped that Douglas could come to New York and become one of the editors.

work. Incidentally, I am not sure, but I have the feeling that Anderson will stay. At least, I have tried to persuade him so to do.

I wrote you about David Stern and the *Evening Post* here. I would like him to know of you and your work and to have you connect up with him editorially, and I am writing him to that effect.

Beyond that there is no more news. We have had a cold snap here and pulled through it, and Mt. Kisco is as good as ever.

Do not fail to write me regularly, and the moment I hear of any connection that will be of any value to you, I will let you know. For my part, I am thinking of contributing such sociologic and economic stuff as I am moved to develop to *Common Sense*,[5] which strikes me as a better medium for my social thoughts than anything I have ever read.

Best wishes, always.

Dreiser

To Frank S. Neff
[CC]

Hotel Ansonia
[Broadway at 73rd Street]
New York, [N.Y.]
January 12, 1934

Dear Neff:

You don't have to ask me to please remember "Blacky" Neff, because I remember him very well, and also his companionship with my brother Al.

Where Al is at this time, I have not the faintest idea. The last time I saw him was in Chicago in 1894 or 5, at which time he was living with a newly married wife in West Polk Street. After that, silence, until about 1929 or 30, when I received a letter

---

[5] A magazine edited by Alfred M. Bingham and Selden Rodman.

from him postmarked Corona, California. In it, he told me that he was studying short story writing, and wanted me to market some of his wares. I wrote and told him that I would be glad to examine them, and give him such advice as I could, but I must have made some unsatisfactory side remark of which I was not conscious, for I have never heard from him since. Inquiries made through friends of mine, at the address given in Corona, developed that no such person lived there, so I have no further information.

As to Warsaw, I have travelled through there several times, and noted the changes. The last time was in 1917, at which time the old house with the beautiful trees which you describe was entirely swept away and replaced by small cottages. The pond and the sawmill at the foot of the house had also disappeared, the pond having been filled in, and the sawmill furniture factory having removed to some other place.

Eagle Lake, which was just a lone outlying lake when I was in high school, had changed its name to Winona, and developed a Christian Conference and God knows how many Christian cottages, to say nothing of a hotel, and a five- or six-thousand capacity public speechifying hall, and things like that. It had become a place where religious people go to spend the summer and to be together.

Also, the town, in some ambitious mood, had decided to connect Pike Lake with Center Lake, by a canal, but in so doing, had so reduced the level of Center Lake (the other being lower, I suppose) that they had dried up the source of Tippecanoe River, to which you refer, and now it begins at some town fourteen or fifteen miles away, where some other little stream had entered it, and all the lovely marshlands and the rice birds and black birds, coming to feed on the wild rice, and the ducks had all disappeared. Warsaw had grown considerably, and was inclined to be industrial, and so I thought that it was time for me to move on, and so did. I was passing through in a car.

But you and the old school house and all that related to the period when Al and you and my brother Ed and Claire and my-

self were in school there, is as clear as it was the day I left there.

I cannot tell you what a warm feeling it gives me to have you write me after this long time, and how pleased I am to see that your son Nelson is State Representative and that he looks so much like you. When I first looked at the picture, I thought you were sending me a photograph of yourself as you were a few years after you left Warsaw. Certainly I will be glad to be proud of the father of Nelson Neff and equally glad to be proud of Nelson Neff when the time comes.

I am glad to see that Nelson favors old-age and unemployment insurance, reduction of the cost of state government, and preservation of natural resources. I wish he had gone further and accepted the need for complete social change, with the capitalistic class eliminated and the people brought into such a friendly relationship as now holds in Russia, if nowhere else.

I will be glad to hear from you at any time, and if I ever hear anything in relation to Al, and you keep in touch with me, I will let you know where he is.

To Max Eastman
[CC]

Eastman and Dreiser had recently conferred concerning the possibility of unifying various dissident leftist organizations.

> Hotel Ansonia
> [Broadway at 73rd Street]
> New York, [N.Y.]
> February 6, 1934

Dear Eastman:

Following your conversation with me, I had a talk with both Alfred Bingham [6] and A. J. Muste,[7] not only in regard to taking

[6] Co-editor of *Common Sense* and executive secretary of the Farmer-Labor Political Federation.
[7] Former Dean of Brookwood Labor College; chairman, American Workers Party; and leader of the Conference for Progressive Labor Action.

over the *Modern Monthly*,[8] but of joining it with *Common Sense*.

As a matter of fact, my thought was what it has always been, that these different quarreling elements might possibly be brought together and to that end, I asked Bingham for a statement of his principles, after the manner of Muste's. Here is a copy of what he sent me. After reading this, and re-reading Muste's statement, I decided that their differences were exactly those between Tweedledee and Tweedledum. They both want to reach the general mass. One feels that the emphasis should be put on the worker and the other feels that it should be put on the farmer, but both agree that the white collar class must be included regardless.

Then I got them, Muste and Bingham, up here separately, and both agreed that there was no important difference, and that they might harmonize. Much to my surprise, Bingham said he thought it would be an excellent thing if they could get together not only on a representative magazine, but on political work, Muste handling his workers and Bingham persuading his farmer-laborers, but with some central office and some central direction.

Also, in regard to this proposition, Bingham was so interested by the idea of a group that he sent me the following list of names which he thought should be included in this conference.

He lists:

A. J. Muste,
J. B. S. Hardman,[9]
Archibald MacLeish,[10]
John Chamberlain,[11]
Lewis Mumford,[12]
Harold Loeb,[13]

[8] Edited by V. F. Calverton, author of *The Liberation of American Literature* (New York, 1932), *For Revolution* (New York, 1932), etc.

[9] Editor of the *Advance* (organ of the Amalgamated Clothing Workers of America) and vice-chairman, American Workers Party.

[10] He had recently published *Frescoes for Mr. Rockefeller's City.*

[11] Author of *Farewell to Reform* (New York, cop. 1932).

[12] His *Technics and Civilization* appeared in 1934 (New York, cop. 1934).

[13] Director of the Continental Committee on Technocracy.

and, of course, yourself and myself, making ten in all with Bingham and Selden Rodman.[14] He also suggests that Stuart Chase [15] might be added, and possibly William Harlan Hale.[16]

Bingham was anxious to have a meeting take place then in regard to the same idea, and, after my talk with Muste, he, too, agreed to send me a list of names of those he thought should be included. As yet, I have not heard from him, but I feel that a conference of this kind would be exceedingly worth while, and might possibly start a union of these two warring elements. For instance, I notice in a paper called, I believe, the *Class Struggle,* a left-wing organ, that they are constantly talking about co-operating with the right-wing Communists, but apparently without success. Under the circumstances, I cannot see why they should not be persuaded to co-operate with this group.

I am compelled to leave New York, to be gone until the 25th, but I cannot see why, when I return, we should not really hold this meeting here at the Ansonia, if that can be agreed upon, or anywhere else that will make the rest of them happy.[17] Can't you use your influence to bring this about, for I think it might lead to something very much worth while.

Regards.

To Evelyn Light
[ALS]

Miss Light, Dreiser's secretary, was in New York.

14 Co-editor of *Common Sense.*

15 Author of *A New Deal* (New York, 1932), *The Economy of Abundance* (New York, 1934), etc.

16 Author of *Challenge to Defeat* (New York, cop. 1932).

17 Each of the principal factions wished to avoid letting another have the supposed advantage of being host. For an account of other difficulties, see the two letters immediately following.

The Monticello
Norfolk, Virginia
February 10, 1934

Dear E. L.

Muste & Bingham were to present each a list of important names from whom 10 were to be agreed upon by both as the most important. Bingham sent his. Muste didn't. Muste should furnish his to me. And I was to submit Muste's list to Bingham just as I submitted Bingham's to Muste. After they checked their preferences for the final 10 I was to do the inviting. Now along comes Calverton with some rush proposition about meeting in the office of the *Modern Monthly* in Morton Street. I have no objection to the place. It could be Muste's office or Bingham's or the Ansonia. The one thing understood was that the proposed names were to be checked back to me and I—as an intermediary between Muste, Bingham & Eastman was to do the inviting. In fact Bingham wanted that so as to keep things balanced between himself & Muste. Calverton was to have no particular hand—in fact Eastman said to me that in any new magazine Calverton would be dropped—if I thought fit. I know that Bingham & Rodman consider him a false alarm. I do not know what Muste thinks— but he should be asked—not in writing but over the telephone— or in person. However I do not want a vast amount of ado about all this. Calverton should not step in as a central manager. Neither should Eastman. All Eastman said is that if I would join an editorial group & get the direction of it agreeable to me (i. e.—see that the paper was made a strong one[)] he would raise the money. But he wanted me to get the Muste & Bingham groups to join, at least to the extent of backing this one paper. Calverton as he said could be dropped. It was to be up to me. The conference is to decide

1—on backing a new single paper

2 as to whether the Muste-Bingham groups can be joined politically or if not that whether they can be made to agree [to] help each other to work in their respective fields. Also—and most important a general statement of not only objects but the actual ways

in which the citizen will be benefited by the changes *these groups* advocate is to [be] written out & distributed not as a pamphlet but a *poster*[.] Once the names were agreed upon I was going to have you do the inviting for me. And all were to await my return. If this program gets balled up or ends in any argument I will drop out.[18] The substance of this letter you can convey to Eastman, Calverton, Muste etc. You can say to Eastman, Muste & Bingham that I feel that Calverton might pass into the background unless Muste insists on retaining him[.] I forget whether Bingham said he did not want him at the meeting but he did say that he was not important.

T. D

To Max Eastman
[CC]

Hotel Ansonia
[Broadway at 73rd Street]
New York, [N.Y.]
February 26, 1934

Dear Eastman:

Just now I have the telegram from you and Calverton in regard to *Modern Monthly,* asking me to speak in order to raise money for it.

This is not my understanding of the proposition you put to me. As I understood it at that time, *Modern Monthly* was on the verge of failure and my suggestion was that the Bingham-Muste forces join to produce, editorially and in other ways, a paper that would be representative of a united front. This is specializing again, instead of joining, and since it is not what I am interested in, I will not do it.

---

18 March 1 was set as a meeting date, but it had to be cancelled when it seemed that Dreiser would not return from the South in time. Meanwhile, other developments doomed the project (see Dreiser's letter to Max Eastman immediately following).

As I understood it, the assembling of representative people selected by Muste and Bingham was to deal with this very question.[19] Obviously, there has been some change of program, and until it is straightened out, I really cannot proceed with either publication, because I do not believe in this divided front. You yourself emphasized this and for that reason, I do not understand this separate appeal from *Modern Monthly*.

At your convenience, if you wish, I will talk the thing over again, but only with a view to a united front on the part of the various organizations.

To I. E. Chadwick
[CC]

Chadwick Productions, Los Angeles, had become interested in the moving-picture possibilities of some of Dreiser's works.

> Hotel Ansonia
> [Broadway at 73rd Street]
> New York, [N.Y.]
> March 17, 1934

Dear Mr. Chadwick:

I feel that the *Gallery of Women* script would make a standard Hollywood picture, but no more. The happy-ending story which encloses the dramatic story is all right as a device, but there is no novelty about it. I feel, for instance, that using the old opera dancing setup is too hackneyed for current use, and the return to the young lover at the end is not substantially based in anything that happened before. It is so obviously a device to overcome the sadness of the real story.

The best idea in it, of course, is the actual gallery of women, but, of course, the most valuable thing to you is the title. In a rough way, the story parallels the story of Edith Adams Wrynn,[20]

19 See preceding two letters.
20 "Ellen Adams Wrynn" was Dreiser's actual title for the story: in *A Gallery of Women* (New York, 1929), I, 131-178.

one of the fifteen, but, as indicated here, even the realism of that is not very definitely handled.

One feature of the story that, to me, lends it a real distinction, is the outline of the psychologic effect of the women on the man. In the first arrangement, Edith Wrynn dominated her artist lover to such an extent that with her his art was weak, and hers strong, powerful. In the second arrangement, where the artist dominated the dancer who came into his life, and once he was rid of the personality of Edith Wrynn, his art came to its full strength. I do not say that hers deteriorated, but certainly it did not improve once she was separated from him. It is a phase that might well be dramatically developed.

As yet, I have not been able to think of a story in this book, other than the one here which would carry that title. It is possible that one could be thought up, but frankly, unless this thing could be made something more than the standard movie, I could not sign it. It is possible that I might sell you the title without any right to my name in connection with it, but it may be that something could be thought up, or some change could be made in this that would make it satisfactory.

It is possible that if I could confer with Miss Mitchell,[21] or someone else here, we might develop something. Personally, I have been so busy in the last several months that I have not been able to give it a thought. In order to do anything, I would actually have to sit down and go over it, either alone, or with someone, with a view to finding the proper solution.

Is it not a fact, though, that stories and even some tragic plays are doing much better than they have done in the past? Here in New York, at least on the legitimate stage, very serious plays are doing exceedingly well this year. Would it not be worth while to try a serious ending for a movie of mine? The two I have produced so far have had serious endings, and both of them have been successful.[22] Let me know what you think.

The script you sent is being returned to you under separate cover.
                                                    Very truly,

[21] Unidentified in Dreiser's files.
[22] *An American Tragedy* (1931) and *Jennie Gerhardt* (1933).

To John H. Chase
[CC]

Hotel Ansonia
[Broadway at 73rd Street]
New York, [N.Y.]
May 14, 1934

Dear Mr. Chase:

Your letter was received some days ago, and I can assure you that it was not lack of interest in what you write, but merely some special work before me, which delayed a reply not only to your letter but to all correspondence.

Your question is very interesting and, curiously enough, really adumbrates a second article which I have in mind to follow the first.[23]

Your question is, "Is all progress the gradual awakening into consciousness of a dormant Eternal Individual? Did it mean that the Eternal Individual for the first time knew that water could be split, when one of its parts got the ax?"

It may be, and yet I do not think so. It seems to me that what we call progress—our seeking for some clue to our origin or identity, even, and the celebration of what we call discoveries—is not so much an awakening of the Eternal Individual as an expression of it. But whether that expression is directive or definitive or not, I do not think we are permitted to know. It may be, or it may be indifferent—the gesture, willed or unwilled, of an omnipotent, omnipresent force which, embodying the possibilities of all forms, conceivable or inconceivable to us, extended itself, expressed itself, into what we see. And which may, conceivably, whether through intention or indifference, withdraw that expression, perhaps temporarily, perhaps permanently, while yet continuing to embody the possibility of its renewal.

Of course, a discussion of this through correspondence is neces-

[23] "The Myth of Individuality," *American Mercury,* XXXI (March 1934), 337-342, is "the first," which had prompted Chase's letter.

sarily limited, but I think my trend of thought on the matter will be plain to you. I am very much interested by your inquiry, and if you have any comments, I shall be pleased to learn them. The article which I intend to do, of course, will be much more comprehensive.

Let me tell you how very much I appreciate the spirit of your inquiry.

Very truly,

To L. Cherniavsky
[CC]

He was Chief of the Science and Art Section, the U.S.S.R. Society for Cultural Relations with Foreign Countries, Moscow.

Hotel Ansonia
[Broadway at 73rd Street]
New York, N.Y.
July 6, 1934

Dear Mr. Cherniavsky:

This is in answer to your letter of June 21, 1934 inquiring after a scenario by myself entitled *Tobacco* and also the play *Tobacco Road,* which you assume to have been written by myself. *Tobacco Road* is a play written by Jack Kirkland, based on Erskine Caldwell's novel, and has nothing to do with me whatsoever, neither has it anything to do with the subject of the scenario entitled, *Tobacco* which I have prepared for use in this country.

The play, *Tobacco Road* concerns the tragedy of a poor white family living in a tobacco belt in Virginia, but does not concern itself with anything outside the social difficulties of that particular family.

My scenario relates to what amounted to a tobacco revolt on the part of several thousand tobacco farmers, which occurred in

eastern Kentucky and western Virginia some twenty-five years ago. My scenario is the result of a personal investigation, not only of the history of the case, but of the actual conditions in Kentucky and Virginia at that time. It cost me in the neighborhood of about $2000.00 to prepare and has not yet been sold to any moving picture company in this country. However it is protected by copyright here and cannot be used without arrangements being made with me.

I would be really very pleased to see this script done by one of your film organizations, but not if it were to disadvantageously affect the prospects of the film here, for I think it is a picture that needs to be shown in America. Neither would I be willing to turn it over to you without some financial consideration, for the simple reason that up to 1928, when I visited Russia, most of my books had already been published in Russia without my consent and without any notice of their use or any financial return whatsoever. It is true that since then in connection with certain books of mine they have paid me what they say is 10% on the number of copies sold. My information as to the correctness of that is nothing more than a letter from someone over there saying that this is the case.

At the same time, as I have repeatedly stated to the Cultural Authorities in Russia, I have been called upon by the militant communists of this country to perform every known service from writing and speaking to entering dangerous areas in order to bring about favorable results for mistreated and injured American workers, and always at my expense. At the same time, as your American Ambassador and New York Consulate will inform you, I am constantly being called upon by Russian newspapers and various organizations to submit opinions, articles, and what-not to their publications and causes without any return to me whatsoever. Accordingly now I feel that if further material of mine is to be used, it should be paid for in order that I might recapture at least a fraction of the money that I have expended on Russia's behalf here and in Russia.

I am not asking for any exorbitant return, but I am asking for

an equitable agreement in case this manuscript is turned over to you. Before turning it over, however, I propose to forward your inquiry to our American Ambassador in Russia as well as your American Ambassador here in order to discover what way I can protect my American rights at the same time that I yield the use of this picture in Russia, assuming of course that once you see it you will be interested to do it in motion picture.

Do not imagine that I am not pleased by this inquiry. I am. But the conditions which I explained are as stated, and I think they should be covered and adjusted as favorably to myself as to you.

Very truly yours,

To Warner Clark
[CC]

Hotel Ansonia
[Broadway at 73rd Street]
New York, N.Y.
July 9, 1934

Dear Warner:

I am really very much obliged to you for informing me of the nature of the work being done by the Peace and Home Service Section of the American Friends Service Committee. It seems to me that it should prove a very illuminating chapter in your economic and social studies.

As I see it, I find very little difference between what the Friends are seeking to do here and what the communists are seeking to do in Russia. Both are laying aside the profit motive in order to help mankind to a better level and a happier life.

The Orthodox Friends base it on their interpretation and faith in Christ. The Hicksite descenders, if I read their book of discipline correctly, base it on some ethical and equitable light shining in the brain of man—not deriving from any religious

teacher in the past. Whatever the source, it is a very beautiful work that the Friends are doing. But, I can tell you one thing, that if this work, insofar as the Capitalists see it, were not an out-cropping of an established religion or sect of religion, they would be against it. Then they would see in it nothing more than a crack-brained socialistic or communistic attempt to upset their profit. In other words, the right to make the mass yield to them a profit, and not only a profit, but the largest possible profit. Being backed as it is by the Quakers, it will even obtain their respect—at least it will compel their awe.

If you were to read any of the writings of Lenin or our own Edward Bellamy's *Looking Backward,* you would more fully realize what I mean.

I think I mentioned to you *The Economy of Abundance* by Stuart Chase. That is one book you should read. If, after you have read it, you do not see the profit system as an anomaly, I will expect some sort of thesis from you explaining why.

Regards,

To Marguerita Davis
[CC]

Her husband, Hubert Davis, had painted some panels for Dreiser's house in Mt. Kisco and made drawings to illustrate An American Tragedy. *On June 8 Mrs. Davis had sought Dreiser's advice concerning her husband's career: would it be best if he continued working for the government in the Civilian Conservation Corps camps, or completed work begun in the Pennsylvania coal fields, or withdrew to a farm in New Jersey to make paintings of some scenery in a valley where an old canal ran? Because of his sensitivity, the social ills he would confront in the first two alternatives would upset him and lead to paintings less pleasant and salable than would the calming atmosphere of the third.*

Hotel Ansonia
[Broadway at 73rd Street]
New York, N.Y.
July 13, 1934

Dear Marguerita:

Your letter to me about Davis' work only reached me last night. I don't know where it has been all this time. Anyhow, late or early the question you raise deserves an answer, because it is the kind of thing Davis ought to do which has been in my mind for a long time. I feel strongly that Hubert should bury [<vary>] his painting more than he has.

Whenever I go to Mt. Kisco I am always enormously impressed with the three or four flower panels that he did on wood, in the dining room. They are really marvellous in the subtle response to nature—delicate, sensitive and vitally true to the spirit of the life and the flowers which he is contemplating. Again, I have one or two passing sketches that he did down in Tennessee, but that had nothing to do with the tragic social life that always interests him so much, rather, they are just casual pencilings of passing scenes that just for the moment happened to attract his eye, and they are wonderful.

The truth is that Davis is so sensitive to everything about him that anything that he troubles to do extracts from the thing that he is looking at all of its values, lovely or terrible. Just now for some reason, he seems to be inclined to picture the grim and somber. I would like to see him just deliberately turn his mind to lighter, gayer, more colorful things and do those for a time. They will have all the value that his genius bestows upon anything, and I am sure that they would sell more quickly. You know, I think so much of his work, I think his temperament is so rarely sensitive that it is almost ethereal.[24] Sometimes I wish almost that

24 See Dreiser's Foreword to *The Symbolic Drawings of Hubert Davis for "An American Tragedy"* (New York, cop. 1930). On December 5, 1933, Dreiser had complained to Henry Allen Moe, secretary of the John Simon Guggenheim Memorial Foundation that twice had his endorsement of Davis been ignored and suggested that if the Foundation wanted his recommendations in the future it should heed his judgment of Davis's genius now. See also Dreiser to Leonid Tolokonski, July 21, immediately following, and Dreiser to Earl Browder, September 26, 1934.

it were possible for him to live with me or nearer than he does so that I might try to inspire him. By all means let him do nature scenes, but not so much wide landscapes, but just intimate reactions to limited subjects and moments.

Where are you now? If you are in town I wish you would call me up or have Hubert do it and let's go out to dinner somewhere.

Cordially,
T. D.

To Leonid Tolokonski
[CC]

Tolokonski was Consul General of the U.S.S.R. in New York City.

Hotel Ansonia
[Broadway at 73rd Street]
New York, [N.Y.]
July 21, 1934

Dear Mr. Tolokonski:

I am a little ashamed of the way I have bothered you since your arrival in this country, but there are so many angles to my own personal relations to Russia, and then again, so many people want to get in touch with the authorities of Russia for one purpose or another.

The reason for my writing you again at this time is to see if I cannot do something for a really distinguished young American artist, who will never, in my day at least, find his hopes awarded in America because he is naturally of a humanitarian and for that reason proletarian point of view. Nevertheless, without any return of any kind to speak of he has done remarkable things. An astounding series of drawings, for instance, illustrating the works of Edgar Allan Poe, drawings really full of symbolism, mystery and imagination.

When my *American Tragedy* came out, he became greatly interested in that and did a series of black and white drawings which constituted absolutely the soul of the book. They are at once terrible and beautiful and they were eventually published in a rare edition by Horace Liveright solely because he admired them so much and wished to see them preserved. However, of course these rare copies have not been sold because the American public is not interested in the terrible and the beautiful.[25]

From that, he turned to Dostoyevsky's *Crime and Punishment* and did [the] [26] most remarkable series of illustrations of that book that I have ever seen. For some time he has carried the thought that if he could just get in touch with Russia, either go there or talk to someone to whom he could show his drawings, that maybe some department of that vast organization that is so interested in the masses would be interested in him and his work. Needless to say, I sympathize intensely with his feelings and desires in this matter.

Why I am writing you now, is to ask if there is any way in which this man's art and his dreams in regard to Russia and what he might do for the Russians over there and what the Russians might do for him of course, may be realized.

I assure you that he is one of the most distinguished artistic temperaments I have ever encountered. He is genuinely a great artist.[27] As great in his shy retiring way as Diego Rivera in his powerful physical and mental application to his problems.

I do not ask you personally to solve this problem for Hubert Davis or for me, but it is possible that you know someone or can hand this letter to some Russian of official distinction in the fields of art, who could seriously consider what I have here dictated.[28]

Very cordially yours,

[25] *The Symbolic Drawings of Hubert Davis for "An American Tragedy"* was published, with a foreword by Dreiser, in an edition limited to 525 numbered and signed copies and priced at $10.

[26] Dreiser's copy reads, "a."

[27] See also Dreiser to Marguerita Davis, July 13, immediately preceding.

[28] See also Dreiser to Earl Browder, September 26, 1934.

To Esther McCoy
[CC]

Hotel Ansonia
[Broadway at 73rd Street]
New York, [N.Y.]
August 1, 1934

Dear Esther:

Back in 1921 in Los Angeles, a woman by the name of Mada-lynne Obenchain was tried for instigating murder, and there was a fellow by the name of Burch who was also tried. He was the man whom she instigated to kill a young man by the name of Kennedy, and Burch was convicted. I don't know whether eventually she was let loose or not.

The murder was committed, I think in the summer of 1921 and ran through that Fall. Now this is what I want:

I want you, if you have the time, to go through the files of the *Times* and the *Examiner* of that period from the beginning of the case to the end and copy out for me the data. I am particularly interested in all of the data that relates to Madalynne Obenchain and also everything that relates to the District Attorney—Wool-wine, who was the prosecutor. I don't know whether it appeared in the papers there or not, but I heard from newspaper men that after Burch was convicted and at the time when Woolwine was getting ready to prosecute her, he fell in love with her while she was in the jail and threw the case over, that is, he decided not to conduct the prosecution himself but appointed his assistant Kees to do the prosecuting, and I think she got off. Then some data in regard to that, his making love to her, or her seducing him, got out and he was finished as District Attorney and also as candidate for Governor, because I believe the Republicans were planning to run him for Governor.

Then she came down, so I heard, to Staten Island here in New York and he followed her and tried to get her to marry him or to live with him, and when he found that she had double-crossed

him he took to drinking and was finished politically and in every other way, so far as I know. After that I could never find anything out about her, where she went, what she did. But now this work, as I know from personal experience may take weeks of your time. As you know, I am perfectly willing to pay for it. I want you to tell me how much time you can give to it, what you want a week and anyhow let me know immediately whether you can or can't do it.

If you can't do it, I have my friend George Douglas on the *Examiner* who probably could get the work done, or maybe you know some thorough-going person, as thorough-going as yourself who could give the time to it. Let me know.

Of course it is understood that you are not to mention this to anyone. This is personal and private between ourselves.

Affectionately,

T. D.

To Arthur Carter Hume
[CC]

Dreiser's lawyer was trying to secure for Dreiser an agreement with the re-formed Liveright Publishing Company, whereby Dreiser could exercise his contractual privilege of buying the plates and unsold copies of his books when the original publisher became insolvent. Arguments concerning the price had been in progress for more than a year.

Hotel Ansonia
[Broadway at 73rd Street]
New York, [N.Y.]
August 7, 1934

Dear Hume:

I understand you will be back this morning. With no desire to annoy you in connection with the Liveright settlement, I do wish to present my situation so that if there is any way to close it up quickly, you will do so.

Just this week as you have seen, a murder paralleling the story of *An American Tragedy* was carried out in Wilkes Barre, Pa.[29] In one way it has created a sort of furor, particularly because it seems to parallel the story of *An American Tragedy* and possibly the technique, or at least some papers have hinted that such is the case. There have been notices, interviews, and telegrams for permission to reprint portions of the book that bear on the psychology of the case, and of course, there will be more, but you see, so long as the book is tied up with Liveright in this way, I am in no position to take advantage of this chance to revive the sales of the book. As you can see, if the case had been wound up, and a publisher now had my works, he would automatically have proceeded to capitalize the publicity and sale of the book. As it is, nothing can be done unless this thing is settled, as quickly as possible.

Again, only last week I had an invitation from the Russian Government to go to Moscow and sit in at a literary conference with Maxim Gorky and others, with a view to outlining the appropriate literary procedure of the Soviet Union from now on. The conference really begins on the 15th of this month, but if I had gone, they were willing to hold it back until the 20th, which would give me time to leave this Friday and still be there in ample time to take part in the conference. As it is, with this case in this position, I have been able to say only that I cannot go. True, with this *American Tragedy* business in the air, even if it was at that time and is now, if this Liveright business were closed up, I could advantageously use my time here to make a new connection and have some action taken in connection with the *Tragedy*, as well as this proposed suit against Universal.[30] Both situations are important to me as you can see, but they hang on

[29] The Robert Edwards-Freda McKechnie case, which Dreiser wrote up briefly in a series of articles for the *New York Post* and *Philadelphia Record*, October 2-4, 1934, and at length, under the title "I Find the Real American Tragedy," for Tower Publications' *Mystery Magazine*, XI (February 1935), 9-11, 88-90; (March), 22-23, 77-79; (April), 24-26, 90-92; (May), 22-24, 83-86; (June), 20-21, 68-73.

[30] Dreiser was proposing to sue Universal Pictures for what he construed as the plagiarizing of *Jennie Gerhardt* in the production of Fannie Hurst's *Back Street*.

closing this case. If you can do anything to speed it now, I will certainly be grateful.

I don't want to put myself in the role of a complainant because you have done so much for me, that it would be ridiculous for me to do so; however, because of these matters, I feel tied hand and foot, and have felt so for so long. I would like to go into a conference now with some publisher in regard to the mentioned cases, and if possible, make a deal which will cover this *American Tragedy* opportunity plus other things which certainly should prove to my advantage within the next six or seven months, if the case will be closed. I know you will do it. Please let me know as soon as possible what the chances are.

You needed a rest ever so much, and I am glad that you had one—I am only sorry that I have to greet your return with an explanation of this kind.

To Esther McCoy
[CC]

Hotel Ansonia
[Broadway at 73rd Street]
New York, N.Y.
August 9, 1934

Dear Esther:

I feel that the Obenchain case shouldn't require the amount of data and typing that you suggest. What is important is that you get hold of all the material and read it carefully. I have some of the material up to the end of Burch's first trial. What I need is all the data concerning Burch's second trial and Madalynne's own trial.

A great thing would be to selectively condense the material before you, presenting of course, all the important thoughts and actions of Burch, Madalynne, the District Attorney, his Assistant

Kees, interpretations of the mood of the public at the time as it is reflected in comments by the newspaper critics said to psychologize the trial. I would be glad, after you have examined the material if you would psychologize the case yourself and give me your interpretation of the motives of the different people. Above all things, if there are touches of character or procedure of any kind in connection with the District Attorney, lawyers and the inmates of the jail, I would like those pointed out, and if they are good incidents, copied out, because what I want is the character of the life in jail and how that surrounded Madalynne, Burch and whoever else was connected with it at that time. I hear for instance that the District Attorney allowed Mrs. Obenchain to employ a Mrs. Peet, a convicted murderess who was in the same jail at the time, to act for her as maid in order to keep her in good formal appearance. If there are any other details of that kind I certainly would like to have them.

If you think it would take four weeks, well and good, get on the job. It is nice to hear about George Douglas, and I see you understand him and his predicament exactly. It is really terrible. Give him my love. I will arrange to pay you for the work to your satisfaction.

T. D.

To E. S. Martin
[CC]

On August 28 Martin had asked: "How did a swashbuckler like you who goes through the world making all these bellicose noises —how did you ever come to write that lovely story 'A Doer of the Word'? It was published, as you may know, by Robert Collier in a small magazine Mind, Inc., *December, 1929 [I, 23-52]. I have given away dozens of them and can't keep them in stock."*

Hotel Ansonia
[Broadway at 73rd Street]
New York, [N.Y.]
September 4, 1934

Dear Martin:

Do I seem to you to go through the world making bellicose noises? If so, perhaps it is based on not [sic] the inequity of life, which in a general way in the larger sense no one can remedy, but which in a lesser sense such as that which relates to a family, a corporation, or a State or a Nation, can be to a considerable degree modified. I object to stupidities which can be really easily swept away and which are tolerated by the smug, calm-minded, precedent-minded, traditional and authority-minded superior so-called classes. Under those circumstances if I make bellicose noises I feel fairly well justified.

"A Doer of the Word," if you were to examine it more closely, is really a bellicose noise disguised as a soft word. In other words, it is an illustration of the vast inequity about which one single-handed man was trying to do something, and you will note that he was not an intellectual or a captain of industry or a senator or a President or any ruling authority, outside of Russia, the World over.

Does this sound bellicose? You know that I have only admiration and the warmest personal feelings towards you. Exactly those. But I have to say the above just the same. Incidentally, I am gratified by your interest in "The Doer of the Word." After all you are on my side of the fence if you are giving away dozens of copies. In addition, I am grateful to you for letting me know that Mr. Collier has printed and used that particular thing without my knowledge or consent for I have no record of the same anywhere.

I am here at the Ansonia Hotel, Suite 14-54. You are over at 179 E. 64th Street. Invite me over there some evening or come and have dinner with me. Come a little early and I'll give you a drink.

To [———] Mathias
[CC]

Hotel Ansonia
[Broadway at 73rd Street]
New York, [N.Y.]
September 6, 1934

Dear Miss Mathias:

Your letter holds real interest for me. Seeking minds are not numerous. Comprehending ones still less. For a man to encounter a woman of real mental force, or a woman a man, is an accident of no little value. It is even so when it produces nothing more than one letter. At least one knows that somewhere there is such a mind which is comforting. One charm of this letter is that it presents your refusal to accept the "Have Faith" of the religionist—or to obey the order to go to the chapel and pray.

I hold a thing like the Catholic Church—also the Mohammedan faith and others to be no more nor less than religious despotisms—independent Empires really permitted to exist in and under governments which pretend and really believe themselves to be democracies or libertarian lands, and for my part, of course, I would [up]root them. Their sectarian dogmas could not be taught to children and least of all could they hold vast bodies of property and wealth. To their demand of right to worship I would say truly—Worship if you will but at your own expense and paying taxes as well as license so to do. Furthermore no person under twenty-one can assemble with you. He or she must wait and attend public forms of education before being permitted to subscribe to your dogmas. If at that time he or she wishes so to do they can assemble and worship with you.

As to my attitude toward—is one of suspended judgment. I recognize its superhuman powers of control but whether for good or ill I am not able to say. I enclose two things which to a degree clarify phases of my thought on the matter.

To Edward B. Rowan
[CC]

The Assistant Technical Director of the Public Works of Art Project, Treasury Department, had on August 25 asked for suggestions as to how federal and state governments and local organizations could "best materially help individual creative writers in need and the general cause of their field of expression."

Hotel Ansonia
[Broadway at 73rd Street]
New York, [N.Y.]
September 7, 1934

Dear Sir:

I have not been completely informed as to what disposition was made of the various drawings made by artists for the government, whether they were retained in galleries, belonging to the government, or were presented to local galleries, or are sold. I know that the artists were given salaries in return I believe for drawings or paintings made by them.

Concerning the writers whom you wish to aid, I do not know whether the government means that they shall do actual manual work of some kind in or out of doors, in return for pay, or whether they are merely to write things to be turned over to the government and to become its property. Whatever the plan, I assume, of course, that the official basis of any help for writers is premised on the ground that a writer is a person who for some time past has made his living writing for magazines, newspapers, publishers. If this is not true, then all "would be" writers and people who have held or are holding other jobs and consider writing their avocation, would automatically be included. I doubt whether the government contemplates any such broad interpretation.

If it is to deal with writers such as I have described, perhaps the government could publish a magazine to be distributed free

in their various camps and also the public at large.[31] Of course the question of what literary standards should be applied and who should be the editor or editors might make this a difficult thing to handle. Perhaps a group of people representative of the various trends and levels and phases of contemporary letters should be entrusted with the management. Whatever the sums paid for contributions they should be uniform for all.

A better plan, it seems to me, would be to exact of each writer, whether he achieves publication in a government magazine or not, either a short story or an essay or some creditable description of his experiences in connection with the government work, if any, which he is doing, or of the region or some phase of the region in which such work as he does for the government is laid. Of poets, certainly one or more poems should be exacted.

Again, the direction of this department might demand and accept, in lieu of any of the above, either an historical account or folklore story of some part of the area in which the writer is or has been employed.

To stimulate genuine effort on the part of all writers, it seems to me that apart from a magazine and its standardized awards, it would be advisable to arrange some scale of honorable mention in connection with such papers or stories, or whatever, submitted by the writers to the government. Also, and apart from honorable mention as well as in addition thereto, there might be prizes of the first, second and third class for really meritorious work. In very exceptional cases, there might, in addition, be given to the writer the right to sell for either magazine or book publication the particular work so honored. All writers of course are seeking distinction for their product, and any avenue such as this which would lead to recognition and distinction, would naturally, it seems to me, tend to extract from them their best efforts for the government as well as themselves. Exceptional works should remain the property of the Author.

The only other possibility for service on the part of writers

[31] This suggestion is one that Dreiser had elicited from Erich Posselt, of the International Literary Bureau.

that I see is that their services might be utilized in propaganda work, though personally I am opposed to that. I think that whatever is written should be free, unbiased, untainted by any influence whatsoever, whether emanating from the government or other sources.

If you find these suggestions of any value, you have my permission to use them over my signature.[32]

Very truly yours,

To Arnold Gingrich
[CC]

The editor of Esquire *had on September 10 asked whether Dreiser would like to do a piece on Upton Sinclair, then active in the formation of the EPIC (End Poverty in California) league.*

Hotel Ansonia
[Broadway at 73rd Street]
New York, [N.Y.]
September 14, 1934

Dear Mr. Gingrich:

I would like to write the thing about Upton Sinclair very much because I know his books and I know that he was twenty years ahead of the rest of the critics of America who are now so loud in their condemnations. His foresight, in my judgment, is only to be matched by their vociferous hindsight.

On the other hand, only three times in my life have I met Sinclair and never have I seriously discussed anything with him. If he, or you, through one of your devils, will furnish me with a little intimate character data about him I could take care of the intellectual and other phases and imports of his work in America so far. Let me know as to this.[33]

Very truly yours,

[32] On September 17 Dreiser wrote Rowan again, proposing that deserving authors at work on, for example, a novel or a play could be helped to complete their work by a small subsidy.

[33] Supplied with the requested information, Dreiser wrote "The Epic Sinclair" (*Esquire,* II (December 1934), 32-33, 178-179).

To [X]
[CC]

[Hotel Ansonia
Broadway at 73rd Street
New York, N.Y.]
September 24, 1934

Dear [X]:

The trouble with you is that you are not a bad girl but rather an unthinking and indiscreet one. Granting that you are a pagan and that you feel that you can do as you please, sexually and in every other way, it might occur to you that you cannot just plunge madly into every man's life and assume that because of your physical and mental charm you can have your way. For instance, before boldly assuming that a word or look from you will accomplish what you want, I should think that you would stop once in a while to consider how deeply and permanently you can wound people without gaining anything more than a little passing entertainment for yourself which you do not value after you gain it.

Take the case of that young fellow and his wife that you visited with here in New York. I can't for the life of me understand the offhand cruelty which you must have inflicted on the wife through your open relations with him in her presence. Obviously it didn't make very much difference to you; you had your fun with him and then departed, but you must know yourself that you have probably wounded her for years. And to what end? You can always get plenty of men, why trouble to hurt someone that was not able to hold her own against your personal charm? The World is full of men. Isn't it better to take those who can't be hurt by dealing with you, rather than one through whom you are certain to hurt another, for instance, who, for lack of charm, is in no position to contest with you?

Take another instance. The night that you waited here in the hall for me, and that without any invitation on my part whatso-

ever. I might have come in with someone who would have been deeply hurt if she had assumed that you were waiting for me, yet evidently that never occurred to you, or, if it did, it didn't make any difference.

Furthermore, think of the note that you slipped under my door without even an envelope, and without any invitation on my part whatsoever, wanting to come in and giving the impression that you and I had some affair which permitted you to come and stay, when, as a matter of fact, nothing of the sort existed. I had never given you the least indication that I wanted or would permit such a thing. The note was found, but by me fortunately, but assuming it hadn't been—how unfair. You know that you have no business doing a thing like that whatever your charm or mental gifts. It is unfair, because if you do that to me you will do it to others and God knows what harm (that you might even never hear of) you might bring about.

Again, take this present invitation. I am to call you up or make an appointment and we will be together instantly. But don't forget that some men are a little shy of a person, however attractive, who goes with everyone. After all, there is such a thing in this world as disease. There is such a thing as a person passing from one to two or three persons in the same night. Do you really believe that an intelligent man is going to plunge into such an arrangement or accept such an invitation without some thought as to what might follow purely from a medical point of view?

I admit that you are interesting, that you are entertaining and witty and a lot of things that men like, but there is really such a thing as common sense and fairness to others underlying even free love. And I think it time that you took some thought as to this. So far I know that you haven't and that's why I am writing this letter. I feel at liberty to write it because you feel at liberty to do the things that you do. I don't dislike you. This is not written in anger. But I do think you ought to give the matter some thought.

If ever you get your mind in sufficient order to see how unin-

telligent this program of yours is, and into what it is likely to lead you, you will probably turn out to be as charming a person as anyone would want to know. The way you are going now you will likely wind up in some tragedy, which will be more disastrous to you than you have ever dreamed of.

Regards,

TO EARL BROWDER
[CC]

Hotel Ansonia
[Broadway at 73rd Street
New York, N.Y.]
September 26, 1934

Dear Browder:

These letters [34] are self-explanatory, but I want you to read them carefully.

Davis is a temperamental radical. With the usual exceptions that always go with men of genius, he is heartily in sympathy with everything that the Communists are struggling for. As I say in my letter to Tolokonski, there is almost no chance for the full force of his symbolic art in America.

If he could go to Russia and be shown the social procedure in effect there and the enormous changes it has brought about, I think it would clarify his own program for him. He is so serious and so powerful in his depiction of the struggle for existence that once the Russians saw his work I believe they would get excited about it and perhaps wish to use some of it there. Anyhow, whether they did that or not, he would come back here fully armed to do the work that I believe he should do and think he will do.

---

[34] Probably copies of Dreiser to Leonid Tolokonski, July 21, 1934 (*q.v.*), and Tolokonski's reply, July 25, 1934, suggesting Davis write VOKS, in Moscow. Perhaps there was also a copy of a suggested itinerary that Tolokonski had sent Dreiser, August 3, 1934. See also Dreiser to Marguerita Davis, July 13, 1934.

What I want is for the Communist Central Committee—you and Foster as a matter of fact—to arrange for some sort of an invitation that will give him a trip free of charge to Russia.

However dubious you may be about these things now you will have the satisfaction of knowing later that you have brought about something of real artistic importance in connection with this great cause. Look into the matter carefully and let me know what you can do.

To Clifton Fadiman
[CC]

Simon and Schuster, having just become Dreiser's publishers, were considering publishing a one-volume selection of Dreiser's works and had assigned to Fadiman, one of their editors, the task of working out details.

> Hotel Ansonia
> [Broadway at 73rd Street]
> New York, [N.Y.]
> October 12, 1934

Re:-*Dreiser Omnibus*

Dear Mr. Fadiman:

My suggestion for selections from the various books is as follows: (This does not mean that other selections should not be made. As a matter of fact, I would like the co-operation and the advice of the editor of the book in regard to these.)

The Color of a Great City:
  "The Log of a Harbor Pilot"
  "The Toilers of the Tenements"
  "A Vanished Sea-Side Resort"
  "Whence the Song"
  "The Men in the Dark"
        (any 3 or 4)

Twelve Men:
"My Brother Paul"
"A Doer of the Word"
"The Mighty Rourke"
"Culhane, the Solid Man"
(any 3)

Hey Rub-a-Dub-Dub (essays):
"Hey, Rub-a-Dub-Dub!"
"Equation Inevitable"
"Change"
"Life, Art and America"
(any 3)

Plays of the Natural and [the] Supernatural:
"Phantasmagoria" [35]
"The Dream"
"The Girl in the Coffin"
"Laughing Gas"
"The Blue Sphere"
"In the Dark"
(any 3 or 4)

A Gallery of Women:
"Reina"
"Olive Brand"
"Lucille" [36]
"Rella"
"Ida Hauchawout"
(any 3 or 4)

Dreiser Looks at Russia:
"Women in Present-Day Russia"
"Religion in Russia"
"Three Moscow Restaurants"
"Some Russian Vignettes"

[35] Originally published in *Hey Rub-a-Dub-Dub.*
[36] Dreiser meant "Lucia."

Chains:
   "Sanctuary"
   "The Hand"
   "St. Columba and the River"
   "Chains"
   "Typhoon"
   "Convention"
        (any 3 or 4)

Free and Other Stories:
   "The Lost Phoebe"
   "Will You Walk into My Parlor?"
   "Married"
   "McEwen of the Shining Slave Makers"

A Traveler at Forty:
   "Lilly: a Girl of the Streets"
   "A London Drawing Room"
   "London, the East End"
   " 'The Poison Flower' "
   "Monte Carlo"
   "The City of St. Francis"
   "Venice"
   "My Father's Birthplace"
   " 'Spotless Town' "
        (any 4 or 5)

Tragic America:
   "Present-Day Living Conditions for Many"
   "The Position of Labor"
   "The Growth of the Police Power"
   "The Abuse of the Individual"
   "The Church and Wealth in America"
   "Crime and Why"
   "A Suggested Phase of Education"
        (any 3 or 4)

Moods: (here I prefer to check with Mr. Schuster).

Sister Carrie:
    Chapter 1
    Chapter 19
    Chapter 29
    Chapter 52
    Chapter 40
        (any 3 or 4)

The Hand of the Potter:
    (complete)

A Hoosier Holiday:
    Chapt. 11—"The Magic of the Road"
    Chapt. 19—"The Rev. J. Cadden McMickens"
    Chapt. 26—"The Gay Life of the Lake Shore"
    Chapt. 35—"Warsaw at Last"
    Chapt. 45—"An Indiana Village"
    Chapt. 51—"Another 'Old Home' "
    Chapt. 52—"Hail, Indiana!"
    Chapt. 56—"Evansville"
    Chapt. 59 & 60—"A College Town" [37]
        (any 3 or 4)

Dawn and *Newspaper Days:*

    I would like to check over these two with the Editor of the *Omnibus* because there are illuminating autobiographies as well as social and economic pictures, a selection of which would be interesting. These selections might even open the book and for that reason I would prefer to discuss the books after they have been examined by the Editor.

    As for *Jennie Gerhardt, The "Genius", The Titan, The Financier* and *An American Tragedy*, I would like to know whether it would be worth while to include a chapter or two from each book. This did not come up in our discussion and it may not be considered worth while, but if you will let me know I will check on these also as I have on *Sister Carrie*.

[37] Dreiser omitted the title of Ch. 60: "Booster Day and a Memory."

To T. S. Stribling
[CC]

Hotel Ansonia
[Broadway at 73rd Street]
New York, [N.Y.]
October 23, 1934

Dear Mr. Stribling:

Some time ago I was asked by Doubleday, Doran to read your entire trilogy, beginning with *The Forge, The Store,* and *The Unfinished Cathedral.* I so did, and you probably have had a copy of what I said.[38]

It has struck me since that in the general summary, I did not make as much as I so greatly wished to at the time, of your book *The Forge.* Frankly this is the only novel of all those attempting to cover either the Southern or the Northern point of view, that I think is worth a straw. By that of course I do not imply that yours is in anywhere near the straw category. As a matter of fact, it is as fine an American realistic novel as I know of. There is something so truly human and real about every line of it. More than that, it is fair to life and to the individual in the South who found himself placed as he was at that time. Really, it is a beautiful book—dramatic, amusing, sorrowful, true.

I congratulate you and I hope you live to do others like it.

Very truly yours,

38 Dreiser to Daniel Longwell, July 6: "*The Forge* is really a fine piece of work. All the period that he deals with is properly understood, the data with regard to it effectively assembled, his mental, particularly his sympathetic reactions adequate." But it was often Dreiser's practice to give to a friend or secretary a book on which he had been asked to comment and then to sign a letter that was largely a transcription of the report made to him. There is evidence that the letter to Longwell was based on such a report, although Dreiser might himself have actually read *The Forge* at that time; and therefore it is the letter to Stribling that seems more accurately to present Dreiser's view.

To Arnold Gingrich
[CC]

Hotel Ansonia
[Broadway at 73rd Street]
New York, [N.Y.]
October 26, 1934

Dear Gingrich:

The first title for "Kismet" [39] was "To Be or Not to Be." It was intended as a refutation of Shakespeare's inquiries through Hamlet, which presupposes that suicide is a matter of personal choice. In some way in connection with this essay, in the title or in a small box, I wish you would get this thought over.

I think to a degree it will startle the average reader if you tell him that when he thinks he is personally committing suicide that he is doing nothing of the sort, that there is no real choice involved. I may think of just the way to say this and send it on, but if I don't perhaps someone on your staff can work it out. I know it will add a lot of editorial and reading value to its publication.

Regards,

To Sulamith Ish-Kishor
[CC]

Hotel Ansonia
[Broadway at 73rd Street]
New York, [N.Y.]
October 26, 1934

Dear Miss Ish-Kishor:

I have been intending to write and tell you that after talking with Schuster of Simon & Schuster one evening, I got him inter-

[39] *Esquire,* III (January 1935), 29, 175-176.

ested, very much so, in *Hadrian*. He had never read it personally but wanted me to have it sent to him. By that time I had received Harrison Smith's letter and I felt that to a degree he was right about the general introduction of Hadrian as a person.

There must be a number of interesting things about his youth and the circumstances which surrounded him, and some of his characteristics which could be introduced before ever you begin the wide sweep of his travels. I say this because in your text even I notice little instances about him here and there that are fascinatingly human and amusing. There must be others, and if they came in their proper order they would of course interest the reader in him greatly.

Not only that, but there should be a short picture of maybe not so much the Roman world, although I think that should be there, but of the Imperial setup just before he arrived on the scene and after. Any period of Rome is interesting but I think that which preceded him will <involve>[40] just what you want for the purpose of giving a gripping start to the volume. When it is time I believe Schuster would be interested. As a matter of fact, I know this book will eventually be published.[41]

I had no idea you were working on a volume in connection with me but since you are, good luck with it. I think I have a copy of my radio talk on war which you can have. As a matter of fact, I have a lot of economic stuff, piles of it, which I wish someone sometime would examine with a view to its social worth.

To Henri Barbusse

[A&CC]

The French novelist and propagandist for peace and communism had on November 1 written Dreiser of conditions in Spain and asked him to use his influence to rouse public opinion against

---

[40] Dreiser's typed carbon copy reads "unsolve."

[41] *Magnificent Hadrian,* with an Introduction by Dreiser, was published by Minton, Balch & Co. in 1935.

fascist dictatorship, to sign an enclosed protest, and to become a member of the Defense Committee for the Victims of Spanish Suppression.

Hotel Ansonia
[Broadway at 73rd Street]
New York, [N.Y.]
November 15, 1934

Dear Barbusse:

All that you say about Spain I really know. From the days of Ferrer and his schools [42] until now. I have followed the machinations of the idle, brutal, grafting, leisure-loving nobles and their allies the grandees and loafers of the Catholic Church. In fact, ever since I was old enough to study the conditions of the peasants and workers of Europe, sweating to make their own meager living and at the same time carrying on their backs the various leisure classes of Europe I have been tormented by the thought that not only should something be done about it, but the how of doing it.

When Russia came along with its Dictatorship of the proletariat, I was cheered beyond measure. And my visit to Russia in 1927-1928, as you may recall, was made delightful by the vision of the workers and peasants actually arranging a life which was fair to all who were willing to work, and that held nothing in store for either idlers or wasters. Since that time though, I know, as you know, that things have gone amiss.

In all the long career of Mussolini with his shouting about what he has done for Italy, the first note of anything decent in his program was sounded the other day, to be exact, November 11, when, according to the papers here, he announced that there was to be no leisure class in Italy, that all individuals capable of

---

[42] Francisco Ferrer Guardia, a socialist, founded an anti-clerical, anti-militaristic school in Barcelona, 1900. Later accused of complicity in an attempt to murder Alfonso XIII, but released, he was eventually, in 1909, convicted of participating in a violent uprising in Barcelona and executed, the victim of what liberals regarded as judicial murder.

working were going to work, and that he was going to narrow the distance between the minimum and maximum living conditions of all. Well, I shall wait to see what comes of that.

In all the activities of the erratic and dictatorial Hitler, I have noted but one thing that I thought respectable and probably important, and that was where once in some speech he said that he intended to teach the leisure class to respect the soiled hands of the worker. Just how he is doing that, if at all, I cannot learn.

In regard to Spain, our American Ambassador, Mr. Claude Bowers, is an old friend of mine, and while Bowers has not in any way officially commented on favorably or unfavorably, the doings of the Fascists and the Catholic Church in Spain, he has communicated to me certain facts in regard to the struggle, and from these, supplemented by what has been brought out in the papers here—more particularly in the radical papers—I have learned how the Fascists and the Church have fought labor in favor of Spain's brutal, idle, ignorant, gluttonous, money and power-mad church and nobility.

I do not happen to know what your religious convictions are, if any, but my own attitude toward the Catholic Church and its program as I see it operating in Italy and Spain and Mexico and our South American countries, is one of unqualified contempt and hatred. It seems to me nothing more or less than a giant, demon-like octopus, or perhaps I had better say, cancer, which has fastened itself on the world and seeks nothing except the domination and mental destruction of the working class, in order that its princes and bishops and clergy and its idle, loafing, leisure-loving associates of the ruling titled classes may remain comfortable and dominant, while all that they prey on grovel and starve.

If I have a battle cry, it is this: Destroy the Catholic Church in every land on the face of the earth. It seeks only domination for itself in all the countries of the world. And in order to achieve that it is intent upon darkening the minds of all the citizens of all the lands that it invades.

I hold that Spain's ills are not partially, but chiefly, to be laid to the machinations of the Catholic Church which has no brains wherewith to prosper a country but only the cunning that seeks to appropriate what little wealth the laborer and thinker seeks to create. In Mexico, in Chile, in the Argentine and wherever, it seeks to control and use the mass in order, as I said before, to support such others as will aid it to rule.

But what to do about this is really beyond me. In short, I wonder if you have a definite program that you know, or believe, will yield useful results. I have written against the Catholic Church here, and not only written against but spoken against it throughout my life. As a matter of fact, my attitude toward it and its program is quite well known in America. I have written and spoken, and not only that, have actively campaigned in different parts of this country against the various powers that are inimical to the workers' welfare. That also is well known. I have been asked to help the cause of labor and of Communism in almost every country where a battle has been staged, from Chile and Germany to Italy and Spain. But what to do, and how to do it?

You say you have documents which you think would help in some sort of fight and that you would be glad to submit them to me. But apart from documents, unless they are documents which expose very thoroughly and accurately the anti-labor campaign in Spain, I don't see of what use they will be to me. If you have vivid and arresting proofs of the horrors that have been so brutally enacted in Spain, of course I would like to have those and I might make some use of them here in our radical press. But having done that much, then what? How is one to strengthen the courage of the workers in Spain, and more, definitely aid them? For words uttered in the United States, or England or Australia, unless they result in bringing to the workers in Spain actual material as well as mental aid, will most certainly fail of any result. Perhaps you could tell me how that is to be done.

As far as writing, surely I will write whatever I can. And in-

sofar as this particular letter is concerned, *with the exception of the use of Mr. Bowers' name, which I cannot permit,* you are at liberty to use it in any form that you please and to sign my name to it.

Tell me what else.

Cordially yours,

To Langdon W. Post
[CC]

Post was Tenement House Commissioner of New York City.

Hotel Ansonia
[Broadway at 73rd Street]
New York, [N.Y.]
December 14, 1934

Dear Mr. Post:

I attended the dinner of the New York State Division of the Continental Committee [43] last night. I was very much interested in the explanation of the investigations of the Continental Committee and in the earnestness and sincerity of the men who did the work. Also I was particularly impressed with your comments on Technocracy and your admission of conviction that the idea or plan had not only arrested the attention of the American public, but because of their immense interest, had encouraged President Roosevelt to develop his N. R. A. plans. I myself suspected as much because at the time I noticed the speed with which Mussolini of Italy seized on the idea and spoke, at least according to the papers, of his intention of studying its technique with a view to applying it in Italy.

The one thing that puzzled, and in a way troubled me was why neither you nor any of the men, who studied out the material and technical resources of this country, [. . . mentioned] [44]

[43] An organization devoted to Technocracy.
[44] Dreiser's copy reads, "failed to mention."

the name of the man from whom the idea of Technocracy sprang. I felt sure as you spoke that you were going to mention Howard Scott by name and properly attribute the origin of the idea to him with appropriate acknowledgements.

Actually considering the amount of work that Scott did, the enthusiasm he brought to it, and the many years of unrecognized labor in connection with it, it would seem to me that the group that was so inspired that it could persuade the government to found and authoritatively develop it, might have had the courtesy to acknowledge the source of its inspiration. I know that it is difficult sometimes for beneficiaries of any valuable thing to bring themselves to acknowledge the sources of benefit, but in this case the source is so plain that the passing over of the name of the author becomes preposterous.

Present in the room were the Utopians of California, whose sole reason for being is Howard Scott. I do not believe that any of those who spoke and set forth their labors would deny the source of their inspiration. The anomaly of it all was so great that at the close of the meeting when you called for comments I was on the verge of rising and saying in some fashion what I am writing to you here. Only the thought that it might inject an element of controversy and so result in ill feeling caused me to be silent. Just the same I want to say to you that personally I was grateful to you for re-presenting and emphasizing the true source in the way that you did. I say this because I still think that the Technocratic idea lacks leadership. The name of Howard Scott is still identical with Technocracy. Whether he is the ideal leader or not, I still cannot see how any subsequent leadership can possibly win in respect let alone enthusiasm without in some way acknowledging the true author of "technocracy" and in some way rewarding him with its respect and gratitude.

Cordially,

To George Douglas
[CC]

Hotel Ansonia
[Broadway at 73rd Street]
New York, [N.Y.]
December 15, 1934

Dear George:

I am truly grateful for your letter—you write so rarely. I know that you care as much for me as I do for you, but you have a "Scotch" way of showing it.

You're right about my being engaged on a serious work and your apparent hunch that it isn't a novel is equally true. It happens to be a book of Philosophy which I have long had in mind and parts of which from time to time I have written, or at least outlined. Now it is to be in extenso. It is not exactly a new slant on the whyfors of our existence but it is relatively new in this sense: That item by item and function by function it will take up the unreality and the mythology of the individual and even of the race. Of course I know and you know that anyone who has examined the theory of evolution in detail can work this all out for himself, but at least in the form that I am using it has not been done—not at least in its entirety. So when in your letter you say that you would love to be with me reading the manuscript, and checking against minor slips of fact, I seized on it as something not only of enormous advantage to me but something that I want to arrange for with you if I possibly can.

So far out of a total of fifteen or sixteen chapters or separate discussions I have eight. One of them entitled "The Myth of Individuality" [45] you will find to be the leading essay in a book published on December 12th by Doubleday, Doran. It is called *Molders of American Thought, 1933-1934*. It probably has come to your desk. However, that essay in my book is to be extended somewhat.

I published two others in the *Esquire Magazine;* one was called

[45] Originally printed by the *American Mercury*, XXXI (March 1934), 337-342.

by the magazine "Phantom You," [46] and there is another one I believe in the December number.[47] But again neither of these are in their final shape. I want to wait just a little longer until I have the opening essay and one entitled "The Myth of Death," and then, if you agree, I will send you the complete outline with duplicate copies of the thing so far and have you tell me what you think.

As a matter of fact, I wish very much that I could have a personal conference with you about this whole business, but I do not see just at the moment how it is to be done. I don't know what your situation out there is; how tied up you are with work, or whether I could consult with you there or here, but I have said enough of how I feel about this and you can tell me how the co-operation that you suggest can be worked out.

What you say about Mencken interests me because it is so very true.[48] He has always been the critic with a purely materialistic approach to the world about him. I have told him so, and we never really agreed mentally on anything and we still do not. We are friendly again of course. He was over here the other day, and we will have further talks from time to time, but your analysis is absolutely correct. In a way I feel sorry because the man has enormous force and a personal appeal for a great many people, but in his case a wall is a wall and a chair is a chair, and that's that.

Herewith go my best wishes for everything in connection with you—your work, your family and your literary labors. One thing that you ought to do is to prepare and publish a series of essays, and if you don't or can't do it in your lifetime, you ought to leave them in some form so that someone else could look after them and see that they are published. I believe a series of essays by you would make you overnight.

46 "You, the Phantom," II (November 1934), 25-26.

47 "Kismet," III (January 1935), 29, 175-176.

48 On December 6 Douglas had written: "Mencken, now that he writes for Hearst (see *Cosmopolitan* January 1935) is sneering at authors with economic ideas and theories. Well, he isn't a creative author and has long since run out of ideas. Thomas Craven (see *Modern Art*) promises to make Mencken look small potatoes to his followers of whom it was once said that, but for free attendance at a state college, they would have been worshippers of Arthur Brisbane or Elbert Hubbard."

1935

To George Douglas
[TLS–RHE]

Hotel Ansonia
[Broadway at 73rd Street]
New York, [N.Y.]
January 11, 1935

Dear George:

In your last letter (January 7,) you argue that you can be of very little help to me because I reason things out fairly carefully.[1] This is not so. The two preceding letters were literally stuffed with suggestions for me, and not only that, quotations and phrases of your own which are enormously suggestive and along the very lines that I am thinking.[2] As a matter of fact, yours is the only intelligent response that I have had so far. Intelligent in this sense—that it is *completely* understanding.

Psychic osmosis, almost a mystical form of it, characterized your very first letter; for at the mere hint that I was attempting

[1] Douglas had said:

"['The Myth of Individuality'] . . . is a powerful essay and confirms a conviction of long standing that you are most lucid when most philosophical. As a controversialist you hit hard, that being your purpose, but as a thinker purely you argue with yourself and thoroughly before setting forth your conclusions. In controversy there is always the temptation to give victory precedence over truth, but in what we think out for ourselves it must be truth only and silence until satisfied that we have it.

"If you carry more conviction as a thinker than as a fighter it is because as a thinker you fight out everything to and for yourself and if there remains a doubt that has not been conquered, it is frankly admitted.

"I mention this in no tone of superiority, but rather in despair of being able in any way to help you in philosophic exposition. I might have helped the fighter by putting him on his guard as to minor slips of facts, but so clear a thinker is not so easily helped."

[2] In fact, letters of January 1, 3, 4, and 6 had all four been nearly equally "stuffed" with references to philosophy and literature, with apt quotations, and with Douglas's own epigrams and verses.

a philosophy you proceeded to interpret the thing I was doing,—the need and place for it under modern conditions,—in a, to me, beautiful, stimulating and at the same time almost amazing way. It is about the same as if a person began, or no more than suggested, a campaign of some sort to a listener, who, before a portion of his thought was out, would spring to a black-board and outline the entire campaign. As a matter of fact, you put in fresher and stronger phrases the very theory with which I have been fumbling for years. And although I have had talks with, and responses from, individuals of considerable weight in this particular field, yours is the only one that means anything to me.

As a matter of fact, I was so fascinated by your response that I began to hint about something—a closer working connection for the two of us which now I want to clarify a little further.

So far as I can see, this work is likely to cover a considerable period of time. I don't see how it can be otherwise, because in the first place I don't want to hurry my thinking, and in the second place, as my secretary can tell you, the amount of revision is enormous. However, it is the only way I can work—thinking out illustrations from my experience, jotting them down, enlarging upon them, finding the proper subject head under which they belong and eventually combining them in some form as essays on the different topics I have in mind. In that connection, I know as well as I know anything, that if we two were together somewhere you would be the most stimulating, illuminating and correcting force that I could have. To bring this about I have thought of several things: For one—asking you to resign your job; come down here to New York, stay with me and work with me to the extent that you are doing now. That is, making yourself available for examining material as it reaches some form and then consulting with me from time to time as to the progress of the idea as a whole. Since I do not feel that this could possibly occupy more than a portion of your time, I figured that the rest of it could be devoted to writing your own essays, subjects which you might have in mind, or which I might suggest to you and which you could work out and not only sell to the magazines

here but later combine in book form after which it would be so easy to get you a publisher. I do not know how much you get out there or how much you would have to have to do this, but I wish you would let me know. In my case, while my finances are not so hot as they were several years ago, still there are one or two things in the air which, if they go through, would permit me, and joyfully too, to finance this scheme—at least until the conclusion of your work and mine. If this were undertaken in the right spirit, I am satisfied you would at least get the recognition which you so utterly deserve. Good God, you are so superior to the current accepted essayist and thinker in the field of belle-letters that there is no comparison. You would be known not only here but throughout the world as unquestionably, if the thing can be arranged, you will be.

This idea failing though, the second one was that presently, in April or May, I would shut up shop here and move out to Los Angeles, provided that I could be in contact with you there and that you would undertake this possibility of working out a book of your own. If, as I say, the financial break I am thinking of should eventuate as I more than fancy it will, I would undertake to subsidize your effort there, or if you were certain that you should not part with your present labors, then to remunerate you in some regular way for your aid to me.

As advantageous as the whole thing is to me, I want you to know, as I believe you do, that your artistic welfare is as close to me as anything outside my individual self could possibly be. There is nothing but the truth here.

Years ago when I first read your articles in the *San Francisco Bulletin* I was not only affectionately impressed but enthused by your viewpoint, and before I knew you, wished that I might know you. And that time when we met in San Francisco [3] was, as I fancy you have guessed from my attitude, one of the most gratifying experiences of my mental life in America.

So with all this in your mind, write and tell me what you think of one or both of these schemes.

[3] Probably early in October 1920.

In a day or so I am going to send you two more of the essays. One of them is in print and appeared in *Esquire* as "You Phantom." [4] It may sound like a further elaboration of "The Myth of Individuality," but it is a little more than that. More likely the Myth of Physical and Mental Existence. I haven't the right label for it but perhaps after you have read it and smoked your pipe a few times you will be able to think for me what it should be called.

The other essay is "The Myth of Possessions." It is, to me, mentally better arranged and better established although possibly you will not think so. I expect to publish that shortly in *Esquire*.

I can't write any more now, but I want you to think these things over and write me.

Your last letter concerning "Individuality" is a mental and temperamental gem.

Dreiser

To George Douglas
[ALS–TEH]

[Hotel Ansonia
Broadway at 73rd Street
New York, N.Y.]
January 14, [1935] [5]

Dear George:

It appears that my books have just been banned in Germany on the ground that they are subversive of morals and character—the morals & character required to erect and continue a worthwhile society. I am wondering if they think I am a Jew. Many, many people for some reason believe that I am! One thing that may have tended to confirm this in their thought is that I wrote

4 "You, the Phantom," II (November 1934), 25-26.
5 Misdated 1934.

a Jewish Tragedy—*The Hand of the Potter*—which had quite a run in Germany. Its social accuracy appears to have misled many Jews. What do you suppose could be done to alter this German viewpoint,—if that is the viewpoint? [6] Of course if my books are being banned because of their psychologic or social merits or demerits I have nothing to say. But I would like to know that I am not being banned for being racially something that I am not.

Regards
Dreiser

To Bruce Crawford
[TLS–ad]

Hotel Ansonia
[Broadway at 73rd Street]
New York, [N.Y.]
January 15, 1935

Dear Bruce:

Naturally I was sorry when you were defeated for Congress last Fall, but it would have astonished me greatly if you with your vision and principles could have conveyed your value to your dreamed of constituents. It is pretty hard for the little man to see his real friend. Almost invariably he is hanging on to the liar or faker who is leading him to the slaughter house. I thought of you the other day when I read one of Will Rogers' squibs in which he said that Roosevelt would soon begin to find out how hard it was to place some of his supposed Democratic followers in Congress. The man that got the Congressional job away from you is unquestionably one of them.

6 In reply to an almost identical letter from Dreiser, H. L. Mencken suggested that Dreiser write Karl von Wiegand, Hearst correspondent in Germany, or Guido Enderes, the *New York Times's* correspondent there.

One reason why I am writing this is because recently I have become interested in Technocracy as a way out; really a better way for American purposes I think than the various isms we have been following. The logic of it is so plain. And the editorial in the last paper that you sent me seems to be written almost from the Technocratic point of view.

I know Howard Scott; he is frequently in the place here and some day when you are in town I would like you to meet him and talk things over. He is really the brains behind the idea, and all that the recent Committee appointed by Roosevelt to investigate our technical resources did was to confirm what Scott had pointed out. The crowd that did that work was the same crowd that tried to throw him overboard after Butler of the Columbia University threw him off. Now they are inclined to come back into the fold and I think a reunion is likely to be effected and perhaps some money secured for really developing this idea throughout the country. By nature of course Scott is a dictator. He has an almost one-track technical vision, but from that point of view it is still a very great vision, far superior to that of anyone I have encountered or read about who is trying to apply technical competence to the problem of supply and demand, or rather, supply and need.

I think if you met him you would be interested in him, and you might even heartily endorse his program, because your mind, if I study your thoughts correctly, runs in very much the same direction.

Personally, I despair of communistic efforts in this country. There are too many groups, too much quarrelling, and the mass sentiment of America seems to be more anti than pro. It would go faster for this other idea if it could be widely explained. As I have told Scott, it needs to be humanized, at least for the mass. Some symbol of what Technocracy really means for the non-thinker must be prepared and provided, but with that I believe it could be popularized. Already the Utopians have a play that presents the idea in a very simple manner which the average fel-

low gets quickly. It has been read to me and it really is a quite Bunyan-like presentation. I am telling you all this because I am going to tell Scott about you, and, as I say, sometime when you are down this way I want you to meet him.

All my best wishes,
Dreiser

To Gobind Behari Lal
[CC]

He was science editor for the New York American *and other Hearst newspapers.*

Hotel Ansonia
[Broadway at 73rd Street]
New York, [N.Y.]
January 16, 1935

My dear Lal:

There is a question that I would like to ask you about gases and their effect on the emotions or mental states of individuals.

Nitrous Oxide as I know from experience produces, in me at least, a laughing and yet somewhat ironic mood. It has twice produced the same effect, for reasons which, once I was under the influence of the gas, I could not remember.

I read the other day in some paper that air, deprived of half its oxygen produces a loss of critical judgment and induces quarrelsomeness. Are there any other established facts in connection with other gases and their power to produce or induce temperamental changes such as these?

I read your column from time to time and find in it matters of no little interest to me. My feeling is that scientific study should be accorded larger space in all of our papers.

Regards,

To George Douglas
[TLS–RHE]

Hotel Ansonia
[Broadway at 73rd Street]
New York, [N.Y.]
January 26, 1935

Dear George:

Your fear that I have no thought-out plan for the book is wrong. I have long had a fairly clear idea of the problem in hand and its necessary subject heads. As a matter of fact, back in 1915 I had a glimmering of what eventually cleared up into a full understanding of the interpretation that I would like to make, and I embodied my early thought in certain essays that are now in *Hey Rub-a-Dub-Dub,* and some of that material I propose to use in this book.

Actually, my theory [7] is that things have to be about as they are if such a scene or social organism as we contemplate here on earth is to function. In other words, I see no way in which it can function differently in the future than it has in the past; change is inevitable, of course but it will be changed not in procedure but in results. In other words, what went on dynamically and structurally in protoplasm is what is going on dynamically and structurally now, but by the process the scene has changed from protoplasm to what we see. It does not follow from that, in my judgment at least, that the game is unprepossessing or horrible except incidentally and in crisis. In the main it must always have been favorable to extension and increase, variety and color, and it looks to me as though it would continue so until some cycle of itself represented by all the activities that we see here is completed. That is one thing that I am going to point out, and another thing is that the prospect of a perfect social order is a myth. There will be a social order; it will be constantly changing and

[7] Dreiser's marginal notes on his carbon copy of this letter label the argument "The Myth of the Perfect State."

probably constantly interesting, even increasingly interesting, but it will not be perfect, because I look on life as a progressive game that is being played for some purpose, probably for self-entertainment. To make the entertainment continuous means that it must change, but regardless of the change, the rules of the game cannot be abandoned and there is no evidence in physics or chemistry or the controlling dynamics that the rules are changing. Incidentally, I hold that there is no evidence to show that this game, as played here, is planned to solve anything. For all we know, such a play process may be in progress under different chemic and dynamic disguises on all of the endless planets and suns.

The opening essay was to be entitled, "The Essential Tragedy of Life." I am not sure whether that is the best title, because what I have in mind is that it has and will have continuously tragic, comic elements which can never be escaped, for it involves a duality which cannot be escaped. That duality can be expressed by such verbal equations as—no evil, no good; no injustice, no justice; no heat, no cold; no weakness, no strength; no ignorance, no knowledge, and so on.

The second essay was to be called "The Myth of Reality," and the thing that was published under the title "You Phantom" [8] was a part of that essay. In the book I was going to make that "A" and a second illustration was to be entitled "B"; then was to follow "The Myth of Individuality," "The Myth of the Creative Power of Man," "The Myth of Possessions," "The Myth of Free Will," "The Myth of Individual Thinking," "The Myth of the Unqualified Evil of Ignorance," "Morality and Immorality," "The Necessity for Limitation," "The Myth of a Perfect Social Order," "The Myth of Death." And then there would be a break, and a second series would be entitled, "Some Attributes of a Creative Energy as Expressed Here on Earth."

    a. "The Reality of Desire."
    b. "The Reality of Change."
    c. "The Reality of Beauty."

8 I.e., "You, the Phantom."

d. "The Quality of Mercy."

e. "The Necessity for Secrecy."

f. "The Compromise called Justice."

In connection with "a," that is, "The Reality of Desire," I have thought that I might have to discuss it under a slightly different title such as "The Reaction called Desire," "The Reaction called Beauty," "The Reaction called Mercy."

The final essay in the book would be entitled, "Equation Inevitable" and will summarize all of the preceding observations and deductions.

Somewhere in this series I want to discuss "The Present Limitations of the Race Mind"—or "Race Thinking" because it is obvious that with the five or six senses that we have and their scientific extensions, we have no power of grasping either the origin of human Life or the origin of Nature, and even if we were to reach the point where we could grasp the exact process by which Life on this earth began, still mentally we would not be anywhere, because all we would have would be a dynamic or electro-chemic or electro-physic explanation of the "how" without the "why." How why is to be answered with the equipment we have is not clear and if it should come about in the long process of change that the why could be discovered by some highly improved organism, that organism still would not be man as we know him now. So I might almost entitle my essay, "The Ultimate Powers of the Race Mind."

However, this will be enough to indicate the general plan which is well in hand. I haven't time at this moment to comment on all of your surprisingly interesting letters, but I can thank you for the suggestions they contain and tell you that I am being guided by some of them. As I told you, I am awaiting a certain development here which, if it comes about, will make possible this scheme of working together, but I will let you know more as to that in a few days.

Regards,
Dreiser

How I would like to discuss personally with you some of these trying obscurities[.] [9]

To Richard L. Simon
[CC]

A revised and enlarged edition of Moods *was the first of Dreiser's books that Simon and Schuster planned to publish. M. Lincoln Schuster had been profoundly moved by his first reading of the poems in October 1934, and Clifton Fadiman had more recently gone through the text with Schuster to suggest cuts and to prepare the book for publication. Fadiman was, however, in the hospital, and Simon, taking up some of the editor's duties, had written on January 31 that since the book as it stood would be almost six hundred pages long it would help sales if Dreiser could eliminate enough of the "less important" poems to reduce the volume to approximately four hundred pages.*

> Hotel Ansonia
> [Broadway at 73rd Street]
> New York, [N.Y.]
> February 5, 1935

Dear Mr. Simon:

The difficulty in connection with your final suggestions in regard to *Moods* is that it leaves me very dubious as to the attitude of the house in regard to the book and to me. If you will read Mr. Schuster's letter of October 21, 1934, you will see that his endorsement is of the manuscript as a whole.[10]

---

[9] Postscript is handwritten.

[10] Schuster had written: "I took *Moods* out to the country [Sea Cliff, Long Island] and want to tell you at once how deeply I was affected by many of the poems in this amplified and revised book. It is an outpouring of selfhood—in your own words, 'The demon out of a secret poet.' What a sweep of phantasms, exaltations, dirges, and defiances! Like all honest contemplations and self-revelations it will inflame some people, frighten many, infuriate others, because of its naked power. I read it right through and at the highest points was moved to go over the cadences again."

It was myself who asked for suggestions as to certain poems which might be objected to, or which might be thought less valuable, or to duplicate each other. No such suggestion was made until January 2, 1935, and then by Mr. Fadiman, speaking for Schuster and himself. By that time, as you will see from his letter of January 2, the poems were divided into three groups, Group A consisting of those which both would like to see in the edition they were contemplating bringing out. But Group *A* contained about one-third of those that were included in the enlarged versions of *Moods* submitted to Mr. Schuster,—incidentally, only one-third of those published in the Liveright edition.[11]

Interesting as that development was, there were eliminated from this proposed new *Moods* a majority of the outstanding pieces of the Liveright volume and some of which had been twice-illustrated by volunteer admirers. Among others discarded were some which had been set to music and a great many that had been published in the *Mercury,* the *Nation, Vanity Fair* and other publications. Naturally, this raised the question in my mind as to what Mr. Schuster's letter really meant; also whether it was not self-evident from this that Simon & Schuster did not approve of the book either as revised by me or as it was published by Liveright.

However, since this revised version represents in the first instance a fair summary of my philosophy in mood form, and in the second, an elaborated presentation of it, I could not see and I cannot see that the book either as poetry or as philosophy has been grasped, or, if so, that it is critically approved of. The evidence seems to indicate the reverse.

To be sure, a clause of my contract with Simon & Schuster provides that a revised edition of *Moods* is to be issued by the firm. That revision, as I explained from the first, was to permit

11 Fadiman had written: "The top section, marked 'A,' consists of those poems which Mr. Schuster and I consider the finest and which we should like to see in our edition. The second section, marked 'B,' consists of poems which we think less good, but from which some might be drawn for final inclusion. The third section, marked 'C,' consists of poems we like least of all. . . . As I understand it, we are to get *Moods* out this spring and I suggest, therefore, that you make your final selection as rapidly as possible. . . ."

inclusion of a number of things written since the volume was issued. But it does not follow that in the face of this critical mis-understanding objection I am willing to have it published by Simon & Schuster. It is my feeling that an author and his pub-lisher should be in fair intellectual as well as critical accord. In this instance the failure to approve of the contents of either the Liveright volume as it stood or this revised version as presented by me, suggests a critical gap which cannot well be overcome. Under the circumstances, I suggest an additional clause be writ-ten to the contract which will state that in case the Publisher finds himself in critical disagreement with a volume of which the Author approves, that volume is to be released to the Author for publication elsewhere. I realize that this complicates the collected edition provision of the contract, also perhaps some other phases of the same, but just how this is to be ironed out can probably be thought out in conference.

Decidedly you can understand that I am not interested in either a forced or half-hearted or anything less than a wholehearted endorsement of any volume that I propose to publish; nor am I to be turned over to minor secretaries with instructions as to what the Simon & Schuster book length for poetry is.

Will you let me know as to the above suggestion? I will be very pleased if you will accept it without argument.

To George Douglas
[CC]

Hotel Ansonia
[Broadway at 73rd Street]
New York, [N.Y.]
February 7, 1935

Dear George:

I forgot to inform you that the man who couldn't understand "The Creative Power of Man" over on the *Mercury* was Charles

Angoff who took charge after Hazlitt [12] resigned. Hazlitt became editor after Mencken resigned and he was the one who bought "The Myth of Individuality." I suppose you have read that the *Mercury* had been sold. Some rich young Jew from Boston has bought it and intends to carry on after some intellectual fashion. Who is his immediate editor I don't know.

I might as well tell you that I have been ailing physically for about six weeks or more. Even now I don't know whether it is my lungs with which, believe it or not, I have had trouble three or four times in my life, or whether it is something else. Just the same in those six weeks I have lost eighteen pounds and for the last two weeks I have been so low that the bed has always seemed the best place, day or night. For the moment I am in bed but in the care of a doctor who is one of the best and I hope to be up and around in perhaps a week. Sick or not, I am going over various volumes and thoughts and writing out my comments on the various subjects listed in the contents of the proposed book which I sent you. Already I have enough material for five or six essays but the job of throwing the material in its proper sequence page by page is still to be done.

I have been waiting for the adjustment of several things in connection with my finances. There is something like 50,000 schillings that belong to me over in Vienna but which my Austrian Jew publishers—Zsolnay—have been holding out on me for the last three years. I finally got a lawyer, and he being a Jew, although I didn't know it, evidently proceeded to make fairly comfortable terms for Zsolnay, but just recently I have dropped him and I certainly expect to close this up and to my advantage, soon. It should mean about $6000.00 in cash when I get it.

Then there is some dickering that is going on in connection with *Sister Carrie* on the part of Universal. If this goes through as I still think it will there will be ample funds for what I have in mind.

Incidentally, I may, because of my present lung trouble, move

12 Henry Hazlitt.

down to Arizona or even Los Angeles or some region near there. If so, I will be in personal touch with you and we could talk out a procedure there.

Regards,
Dreiser

To H. L. Mencken
[ALS–NYP]

Mencken had discussed with Dreiser the ultimate disposal of their manuscripts and papers. Mencken himself was considering giving his collection to the Library of Congress.

[Iroki
Old Bedford Road
R.F.D. 3]
Mt. Kisco, [New York]
February 13, 1935

Dear Mencken

I'm sick up here & won't be in N. Y. until next week. Had a letter from Washington & will answer it Monday or Tuesday. Will you tell me this—exactly what varieties of personal material are you depositing in Washington? It will help me think out my own procedure.

Incidentally I am going to trouble you with a question. It relates to the problem of individual mind as opposed to some form of electro-physical control operative through all minds as mechanisms[.] Back in 1900 Jacques Loeb wrote a book—*Comparative Physiology of the Brain & Comparative Psychology.* In it he dismissed all metaphysical conceptions of mind and presented a mechanistic series of chemical reactions. This dismisses reason—(except the mechanistic semblance of reason)—any such thing as individual creative power—or creative thought etc. Here are my questions. Did you ever read the book? (Published by

Putnam) Have his deductions ever been gainsaid. Has Loeb's tropistic data—his demonstrated heliotropisms, geotropisms, galvanotropisms ever been questioned? Have these been brilliantly enlarged upon or summarized by a particular person? I know there is plenty of work pointing in this direction but are you familiar with any one single luminous work?

Regards
Dreiser

Address me
  Mt. Kisco, New York
The Old Road

To George Douglas
[TLS–RHE]

Hotel Ansonia
[Broadway at 73rd Street]
New York, [N.Y.]
February 14, 1935

Dear George:

There's no use saying thanks for such letters as I have received from you and the invitation to live in your house. You can judge for yourself whether I am grateful or not. There is no question that I have present trouble with my lungs. It springs from earlier attacks; one when I was 18 and another when I was 45, but the second attack was really brought about by a very severe siege of bronchitis which drove me out of New York and kept me out until I was once more okey. This present thing was once more preceded by Grippe and then a plentiful supply of bronchitis and finally a break which has been carefully diagnosed here and I am ordered to get out of New York and really into a sanitarium.

I understand that there is a very good one a little way out of Los Angeles, but I will be the judge as to whether I will enter one and for how long. If I should decide not to enter one direct

I will come on to Los Angeles and would like to take your offer for a few days' stay anyhow until I get my bearings. The chances are that I will ship my car in which case it will occupy one of the two stalls in your garage for the time being anyhow. I will let you know more as to that by letter and if not by letter, by wire.

For the past week I have been in bed at Mt. Kisco and I am only down to the Hotel in New York today in order to transact some very necessary business.

Don't think that I am too seriously afflicted, because such is not the case. While I am pretty much under the weather at the moment, my vitality is not to be sneezed at and with sufficient rest and a different climate I will be all right I am sure.

In regard to Los Angeles, the chief compulsion is identical with my desire to be near you throughout the formulative phase of this book. There are so many and such interesting topics, and while I have the ideology clearly in hand and not a little of the basic and convincing data, nevertheless, study of and discussion with you of the different phases would be not only clarifying but constructive in the best sense, as well as a delight. As a matter of fact, as I told you before, I would like nothing better than to sit opposite you at a table and take up a given topic together with my theories or proofs and thrash it all out with you item by item.

By the way, this change may come very quickly, probably within the next two weeks. If so, you can expect me bag in hand; only not now but when I arrive, I will tell you what my immediate plans are—whether to enter a sanitarium or not and for how long. So until further notice meditate on this.

I suppose you got "The Myth of Possessions." I am expecting to hear something about that in due course.

Regards,
Dreiser

Please do not tell anyone that I am coming[.] I prefer to remain unremarked as long as possible.[13]

---

13 Postscript is handwritten.

To Sulamith Ish-Kishor

[CC]

Dreiser was preparing his Introduction to her Magnificent Hadrian.

Hotel Ansonia
[Broadway at 73rd Street]
New York, [N.Y.]
February 14, 1935

Dear Miss Ish-Kishor:

I have been ill and in bed for the last week and not any too strong at the present moment, but I am taking the data you sent with me to Mt. Kisco and will try to work out my thoughts in connection with *Hadrian.* Personally I wish you would provide me with a brief (that is, much briefer than is here) condensation of the chief points of his career. To that as a backbone I will elaborate from the remainder of the material you provided me. I should think this could be done in 500 or 600 words.

As you know, Simon & Schuster are bringing out *Moods* in an enlarged form; however I know they are dubious about their adventure principally because they do not understand it in any way whatsoever. I think that Mr. Schuster's conception of it is that it is an attempt at lyrical poetry in a non-lyrical form and is the only opinion there that has any value. He does not appear to grasp that what this is is lyrical philosophy and possibly the first conscious attempt to express an individual philosophy lyrically, that is, cadenced and declaimed, which is the modifying line on the cover. I think one of the reasons why the book has a moderate number of enthusiastic admirers and a larger number of dubious inquirers or students is due to the fact that its character and reality as lyrical philosophy has never been grasped.

Someone who understands this and is moved by the achievement could present it in the form of an introduction which would make for understanding of the book and so for a larger audience.

Your grasp of life and your lyrical poetic approach towards your subjects makes me feel that you, in perhaps a thousand words or so, could indicate this that I am saying. If you are in any physical condition to do this, I wonder if you will trouble to look over the enlarged manuscript, check those that most appeal to you and any that you think might be left out, and then tell me how much, if at all, you agree with this point of view and whether you could express it for me in a way which could be used as an introduction.[14]

I hope that you are well, and if you are, that you will stay well.

To Richard L. Simon
[CC]

The publisher on February 9 had replied to Dreiser's letter of the 5the by saying that both he and Schuster were agreed that to secure the widest possible audience Moods *should be condensed. He had also questioned whether the publication of a Dreiser omnibus was the best possible way to increase Dreiser's following.*

Hotel Ansonia
[Broadway at 73rd Street]
New York, [N.Y.]
February 14, 1935

Dear Mr. Simon:

I am obliged to you for clarifying the situation in regard to *Moods.* I still think that the trouble in regard to the book springs from a misapprehension as to the underlying idea and motive of the work as a whole. For instance, I think that Mr. Schuster's conception of it is that it is an attempt at lyrical poetry in a non-lyrical form and that for that reason he feels that a selection would be as valuable as the book in its entirety. The real truth about *Moods* is (in its earlier form and its present) that it is not an at-

14 For her Introduction see *Moods, Philosophic and Emotional, Cadenced and Declaimed* (New York, 1935), pp. v-viii.

tempt at lyrical poetry in a non-lyrical form but an attempt to achieve lyrical philosophy, which, as you can see for yourself, is an entirely different thing. Not only that, but it may be that this is the first conscious attempt at philosophy in this form, but however that may be this book is my attempt to express my individual philosophy in lyrical as well as emotional form. That is why the line *Cadenced and Declaimed* was added and why that line is so very important.

I am sorry now that I did not present this thought in connection with it in the first place but so many particular readers have grasped the truth of what I am saying that I had the feeling that the volume would identify itself as such in the minds of your readers. However, when the question of length came up I began to sense what the real trouble was and now I feel that what is really needed is an interpretive introduction from someone who fully understands this and can express it in such a way as to make the work mentally more amenable and possibly more agreeable to those who come across it and may be thinking of it as an attempt at lyrical poetry. In connection with that thought I have now fixed on the person that I think can write such an introduction.[15] But to do this I must have the volume back in my hands in order that it may be gone over by the writer that I have in mind. Incidentally, in having it reread and an introduction prepared I will have this person take up the question or problem of elimination and have the Moods rechecked from that point of view. When it is done I will, as you suggest, re-present it for publication. At that time if it still appears too long, I suggest that a smaller type, which will bring it nearer to your idea of book size, be used. Of course I would like to see the proposed type as well as the general format. Will you therefore do me the favor to return the Ms. at once and as soon as it can be rechecked and the introduction written I will return it to you.

In regard to the two other suggestions—the brochure about myself and the omnibus Dreiser—I feel that if a brochure has any

[15] Sulamith Ish-Kishor, whose brief Introduction was included in the published volume. See Dreiser to her, February 14, immediately preceding.

value whatsoever that value would be in connection with either the novel or the book of Philosophy [16] and therefore should await the appearance of the one or the other.

In regard to the *Omnibus*, I am principally not sure as to procedure. I think there would be real value to a selection, if it were really a representative cross-section of all of my works because I am satisfied that by far the great majority of those who are familiar with the novels are not at all familiar with the plays, the essays, the short stories, *Moods*, or some of my social papers—economic, political, and literary.[17] Naturally, such a book would help to introduce these other modes of expression and perhaps bring my other books additional readers. I say this with considerable conviction because I had noted that *The Hand of the Potter* both in Germany and England has introduced me to audiences which I could never have otherwise reached. Incidentally, quite recently in America and France "The Girl in the Coffin" has been seized upon by the communists and the socialists as a document illustrating their theories. Of course the play was not intended as such but just the same it is serving as a medium of introduction to thousands who would not otherwise be aware of my several plays. Again I am satisfied that certain stories introduced in this book would bring readers to my other volumes, but just when this is to be done is really for you to say, not me. I would prefer your advice as to this and as to that please let me know at your convenience.

In regard to *Moods* I have just arranged with my secretary, Miss Helston, to call at your office and pick up the Ms.

[16] Both *The Stoic* and *The Bulwark* were nominally in progress, but Dreiser's first interest was the book of philosophy about which he had been writing to George Douglas since December 15, 1934.

[17] See Dreiser to Clifton Fadiman, October 12, 1934.

To Sulamith Ish-Kishor
[CC]

[Iroki]
Old Bedford Road
[R.F.D. 3]
Mt. Kisco, New York
March 5, 1935

Dear Miss Ish-Kishor:

The Introduction is right.[18] It is sensitive and wise and is what the book needs. Most of your corrections are accepted; the others fell before personal preference. In regard to the poems to be left out I did throw out a portion but left others and cast out some on my own judgment. All together I sent you 297 Moods; the book as it goes to Simon & Schuster now contains 248 and the title I have fixed on is *Moods: Philosophic and Emotional* with the under line "Cadenced and Declaimed"[.]

I feel that with this title and your introduction the book really needs no further comment, that is, on any jacket, although if Simon & Schuster of their own accord propose something I will of course consider it.

I would have sent the set back to you for your judgment as to how the philosophic and romantic phases of the book were to be divided but after serious consideration I have decided that it would be a mistake to partition the philosophy and romance. As I see it now it is better to mingle them, holding to variety for interest['s] sake and leaving those philosophically bent to the burden of assembling in their own mind the thoughts meant for them.

Among other things you are really a born essayist and critic. Along with your other writings you should indulge in both. This country certainly needs them and I am certain that after a time the most intelligent magazines will gladly welcome what you have to say.

18 See Dreiser to Ish-Kishor, February 14, 1935.

I will not multiply my thanks in this letter but leave them to be indicated in other ways.

What you tell me about the Priestess of Isis and Osirian Antinous is one of those coincidences which confounds me as it would anyone. If you could only delve into the matter further, what you might not turn up.

Very truly yours
Theodore Dreiser

To Tiffany Thayer
[CC]

On February 26 Thayer, secretary of the Fortean Society, which had been dormant since Charles Fort's death, had proposed to reactivate the group by publication of a magazine to be called The Fortean *and to be devoted largely to printing Fort's notes verbatim. The first number, he had suggested, should feature an article by or about Dreiser as Fort's discoverer, and there should be no room for ghoulish imitators.*

[Iroki]
Old Bedford Road
[R.F.D. 3]
Mt. Kisco, New York
March 5, 1935

My dear Thayer:

Your letter in regard to the Fortean Society is very interesting but I personally decline to have anything to do with its continuation or this proposed magazine venture of yours. At the time the Society was organized I thought that there was some intelligent and constructive work to be done by the members during Fort's life; however, in so far as I know, except for some efforts on my part to achieve publication for Fort and a publisher for his complete works, nothing was done, or if so, I have not heard of it.

At the time of his death I was interested to see the notes that he left in order to estimate their volume and to some extent their nature, but this was blocked for me by your taking them and disappearing with them up to this time. I believe I wrote you for information but received no reply. I don't know what it is that after so great a length of time revives your interest in the Society, but if it is as keen as your letter indicates, you and the other members will not need my name or my direct services. Indirectly, of course, whatever I have or know in regard to Fort is open to any particular inquirer who definitely plans something worth while in connection with Fort's mental achievements.

Incidentally, it strikes me as presumptuous and ungracious for the only person who seized upon his property and disappeared with it, to indulge in thoughts concerning the ghoulishness of developing material in imitation of Fort. Exactly who would be mentally capable of imitating Charles Fort? I do not see any name on the list of the founders that would be likely to achieve anything but a ridiculous imitation—nothing that would in any way interfere with the sound and just progress of his ultimate fame. The remarks are characteristic of your entire attitude in regard to me and this society, and as far as I am concerned I desire to have nothing more to do with this venture as it is at present constituted. If at some time the thing is shaped up in such a way as to make sure the real advancement of Fort's mental interests, I will be glad to do what I can. As it now stands I see nothing but a tentative adventure on your part looking to decidedly undefined purposes of your own.

Very truly yours,
Theodore Dreiser.

To Calvin Bridges
[CC]

Bridges, professor of genetics, whom Dreiser had met at the Woods Hole Marine Biological Laboratory in 1928, was now associated with the California Institute of Technology.

[Iroki]
Old Bedford Road
[R.F.D. 3]
Mt. Kisco, New York
March 16, 1935

Dear Bridges:

Recently I have been rereading Jacques Loeb, *The Physiology of the Brain,*[19] *The Organism as a Whole, Heliotropism* [20] and some other volumes. In part you and Morgan [21] and others working on Drosophila appear to have derived at least some preliminary suggestions from Loeb.

What I want to know is this: Has Loeb's data in regard to heliotropism, chemiotropism, geotropism and others, been superseded by contradictory data? Does your work and that of Morgan and others in any way conflict with Loeb's mechanistic interpretation of life?

Here's another question: Exactly what is meant by the principle of uncertainty in connection with microscopic processes, and does that principle imply a possibly irremediable disorder as opposed to order in the universe? I note the constant use of the phrase "ordered universe," and of course the word "cosmos" as representing the entire universe seems to imply a complete absence of disorder. Is there no room for the word chaos in connection with the universe? Even to the extent of temporary chaos? Is there any evidence in sight so far that the universe has been partially, let alone entirely, chaotic?

Will you answer these questions for me quickly, as there is something I am working on which requires clarification on these points?

[19] *Comparative Physiology of the Brain and Comparative Psychology* (New York, 1900).

[20] *The Heliotropism of Animals and Its Identity with the Heliotropism of Plants,* a pamphlet originally printed in Würzburg, was reprinted in Loeb's *Studies in General Physiology* (Chicago, 1905), Part I, pp. 1-88.

[21] Thomas Hunt Morgan, director of the William G. Kerckhoff Laboratories, California Institute of Technology, an expert on genetics and embryology, recipient of the Nobel Prize for 1933 for discoveries relating to hereditary functions of the chromosomes. Bridges had been one of his collaborators in writing *The Genetics of Drosophila* ('s-Gravenhage, [1925]) and other works.

Incidentally, my love, I am planning to arrive in Los Angeles perhaps within a month. I shall be living somewhere between Hollywood and Beverly Hills, and the first person I will be looking up is yourself. Don't decamp with any Hollywood beauty before I get there.

To George Douglas
[TLS–TEH]

[Iroki]
Old Bedford Road
[R.F.D. 3]
Mt. Kisco, New York
March 16, 1935

Dear George:

I hope you are not entirely discouraged by this development in connection with my health, but until I feel reasonably sure which way I am going, it would be useless to come out there. I believe in my last note I wrote you that I have closed up my place at the Ansonia and have been resting and dieting and doing considerable sleeping here at Mt. Kisco.[22] I find myself improved and if this keeps up for an additional two weeks I shall be on my way to Hollywood.

In connection with the loss of weight and the general depression, there was a sudden probably glandular development which induced, in me, the most amazing morbid fears. These began to descend in periods of from three to seven seconds, at most a minute in duration, but they were really startling and productive of a reflective depression, not an integral part of the seven seconds but the consequence of it. Being of an analytical and philosophical turn I have been mentally startled and illuminated by something for which I have no words. Perhaps I might call it a sense

22 See Dreiser to Douglas, February 14, 1935.

of psychic earthquake as though something abysmal and final were first opening under or splitting once and for all the so-called conscious something which is me. I fancy a man standing on a trap with a noose around his neck might have some such feeling, though I doubt it.

Of course long ago I changed my diet and the character of my general activities and in so doing have steadily benefited by it. So much so that I appear to have stabilized the question of weight and also the question of strength. My physical strength bounced up and down like a thermometer, strong at 7 A.M., weak as a cat at 11, moderately revived at 3 and worn out at 6. Just now I am rapping on a large snake wood table while I report that that is also a thing of the past and that I am feeling much better and plan to do as I wrote you if I am still welcome. We can arrange the matter of finances when I get there.

Incidentally, I am still reading and collecting current scientific data and I swear if nothing else is growing my brain appears to be. Fortunately I am not confused by what I find. But a lot of the things that I suspected in connection with this mortal scheme are being confirmed. I am satisfied that if we could sit down and go over the data I have so far collected you would be delighted, for it is amazingly interesting, ranging from the biologists, and chemists to the physicists, electro-chemists, astronomers and college philosophers.

Write me and let me hear from you as to how you are.

Regards,
Dreiser.

Discharged my secretary. Dictating to a temporary substitute.[23]

[23] Postscript is handwritten.

To H. L. Mencken
[TLS–NYP]

[Iroki]
Old Bedford Road
[R.F.D. 3]
Mt. Kisco, New York
March 16, 1935

Dear Mencken:

I don't know whether I told you, but since writing you I closed up my apartment in the Ansonia and moved up here to Mt. Kisco. Reason—ill health. I found myself giving way under grippe and strains of various sorts. I am staying here and will be for the next two weeks anyhow, after which, if I feel physically okay, I will be moving on to Los Angeles where I will continue with the work that I have in hand.

If you are going to be in New York between now and the first and could find it convenient to spend a night or a day up here, I will be glad to have you. There is plenty to discuss. Of course you noticed that the *Spectator* folded up and you probably read George's bright picture of its profitable history. It did excellently so long as it had the courage to say something, but when I found George too timid to make any radical assertions I withdrew, after which I always anticipated that lack of courage would kill it.—It has.

You know, I still feel that there is room for a very modern light and even gay-mooded philosophic journal, and it was that that I wanted to talk to you about. I feel satisfied that now the intelligentsia could be interested in the mystery of life and it could be attacked from so many angles and at the same time relieved, by the way, by purely play-boy material. In such a matter it seems to me that Nathan would probably be useless, but there are some temperaments drifting around that would provide color and gaiety.

Enough of that for now, but if you come up this way before

I go I would certainly like to talk the matter over with you. By the way, if I am in Los Angeles and you come down that way, I will be living for the time being with George Douglas of the *Los Angeles Examiner.* If you do not know him, I can assure you he is one of the most fascinating temperaments I have ever encountered.

Regards and best wishes,
Dreiser

TO ROBERT ANDREWS MILLIKAN
[CC]

Millikan had been awarded a Nobel Prize in 1923 for isolating and measuring the electron.

[Iroki]
Old Bedford Road
[R.F.D. 3]
Mt. Kisco, New York
March 16, 1935

Dear Mr. Millikan:

From time to time I have read statements of yours in interviews as well as your confession of faith in "What I Believe." [24] I note that you lay great emphasis on the *integrating factor* in the Universe which you seem to identify with mind, ideas and intelligence. In other words, you believe in an ordered Universe.

In the work of some other scientists, not yourself—the late Michael Pupin for one, I find reference to a possible chaos as opposed to cosmos. I would like to know if the result of your scientific labors so far justifies the assertion that the universe as thus far surveyed is truly cosmical, or, on the contrary, there is

[24] The title of a series of articles by various thinkers for the *Forum* in 1929 and 1930, published in a volume entitled *Living Philosophies* (New York, 1931), to which Dreiser is apparently referring.

any evidence of disorder or chaos anywhere. Of course in the human world one finds if not chaos at least from time to time chaotic lesions which in due course are either remedied or pass by way of death—new organisms representing new and non-chaotic arrangements appearing. Is there a place for the word "chaos" in discussing the universe?

Incidentally, there is another phrase of yours which I encountered in one of your discussions. You mention the *principle of uncertainty*. What relation has that to a possible permanent disorder in the Universe, if any?

I would be very grateful for your comments as to these matters.

Very truly,

To Tiffany Thayer
[CC]

To Dreiser's letter of March 5 Thayer had replied on March 11 insisting that Dreiser was just angry, that Thayer was altruistic and doing all the dirty work, and that Fort's will gave the Fortean Society's Secretary possession of all Fort's notes.

[Iroki]
Old Bedford Road
[R.F.D. 3]
Mt. Kisco, New York
March 16, 1935

My dear Thayer:

Your general procedure is egoistic and utterly inconsiderate of any desires or problems other than those that relate to yourself. Your whole course in connection with Fort and myself at least has indicated as much to me. I do not care to work with you. My decision is to remove my name from the Fortean Society and I hereby formally request you to do this at once.

If, as an outsider, at some time or another I can be of service to the Society in connection with Fort and his material I will be glad, if possible, to be of such service.[25]

TO GEORGE DOUGLAS
[CC]

[Iroki
Old Bedford Road
R.F.D. 3]
Mt. Kisco, New York
April 3, 1935

Dear George:

I am still here but I will start shortly. You needn't worry about annoying me with your philosophical letters. They interest and stimulate me so much that I am keeping them together in a file for the purpose of reference. The two poems that you sent me by George Sterling apply most amazingly to this entire theory. I intend to use both of them as quotations at the head of chapters. This last one [26] would apply most exactly to the last chapter or summary of all that this book will contain.

25 In 1937 Fort's widow, through her attorney, sought to get the notes on the ground that Thayer was treating them as his personal property. Thayer declined, and before the argument was settled, Mrs. Fort died and left Dreiser in charge of the estate. Dreiser, wishing to avoid a public quarrel, pressed no further.

26 Douglas on April 1 had quoted Sterling's sonnet "To Science":

And if thou slay Him, shall the ghost not rise?
    Yea! if thou conquer Him thine enemy,
    His specter from the dark shall visit thee—
Invincible, necessitous and wise.
The tyrant and mirage of human eyes,
    Exhaled upon the spirit's darkened sea,
    Shares He thy moment of eternity,
Thy truth confronted even with His lies.

Thy banners gleam a little and are furled;
    Against thy turrets surge his phantom tow'rs;
        Drugged with His opiates the nations nod,
Refusing still the beauty of thine hours;
And fragile is thy tenure of this world
    Still haunted by the monstrous ghost of God.

I am no less impatient to get out there than you are to have me come. By the way, are you familiar with Jacques Loeb's *The Organism as a Whole*? The more I examine the various scientific attempts at an interpretation of life the more I respect and admire Loeb. He has not been superseded—he has not even as yet been approximated. The neglect of him springs either from the inability of some current scientific minds to grasp him or that once fully understood, he will belittle them.

I spent yesterday at the Rockefeller Institute talking with various big shots and most of them found considerable difficulty in grasping the extent of Loeb's deductions. Of all scientific reading that you could do at present, I think the reading of Loeb would prove the most profitable.

Regards

To CHARLES E. YOST
[CC]

On May 2 Yost had reported hearing that the trustees of the Carnegie Library in Angola, Indiana, had ordered the librarian to burn every one of Dreiser's books.

[232 South Westmoreland Avenue
Los Angeles, California]
May 17, 1935

Dear Yost:

Thanks for yours of May Second. I am a little late in answering but in the last three weeks I was preparing to leave New York for the City of the Angels and here I am. What surprises me is the outburst in Angola[,] Indiana. And you are truly kind in letting me know about it. I know that as a spiked-tailed, two-horned specimen I grow in size and weight every minute, the evidence pours in from every direction and I am not surprised. For years I have had ample evidence that the Catholics were doing their

best to stop not only the reading but the distribution of my books and I also know that in a given list of corporation papers the use of even my name is out except for the purposes of attack. The *New York Times* for instance will use the name if it happens to be prominently identified with some public affair but no more; when it comes to an attack, however, I get the first page. As for instance on Tuesday last when they gave full space to what Rabbi Wise had to say about me and my comments on the Jews.[27] I don't know that anything is to be done about it; somehow my affairs seem to take care of themselves. I guess it will all end in a Portrait in Black.

As for us, I wish that I could write you oftener because I think of you often. Your virility and your enthusiasm combine to make a golden example by which I struggle to guide my useless steps. Incidentally this letter of yours would prove useful to me in several directions if I were permitted to either quote it or to use it as is. I do not mean for publication but in connection with a group of individuals who would be glad to have the data. However, if you object, just say so.

My address for the present is 232 S. Westmoreland Avenue, Los Angeles.[28] Let me know as to the use of the letter or parts of it and I will write you as often as I can and I hope you do the same by me.

To Harvey B. Lemon
[CC]

Lemon was a physicist at the University of Chicago.

27 Following recent publication of his correspondence with Hutchins Hapgood (see Dreiser to Hapgood, October 10 and December 28, 1933) Dreiser had been asked to clarify his position. See "Dreiser Denies He Is Anti-Semitic," *New Masses*, XV (April 30, 1935), 10.
28 George Douglas's address.

[232 South Westmoreland Avenue
Los Angeles, California]
May 20, 1935

Dear Mr. Lemon:

I read and understood and what is more enjoyed *From Galileo to Cosmic Rays* which is kindly inscribed to me. Since we had our talk I have been meditating on what you had to say about a standardized form of life origination on millions of possible planets throughout our own little illimitable universe. However, it was not so much the thought of this as the probable standardized process which you described which interested me, and I am writing to know if you won't kindly re-state this theory for me. I ask this because I have always been fascinated by any and every demonstration of the mechanistic nature of life. Occasionally I write and argue for this conception.

You know I asked your opinion as to the probable nature of the bridge between the ultimate physical atom or photon and the ultimate unit of protoplasm or if not that then the physics of protoplasm. If I recall aright, you offered some technical possibilities as to the how of it and if you would be good enough to repeat that I will be very much obliged to you.

Since seeing you I have removed from New York to Los Angeles and my present address is 232 S. Westmoreland Avenue. If by any chance you're coming out this way I would appreciate another conversation because I have the feeling that we might thrash out something of value. I have friends of long standing in the Rockefeller Institute, the laboratories of the New York University and the Institute of Technology here at Pasadena and I would like to join you up in friendship with those.

Very truly yours,

To Simon Flexner
[CC]

Dr. Flexner, the pathologist, was director of the Rockefeller Institute for Medical Research.

232 South Westmoreland Avenue
Los Angeles, California
June 1, 1935

Dear Dr. Flexner:

Thank you so much for the Paper by Professor Morgan.[29] It fills in exactly what I want to know about the latest in genetics, and particularly, in regard to the genes. As in the case of the physics of protoplasm, I notice that the line between matter and energy, is lost or not to be determined. This seems to unite the two worlds, and on the plane of immensely creative intelligence.

I wish I could orient your personal attention to the mystery of the Autonomic System. Something creatively astounding appears to be waiting for proper biological, chemical and physical attention. Is not there someone who has written something of real import in connection with the Autonomic System, and the true function of the Solar Plexus?

I hope you are strong and happy.

Regards,

TO H. L. MENCKEN

[TLS–NYP]

232 South Westmoreland Avenue
Los Angeles, [California]
June 24, 1935

Dear Mencken:

Thanks for the copy of that Harlan County Coal Investigation report. It merely substantiates in part, what I found there. I say "in part," because while I was there, people were murdered by the operating gang, or their sheriffs and deputies, for collecting

[29] Enclosed in Flexner to Dreiser, May 22, 1935, it was probably Thomas Hunt Morgan's Nobel lecture, "The Relation of Genetics to Physiology and Medicine," presented in Stockholm, June 4, 1934, and printed in the *Scientific Monthly*, XLI (July 1935), 5-18.

food and clothing for the workers who were being robbed and tortured by them. But they did not get away with their plans in connection with me—not by several long jumps.

I am glad you are staying on in the old house: [30] it is the sensible thing to do, but if you start wandering soon, wander out this way.

I am planning, one of these days to open an intellectual monastery somewhere in Southern New Mexico. It will have cells and beds, and a long, refectory table which will accommodate wandering apostates from normalidy, wherever they may be. But—!!! they must bring with them the minds that will make the refectory table an escape from the hum-drum cares of the world.

Thanks again for the report.

Regards,

Dreiser

Top honor is to be hailed as Father-Brother. Unlimited stay (with final honors) come with a unanimous vote. I am looking for charter members or brothers. Brother Heinrich for instance. All personal archives to be safely stored in the monastery.

The glorious George Douglas has signed up.[31]

To Sergei Dinamov
[CC]

232 South Westmoreland Avenue
Los Angeles, California
June 27, 1935

Dear Sergei:

Your letter of June 9th reached me June 25th here, in Los Angeles. Since you heard from me last, I was compelled to come out here in order to get rid of Bronchitis, or try to, and I am still on that job.

---

30 Mencken's wife had just died, but Mencken planned to remain in their house and to learn to endure the fact that she was no longer in it.

31 Postscripts are in Dreiser's hand.

I knew you would see the Hutchins Hapgood correspondence,[32] and was wondering why I did not hear from you before. Apart from what I said to the group representing the new *Masses*,[33] I have not changed my viewpoint in regard to the Jewish programme in America. They do not blend as do the other elements in this Country, but retain as they retain in all countries, their race solidarity and even their religion—here particularly. Russia appears to desire to solve the problem by giving them all their race and national rights in a district like Biro-Bidhzan. As I state, I do not underestimate their good qualities, their genius or their usefulness in connection with the world's work, but I do maintain that they have certain social reactions which, as yet, do not seem to blend any too comfortably with the national characteristics which they choose, or are compelled to invade. Whether this problem, as Hapgood insists, could be left to the general cultural advance of the world, is not so easily answered. But, after all, I did not make the Jewish problem, and am not compelled to solve it, but, as all Jews realize, it is a problem here in America, as elsewhere, only they will not discuss it, and they have no programme to offer. You saw one result of their peculiar race drift in their management of the Movies in this Country. The fact that the Catholic Church was finally permitted to capitalize their so-called moral objections to the character of the Movies, was due entirely to the management of the Jews, and it has strengthened the reactionary Catholic Church no little in this Country. There are other temperamental lines pursued by the Jews here, at least, which are steadily building up other difficulties for them, but they cannot see this, and no one who does not welcome their race boycott is allowed to speak. This is confidential and private. If you wish to comment further, I would be glad if you would.

Another thing: I wish you would give me a brief picture of the general state of Russia today—your personal reactions. There

[32] Printed in the *Nation*, CXL (April 17, 1935), 436-438. See Dreiser to Hutchins Hapgood, October 10 and December 28, 1933.

[33] "Dreiser Denies He Is Anti-Semitic," *New Masses*, XV (April 30, 1935), 10.

are so many attacks being launched here by the capitalistic world, that I would like to know how the general Soviet programme is advanced.

Regards,

To John Ford
[CC]

Ford was then a director for the Fox Film Corporation.

4922 Rosewood Avenue
Los Angeles, [California]
August 21, 1935

Dear Mr. Ford:

I was fortunate enough the other night to happen in on your screen interpretation of Liam O'Flaherty's *The Informer.* It is a work with which I am familiar. Because of that, I was all the more impressed by your very understanding, sympathetic and resourceful interpretation. From the beginning to the end, at each point it seemed to me to render sincerely, tenderly, accurately the values which Mr. O'Flaherty was seeking.

I do not know what pains and contentions may have attended your steps throughout this work but whatever they were, you must feel amply repaid by the knowledge that you have presented a very sad, melancholy and brooding phase of life in a tender, poetic and altogether lovely manner.

Mr. O'Flaherty is to be congratulated.

If ever the same understanding and resourcefulness were brought to the interpretation of any of my works on the screen, I should hold myself deeply indebted.

I am cordially and with my compliments

To Joel Stebbins
[CC]

Stebbins was a research associate at the Mt. Wilson observatory in Pasadena.

[4922 Rosewood Avenue
Los Angeles, California]
August 30, 1935

Dear Mr. Stebbins:

That was an impressive as well as a delightful evening you made for me and my friends at Mt. Wilson. I had always wondered about the greatest reflector and how it was constructed and operated. Among scientists, astronomers, because of the all-inclusiveness of their observations and speculations, have long since taken on, to me, a relatively sacerdotal character. From the many idle comments I made you might have judged that I was not deeply attentive and reverent. Only by one thing was I irritated—the non-wisdom of hampering the very important work of observation with the needless mechanical lacks and impediments which I found there. I am still shocked to see that, whereas the trashiest office factotum today pushes buttons and uses mechanical servants to further his brainless and futile ends, quite the first work of the world is still hobbled with discreditable and delaying inconveniences.

Apart from this let me say how deeply indebted I am to you for your courtesy and your time and your labor in making clear so much that I wanted to know. So patent in your brief and clarifying comments was the seriousness and the reverence of your past labors and services in this field. Most of all, after your labors with the great machine were ended, I was moved by your own personal and poetic and affectionate response to the night sky outside, and your illuminating explanations and deductions.

Awe and reverence, as you well know, walk with deep understanding. I felt the three transfuse in all that you had to say.

Gratefully,

To Donald P. McCord
[ALS]

McCord was a brother of the Peter of Twelve Men.

[4922 Rosewood Avenue
Los Angeles, California]
September 10, 1935

Dear Mr. McCord:

What a swell Sunday. I loved it. So did Helen & Douglas.[34] Your home is so <purely> individual and sensible and beautiful. Lust and length of days.

I read Mr. Carew's article. It's very good. But views as brave as his involve danger. He's on the firing line just as Huey Long was—just as Roosevelt is. Just [as] I am all of the time. And to-day—as you see—they're out to get the individual daring enough, kindly enough to sponsor the welfare of the common man as against—not the original creative giant who does things for every body but the second raters—his heirs and assigns who want to be somebody by virtue of inheritance, and by reason of feeling superior because of what they have inherited. They are called conservators. But their real name is loafer. They make the idle rich. You must have read Thorstein Veblen's *The Theory of the Leisure Class.* It's marvellous.

Can't say more now—but I'll call you up & we'll laugh some more.

Regards.
Dreiser

Helen has gone to Portland to see her mother. But I go on as usual.

P. S. I liked the story in the *Sat. Eve. Post.* Colorful & dramatic. But I couldn't hit a building at 15 paces[.]

34 Helen Richardson and George Douglas.

To H. L. MENCKEN
[ALS–NYP]

4922 Rosewood Avenue
Los Angeles, [California]
October 6, [1935]

Dear Mencken:

Are you still in the U. S. A. Suppose you report. I am here but leaving for New York between the 15th-20th of this dear month. Have just been reading a book by Alexis Carrel. If this is his measure, he is smaller than I thought. Have you read it. *(Man the Unknown)* I wish we could meet and talk. Not finding one to suit me I am constructing (drudgingly and trudgingly I will admit) a life picture of my own. It may not even please me but it will, I hope, please me personally much more than the things I read.

L.A. begins to take on the feel of a city[.] It has taken 2,400,000 people to approximate this but now one can find some people—some resorts and not feel the weight of either Iowa or the movies. There are too many internationals here. When it reaches four or five million as it will [it will] I believe be arrestingly different and perhaps—who knows—intellectually gay. Just now it faintly suggests its future. Drop me a line[.]

Dreiser

To Upton Sinclair
[CC]

[Iroki
Old Bedford Road
R.F.D. 3]
Mt. Kisco, New York
November 25, 1935

Dear Sinclair:

You were good enough to put me on your EPIC mailing list and I have since been reading it [35] with great interest. What strikes me as so valuable about it is its very complete grasp of the American situation as disassociated from all other phases of the struggle for equity now being conducted in various lands. I em-phasize this because to me it seems so very important that the American problem in all its intricate American phases should be simply and clearly presented to Americans. Then and then only, will they be able to solve it according to their particular American reactions. I have wished all along that you and your organization would definitely endorse as a necessitous phase of your own work Technocracy, because I cannot see how your program of production for use can be divorced from the technical programs of Howard Scott. It is entirely possible that you personally feel that this is impolitic, but I cannot see how a forthright program looking toward social change as great as this can afford to ignore a plan so distinguished and complete as this. The two movements should be harmonized.

Am I correct in assuming that what you are now engaged upon is a nationalization of the California movement? If so, I am for it and would like to see branches of it in every village[,] town and city in America. If my observation is correct it is the one plan that has gripped the attention of all America, whether they support it or oppose it. As such it will present a source of power which can now be rapidly added to and used to effect the changes

[35] *National EPIC Magazine.*

which all of those suffering from the economic injustices of this day so much desire and need. I am enclosing a check not only to cover a subscription but to help to furnish others with copies. Incidentally, is there now in existence a national EPIC organization? If not, are you contemplating the formation of one? Insofar as I can, I would like to encourage specific branches in this region, but I wish to make it perfectly clear that I am in no position to undertake time-consuming labor in this field at this time. But I am really very anxious to see this movement prosper and wish to do what I can to further it.

Cordially yours,

To Sherwood Anderson
[ALS–New]

On December 1 Anderson had written from New York: [36]
Dear Ted

For some reason I have recently been a good deal haunted by thoughts of you. How are you? What are you doing and thinking?

I came East about Oct. 1st and went to stay up the Hudson, some thirty miles from town on the farm of a friend. Have been at work on a novel. Oh I know Ted that you think the novel is not my field but I may make it yet. I am trying, this time, to get a bit more outside, not quite so much surrender to pure feeling, more observation . . .[37] more mind if I have it.

I haven't been seeing many people. Came into the city about ten days ago and am at that same place . . . 54 Washington Mews . . . until Dec. 15th and then to Marion[,] Virginia until about Jan. 15th. After that I think I'll hit off South and West . . . I'm thinking of Tuscon[,] Arizona, near the Mex. line, probably for Feb. and March.

Are you at work on a novel, or play, or what are you up to?

I remember once speaking to you of one of my favorite books of yours and said *A Traveler at Forty,* when I meant, *A Hoosier Holiday.* I recently reread it with joy.

---

[36] Printed in *Letters of Sherwood Anderson,* ed. Howard Mumford Jones and Walter B. Rideout (Boston, cop. 1953), p. 335.
[37] Anderson's punctuation is followed throughout.

Ted, don't fail to write that part of your own life having to do with Street and Smith, the *Delineator* etc.

And we should have also from you a book of people, pictures as in *Twelve Men* but more general, wider . . . many sketches put down as you can do it.

Do you write letters. I'd like to hear from you more often, your thoughts etc. I've had a notion recently that we men, of our time, do not communicate directly often enough. Often during a walk I find myself thinking of you, or some other man loved and respected, feeling lost from them. My best to Helen. I like that woman.

Sherwood

Did you know about Jerry Blum, gone clear off . . . out to shoot people etc. Poor cuss. He's now in Bloomingdale.[38]

[Iroki
Old Bedford Road
R.F.D. 3]
Mt. Kisco, [New York]
December 6, 1935

Dear Sherwood:

No one could write me a more comradely or more welcome letter. We rarely write each other and even when together do not say a great deal, but you are in mind as Poe is in my mind, as George Sterling is in my mind, as Mencken and Powys and Oscar Wilde and Villon are in my mind. You are first and foremost in all that you write a poet—and as such original, different[.] I think of many things you have written because I love to think of them—or to put it correctly they compel my temperament to react to them. I think you have [a] kindly and a beautiful mind. For proper emphasis maybe I should reverse that—maybe not. You say I think the novel is not your field. I don't know that I ever emphasized that. It may be yet your greatest field. I loved *Many Marriages* at a time when many quarreled with it. The thought and beauty of it is as clear to me today as when I read it.

[38] Jerome Blum, the painter, was undergoing treatment at the mental hospital.

Hearken! Don't go away without coming up here. It's winter but the little house in which we are living this winter is delight-ful[.] I'm working on several things, among them a phase of phi-losophy. But come up and let's talk, for I delight to see you. Helen would underscore this for herself. You know we passed through Marion, Va. late in November. I ran out of money & had to telegraph New York and my bank wired it there. The girl in the telegraph office knew all about you—or seemed to. She said your house was 40 miles away but that you were in New York. Also that a son or "relative" of yours ran the town paper[.] It was five P. M. and we were trying to make a certain camp com-mended to us & so we pushed on.

I'd like to write you Sherwood—and will from now on. But come up,—the two of you. The telephone is Mt. Kisco—5413. How about this coming week? Poor Jerry! What a tortured tem-perament. I wonder is he wholly irrational or knows that he [is] only partly so. And where is Frank[?] [39] Her love has cost her a world of strain and labor.

Will you come[?]

Dreiser

To Clifford Odets
[CC]

The playwright had given Dreiser tickets to see his Paradise Lost *on December 20.*

[39] Mrs. Blum.

[Iroki
Old Bedford Road
R.F.D. 3]
Mt. Kisco, New York
December 23, 1935

Dear Mr. Odets,

I was greatly impressed by *Paradise Lost*—so much so that I have been thinking of it ever since. If I were looking for a cross-section of human life at a certain economic level, I would consider that this play, with some eliminations, would be a splendid picture. If I were desirous of seeing the Jewish people of this day psychoanalyzed, and their aesthetic, economic and social reactions dramatized, and more, done into great tragedy, I would again say that the elements are in your play, movingly and powerfully set forth. If I were looking for the customary indictment of our economic and social order, I would say that here, again, you have included all the materials for it. The only problem that evolved out of all my thrills was whether all this material truly belonged in this crushing indictment of the economic order of the day.

Personally, I would not agree that the neuroses from which a number of your characters were certainly suffering were the result of the economic order alone. My personal opinion has been that they occur in all walks and in all circumstances, as much where there is no economic distress as where there is. Again I am positively convinced that the intense sex drama involved could as well have happened in a Marxian as a capitalistic regime. Lastly I was a little surprised that the various and moving and troubling actions of the characters, expressing as they did, and beautifully, temperamental afflictions, could have brought about the sudden illumination of your leading character, Leo Gordon, with which you closed the play. It seemed to me that such an <illumination, beautiful as it is, could not be explained wholly from the life which you offer, and yet for the life of me,> I could not possibly condemn this play or make light of it, or charge it with being deficient in tragic as well as illuminating material.

It is crowded with it. It would, if continued, cause millions of people to think, and what is more, arrange their thinking to better social and economic advantage, and even if it did not do that, it should still be commended as thrilling entertainment. Yet, saying all these things, picking flaws, you might say, I still wish it to succeed, and have already recommended it to many who will unquestionably proceed to see it.

Yet, all these things said, I still feel that what I have pointed out should have your serious consideration. A man who obviously must be called gifted and with powerful and arresting life tragedies at his finger tips, should not give us three great plays in one, but rather three separate ones, each in its proper field.

My regards and best wishes,

To George Douglas
[TLS–TEH]

On December 14 Douglas had sent a letter consisting mainly of poems and epigrams written by himself.

[Iroki
Old Bedford Road
R.F.D. 3]
Mt. Kisco, New York
December 27, 1935

Dear George,

Your pyrotechnic burst of December 14 entertained me greatly. From one point of view it looks as though you were slowly but surely evolving a rhymed philosophy, *Chemical and Physical Poems* by George Douglas of the Laboratory School of Poets. It will have this very great advantage over ordinary science and philosophy—it will be in turn poetically moving and amusing. That is more than you can say for Spencer, Schopenhauer, or Dr. Kant.

I would write more often but actually I eat and sleep the various problems which I am attempting to solve. But don't think I am lost in any mist. I am slowly but surely lining up the answers to a series of propositions, and though I am still gathering material, I am also formulating it. The result should be presently visible. If you were here I could explain some of the strange angles which have emerged, but to sit down and dictate it would be to write parts of the book, so I am waiting till we meet again.

Daily I think of Los Angeles and the very great difference between that world and this. We shall certainly move back as soon as this place is disposed of. But in the meantime, I am enjoying country winter life, and I confess that I like it just about as much as I like the continuous even weather that holds out there. I am glad that Halley and Dorothy [40] are doing so well. It looks to me as though at last you are a free man. If you are, what are you going to do with your freedom?

Give my regards to everybody.

Affectionately,
Dreiser

TO UPTON SINCLAIR
[CC]

[Iroki
Old Bedford Road
R.F.D. 3]
Mt. Kisco, New York
December 27, 1935

Dear Sinclair,

Sure, use the letter that I wrote you.[41] I mentioned a check but find no record of it in my check book; it must be that I overlooked it before, but here it is.

40 Douglas's daughters.
41 November 25, 1935 (*q.v.*).

Howard Scott was out here yesterday and we talked over Technocracy and the EPIC movement; and today I am mailing him a copy of this letter and of your letter of December 13,[42] not for publication, but for his inspection. The more I talked with him, the more I am satisfied that Technocracy is the method. I am also satisfied that for the time being at least, political methods will be needed to bring about Technocracy's control. It is because of the possible union of not only Technocracy but other movements that I am so interested in EPIC, and in seeing it generally established, not so much as a party but as a method for bringing about a new social order, which would then certainly not need EPIC in its propaganda form, as you know. I read your editorial on your trip, and personally feel that you ought to take a rest and unload some of this work on other personalities. The only trouble with this is that there are no others like yours. If you are the God in the machine, you have to do the work of the God in the machine, or the machine stops.

Regards,

42 In it Sinclair had written: "I would say that EPIC is merely a practical technique for bringing technocracy to pass." He then had criticised Howard Scott for continually spurning political action.

Letters of Theodore Dreiser

A

D1518322